DON'T BOTHER

SUDAN 1959 – 1964

by

Dorothy Isabel Lowe

DON'T BOTHER TO UNPACK
SUDAN 1959 – 1964

by

Dorothy Isabel Lowe

DON'T BOTHER TO UNPACK
SUDAN 1959 – 1964

first published in Great Britain in June 2002 by
Dorothy Isabel Lowe
228 Cambridge Road
Great Shelford
Cambridge CB2 5JU
reprinted October 2002

© Dorothy Isabel Lowe
All Rights Reserved Worldwide
ISBN 0-9542840-0-3

Grateful acknowledgement is made to

The Church Mission Society, 157 Waterloo Road, London, SE1 8UU for permission to quote John Carden: *Empty Shoes*, published Highway Press/CMS 1971, and to reproduce two photographs, duly attributed.

Mrs.Eileen de Saram who allowed me to quote from Brian de Saram: *Nile Harvest*, published 1992.

Penguin Books Ltd. for a licence to quote from Alan Moorehead: *The White Nile*, published Hamish Hamilton, Ltd., London 1960.

James Currey for permission to quote Andrew Wheeler: '*From Mission to Church in an Islamizing State: the case of Sudan, 1946 – 64*' in *Christian Missionaries & the State in the Third World*, edited by Holger Bernt Hansen and Michael Twaddle, published James Currey, Oxford, and Ohio University Press, Athens, 2002.

Printed by The Tavistock Press (Cambridge) Ltd.,
217A St. Neots Road, Hardwick, Cambridge, CB3 7QJ

For

John Bethel Lowe

With gratitude for the love, support and fun
throughout all our years together
within the love of God.

ACKNOWLEDGEMENTS

You will know from a glance at the photographs that this book is a personal account. At first I wanted simply to describe our journey to Mundri for Michael and Katherine who, only twenty months old at the time, remembered nothing of it. Before long I realized that the geography, no matter how interesting, wasn't enough except as the setting for why we went to Sudan and how we lived for the five years we were there. So here it is, the experiences of that time, a special account for our much loved Michael and Katherine and Patrick. It is for others too who may like to read about an ordinary family living in a way which was not always exactly ordinary.

Resources from that time are scant – various letters to our families and copies of reports to CMS in London but, apart from two small notebooks, no diaries or other records. Our photographs, limited because we had to be politically sensitive, and our books about Sudan prodded my memory. News, letters and visits from Sudanese friends keep the Church and people of Sudan in our thoughts and prayers. John and I do not forget how blessed we were to live and work at Bishop Gwynne College of the Episcopal Church of Sudan (E.C.S.). Four decades later the brutal war continues, intensified in recent years by the extraction of oil within the South of the country.

Founded two hundred years ago and still flourishing, CMS, the Church Mission Society, has always been central and important to me. This great company of Christian men and women who are serious about the Kingdom of God made it possible for John and me to serve as mission partners for fifteen years in Africa, and linked us with supporting and praying parishes in Ireland and England. Through CMS we have been inspired, challenged and loved, and we have found wonderful friends within its membership. Thank you CMS.

The *Faith in Sudan* series of eleven books (published by Paulines Publications, Nairobi, between 1997 and 2001) are a rich resource, and I congratulate Andrew Wheeler on his achievement as editor and his contributions. With all his knowledge and scholarship I'm indeed honoured and grateful that Andrew has written the foreword for my book.

I am grateful to my family and friends for their interest; to David Williams and to Katherine (née Lowe) and Richard Howlett for written comments on an early draft; to Elizabeth Bray for never ceasing to encourage me and for her astute and pertinent guidance; to Michael Lowe who insisted I must join the ranks of the computer-literate, and then became my tutor and an enthusiastic scrutinizer of text and format and maps. Without them, as authors so often say, this book would not have been written. But most of all that is true of John. He waited for me to finish before he read a single word and then with sensitivity made suggestions and attended in detail to the shape and accuracy of each chapter. Thank you John for the coffee and meals you prepared for us both; without 'support services' from you this book would still be far from ready for the printer. And thank you Michael for placing the entire text, the scanned photographs and the cover we designed onto that flimsy CD which seemed to be all the helpful Mark Lawrence of the Tavistock Press needed to produce this book by digital technology.

Dorothy Isabel Lowe
Cambridge, 2002

CONTENTS

Acknowledgements

Foreword

Maps

1	By sea with the cargo	1
2	Through the Suez Canal	7
3	Looking back from Port Sudan	13
4	Rattling on the train to Khartoum	23
5	The Tomb of the Mahdi in Omdurman	31
6	The next train to Kosti	36
7	Through the Sudd by paddle steamer	43
8	Juba shopping	51
9	Don't send any lukewarms	59
10	Meeting the missionaries	65
11	The long road to Mundri	72
12	Bishop Gwynne College	78
13	The Doll's house	90
14	Diya's village	99
15	How it began	110
16	Training for ordination	121
17	Lusi died	131
18	The snake in the *tukl*	135

19	Health and hygiene	137
20	The long, long surplice	144
21	Supper parties	151
22	How I fume	161
23	Our first Christmas	170
24	On leave	180
25	Sapana	185
26	Maria	192
27	Omdurman and Arabic	200
28	Can open mouth very wide	211
29	The *Tukl* primary school	216
30	It's hard to belong	227
31	Money for the cooks	236
32	Do you think you'll like it here?	243
33	Arabization and Islamization	250
34	The new Cathedral	255
35	This is the day the Lord has made	264
36	Canon Ezra's blessing	270
	Postscript	

FOREWORD

"Don't bother to unpack", they said to Dorothy and John Lowe as they arrived in Southern Sudan with their young twin children, Michael and Katherine. "Don't bother to unpack" because we don't know how long you'll be here. "Don't bother to unpack" because the political and social situation here is so unstable. "Don't bother to unpack" because you don't belong here. Well, the Lowes did unpack - not only their belongings, but also their hearts and minds, their compassion and their commitment. They made Mundri and Bishop Gwynne College their home for five years until the expulsion of all missionaries by the Sudan Government in 1964. Their lives were filled with Sudanese friends, and shaped by encounter and immersion in a young and vibrant African Church. Mundri became their home and it provided the contours of a lifetime of Christian witness and service that unfolded thereafter in Uganda and in south-east England.

Dorothy Lowe has written a vivid and moving account of these formative years in their lives as a young missionary family. Her account draws together the fine and delicate strands of a young family adjusting to life in a strange and foreign land, exploring it with openness and respect, and the tougher strands of an unfolding political and social drama characterized by fear and uncertainty. The engaging stories of family life stand in stark contrast to the gathering clouds of civil war. Dorothy is aware of both and her account is a remarkable testimony to the simplicity, faith and realism with which Sudanese and expatriate Christians alike faced the looming catastrophe. In 1965, the year after the Lowes together with other missionaries were expelled, Southern Sudan lurched into savagery and destruction as northern troops attempted a ruthless suppression of Southern aspirations. Villages, schools and churches were burned, political, religious and intellectual leaders sought out for elimination. Neither the Lowes, nor their missionary colleagues, were ever able to return.

Caught up as they were in this drama, the Lowes were nonetheless able to relish the opportunity to explore this rich and diverse country with all the resources of their lively imaginations and of the Christian faith which had brought them to Sudan. Nearly forty years after they left, Dorothy still recalls the sights, smells, intricacies and subtleties of their life with extraordinary vividness and accuracy. To read this book is to travel by sea to Port Sudan, by rail to Khartoum, to journey by steamer through the reed-choked channels of the Nile, to toil along the dusty roads of the South, to live in Moru villages as well as in the theological college where they worked. It is to share the exhilaration and sense of discovery, but also the confusions, misunderstandings, pains and sorrows, many of which Dorothy gathered into 'How I fume', her notebook of frustration. Especially moving is the thread of sorrow which weaves its way through the book, that Dorothy, because of Government restriction, was prevented from practising as a doctor in Sudan, despite her lifelong sense of God's call to missionary medical work. When Lusi, two-year-old daughter of Canon Ezra Lawiri, Vice-Principal of the college, died and Dorothy was unable to help, the pain lived with her for many years to come.

As the years pass, political issues and strident voices push more obtrusively into the narrative. Missionary presence in Sudan has always been controversial - from Catholic missionaries in the 19th century countering the slave trade with schools for freed slaves to the missionaries of the Condominium period (1900-56) who were accused of being agents of colonialism, of having introduced an alien religious culture and thus having contributed in a major way to the divisions and conflict in Sudan. In the immediate post-independence period missionaries were perceived by the Government in Khartoum as being a major obstacle to a Sudan united in religion and culture.

But other perspectives also have their persuasiveness: that the missionary contribution to modern education (especially for girls) in both North and South was decisive for Sudan's emergence as a modern nation; that the provision of vernacular education and vernacular scriptures enabled traditional cultures in Southern Sudan to be revitalized and to adapt to modern challenges and survive Government attempts to suppress; that the missionary contribution has enhanced the possibility that Sudan can build its future unity and prosperity on the reality of its pluralism rather than on enforced uniformity.

Fifteen years and a civil war after the Lowes left, another young couple took up residence in the "Doll's house" in Mundri, the Lowes' first home. It was our first married home. We walked the same paths and taught in the same classrooms, now repaired after ruin. We learned from the Sudanese pastors who had been the Lowes' colleagues and students. Our daughter played with the children and grandchildren of the Lowes' friends and mentors. The world they knew in the early 1960s and which is described here, we could still recognize in the early 1980s. A generation and another civil war later, the college has been ruined and restored yet again, and is now a secondary school for a new generation of young people. Will the cycle of war, destruction and rebuilding continue through further generations? Or can the faith, the hope and resilience that the Lowes saw in the 60s, and which is still evident today, in the end have its reward? Will those who love Sudan - both Sudanese and those around the world who have been touched by its special magic - live to see its peace and prosperity?

Andrew Wheeler

April 2002

Andrew Wheeler and his wife Sue have been CMS mission partners with the Sudanese Church in Sudan and in exile for twenty three years. He is the series editor and a substantial contributor to the "Faith in Sudan" series of books (published by Paulines Publications, Nairobi) which chronicle the history and contemporary experience of the Sudanese Church.

More recently he has served as the Archbishop of Canterbury's Officer for the Anglican Communion and is currently Director for Mission Education at St. Saviour's Church in Guildford.

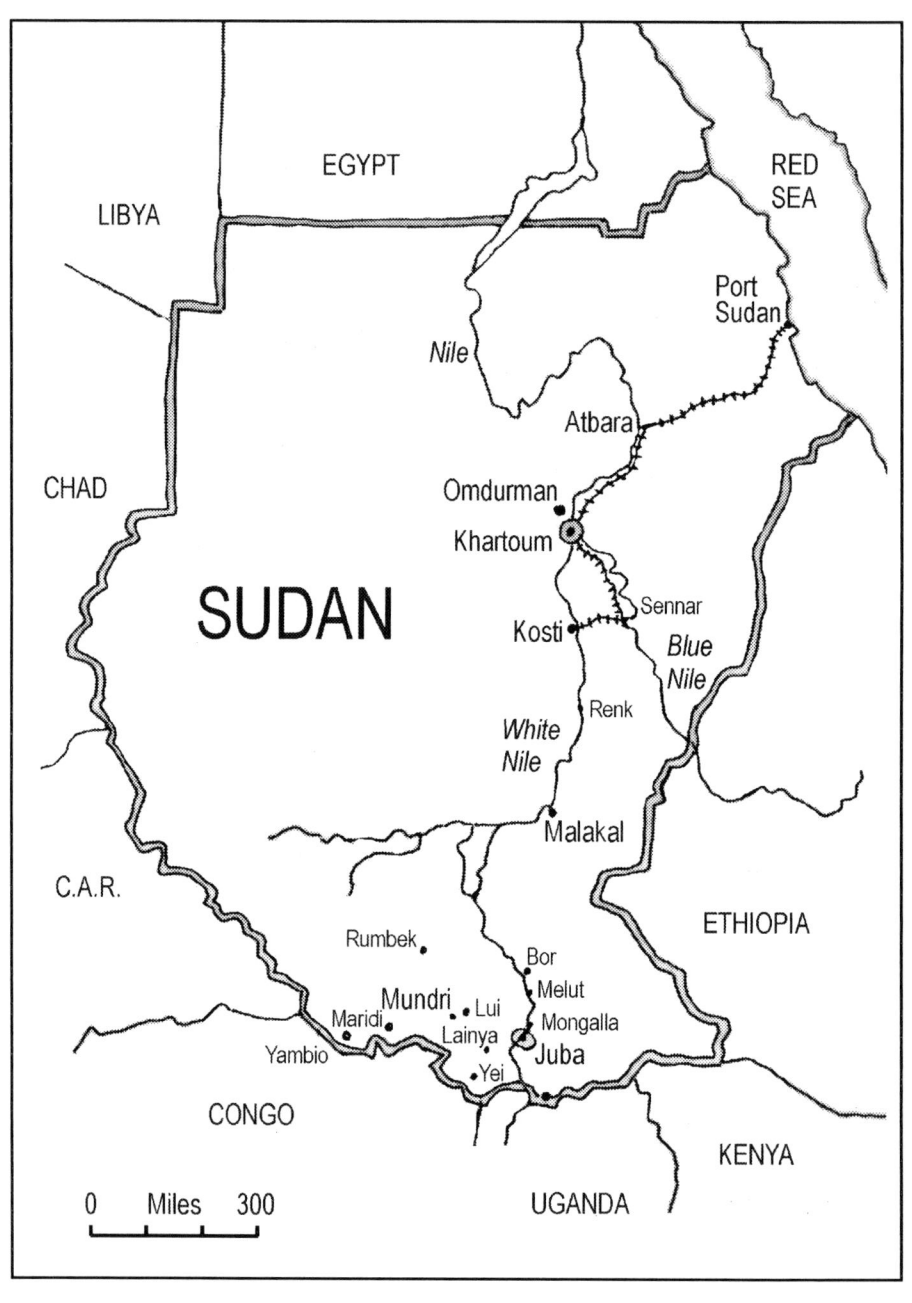

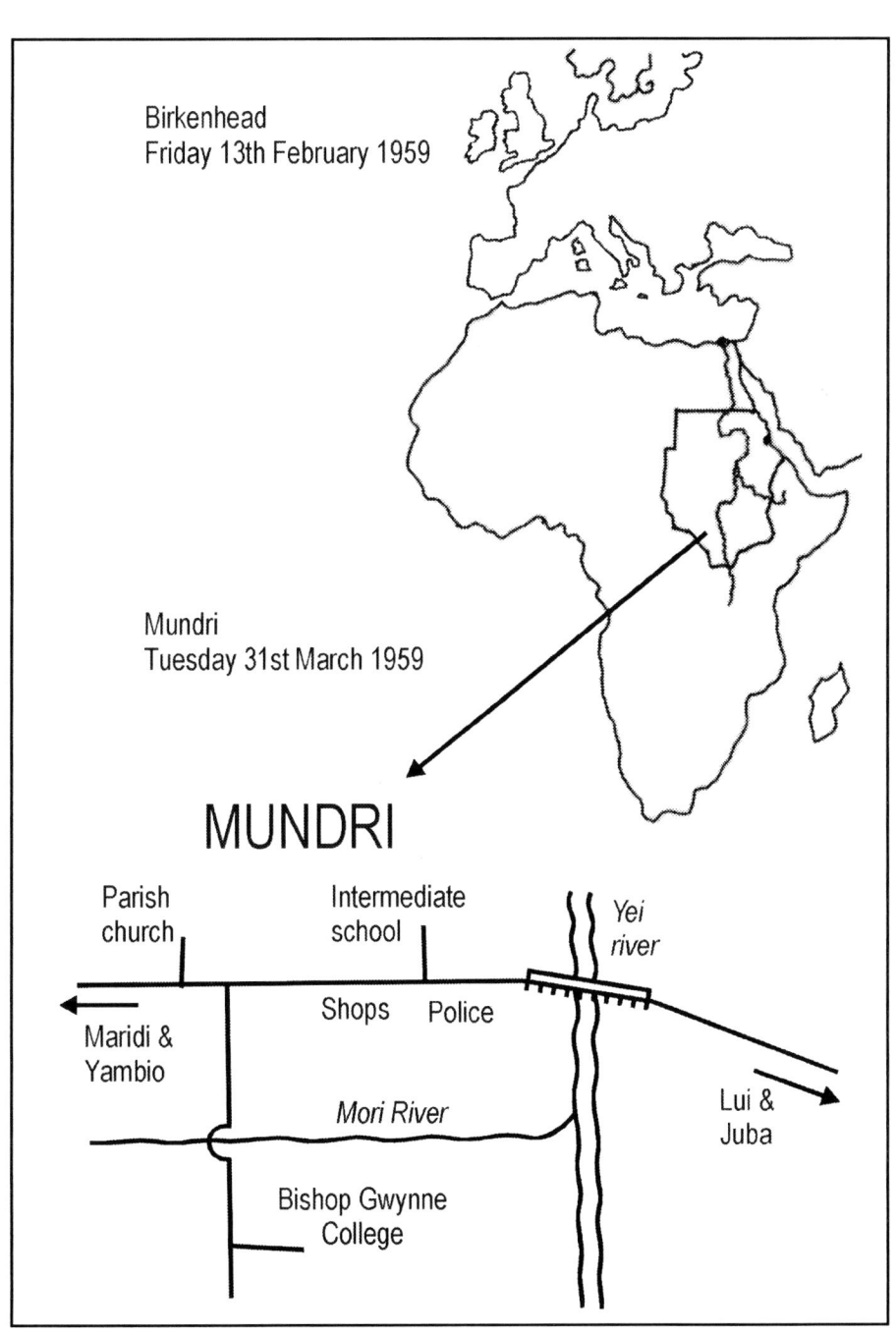

1   By Sea with the Cargo

We woke to an unfamiliar rumble. Not thunder. Not the rains coming early. But the groaning of heavy vehicles less than a mile away. They were on the unpaved main road, then we could hear them coming down the narrow track to the College. We dressed quickly, and through the billowing dust made out the line approaching our house. A number of large trucks, two Bren gun carriers, lots of soldiers fully armed and wearing tin hats who quickly jumped to the ground. There they were, the army had come. Our house was surrounded. What was to happen to us? Would the children be alright? Would we be imprisoned, deported, separated from each other? What would become of the College, of the people around us, of the Church? So ended the five years we spent as a family in a remote spot in Southern Sudan.

I'm not surprised if you ask how we came to be in that remote place, what we thought we could do there, and how we related to the Sudanese people among whom we were living. Read on, travel with us and our children by cargo boat from Birkenhead to Port Sudan, by train to Khartoum, by Nile steamer to Juba and on to Mundri by lorries. Enter our lives as we, John ordained and I a doctor waiting for a licence to practise, observed and adapted, questioned and loved and raged, and more than anything else shared in the hope and joy which the Christian gospel brings. This is my personal account of those formative years.

We were to sail from Birkenhead on Friday 13th February, 1959, on the S.S. Salween of the Henderson Line. And there she was, a shabby cargo boat, tied up in the gloomy docks where a fine mist shrouded the gantries and warehouses and hazy lights were reflected here and there on the dark oily water. We could hear the hum of the city of Liverpool constant in the distance, but this quay felt remote and still except for the sudden clanking of chains, muffled voices, and a flurry of activity as a ship hooted and left port or another arrived. Soon it would be our turn, the point when we moved from our life in Ireland and England to our life in Africa.

John and I with Michael and Katherine, our twenty-month old twins, had come on board in the afternoon, and so had my parents and John's father who wanted to make the most of every last minute before we sailed away. It was odd to be the only passengers embarking at Birkenhead, the only little group that evening to sit in the dimly-lit passenger lounge with its panelled walls and dull patterned carpet, all of us aware of the emotions of a major parting. Two years would pass before we saw each other again and, with no telephone at our remote destination, it would be two years before we next heard each others' voices. Michael and Katherine had been busy pushing furniture around and piling up table mats but now they were settled at last in their bunk in the cabin we would share with them. We stood with their grandparents at the cabin door for hugs and prayers and kisses and, as she always did, Katherine wriggled when Papa tickled her with his moustache. "Oh now, now," said Papa, "dear, dear, the poor little children!"

Conversations at the time of parting are tedious and repetitive. It had all been said already and I just longed for the hooter that would announce we were about to cast off. We sat in the lounge in leather armchairs at a small mahogany table, my mother and father side by side with Papa opposite and John and me, still in our twenties, in between. "You'll write to us when you get there, won't you?" said my mother; I could feel how desperately she was wanting to stay in contact with us. Both grandfathers, formally dressed in dark suits and clerical collars, usually delighted in heated theological discussions when neither of them budged an inch but tonight it was different; I was surprised to see for once they were nodding their heads in agreement. My mother, golden-haired and wearing an emerald green coat, was worrying about our safety and struggling to hide her feelings. Each of them was coping with the situation in their own way. Papa, the Reverend John Bethel Lowe, his name the same as given to my husband John, was finding our departure especially hard, no doubt it put him in mind of Mama's death in 1946, years before John and I had met. My father seemed more detached. He was excited by foreign travel and hadn't forgotten his first venture abroad on his honeymoon, when he surprised and alarmed my mother Emily May (Ludlow) by taking her to France with all its foreigners!

For both John and me this was a special day. We were leaving the places and people we knew and were at the start of an exciting adventure with a purpose to it. Our parents would miss us but we knew they were well pleased we were going to Africa to help the Church in Sudan, that the direction and purpose of our lives was in line with their own.

Our ship, the S.S. Salween, was not a glamorous cruise liner; she was a small cargo vessel which plied between Birkenhead and Burma, with 12 cabins for passengers. Only sixty feet wide and a bit over four hundred feet long, she was badly in need of refurbishment and paint. Her end would come in 1962 when she was broken up in Hong Kong, but in her time she carried many a missionary and other traveller to Africa and further east and she would carry us to Port Sudan. John was to teach in a College for training Sudanese clergy of the Episcopal (Anglican) Church of Sudan and I to make a home for John and our children and practise as a doctor, the vocation at the centre of my life. We would be supported by the Church Missionary Society and were responding to a request from Sudanese Church leaders.

The rest of the passengers joined the ship at Newport in South Wales. Barbara Rogers and Mary Chapman who had been with us for a year at the CMS Missionary Training College, and Ellsworth Balzer, an American missionary we nick-named 'Ebenezer', would all, like us, disembark at Port Sudan, the Dawsons and their two children who were returning to their tea plantation in Ceylon would travel on to Colombo, and Miss Sandles, for many years a missionary in Burma, was going all the way to Rangoon. There were other passengers too but not enough to fill all the cabins. Travel by a cargo vessel like ours, with no social programme, was not chosen so often now that air travel was quicker and becoming less expensive, though it was a decided advantage that on the Salween we could take mounds of baggage with us, and have time to rest and relax during the voyage. The ship's cargo was a mixed assortment - four large tankers for Sudan Railways secured on our deck, forty Land Rovers, enormous supplies of food for the military forces in Aden, tin plate and crates and barrels, as well as the baggage of the passengers. A model ship on the captain's map indicated our progress and every day we climbed to the bridge to inspect it. How far were we from England, how much nearer to Port Sudan?

We could take to this life alright, eating the traditional lavish meals served at sea, and lolling about on deck-chairs in bright sunshine when the weather was warmer, though we had to take shelter from the strong February winds. We read our books while Michael and Katherine played about nearby, safe on decks fitted with rails and wire mesh, and when they needed more attention we played hide-and-seek with them, all of us shrieking with laughter every time we discovered each other's hiding place around the ship's corridors and decks. Most of the time an empty sea was all we had to look at, but near the coast of Algiers there were glorious views of high mountains topped with snow and some days later a spectacular display of porpoises gliding in and out of the water as if they were escorting the ship. I embarrassed John by making a pact with the Captain that he would hoot his big horn for me whenever the porpoises appeared!

We joined in board games with the other passengers. Missionaries, we discovered, were highly skilled Scrabble players, especially 'Ebenezer' though John came a close second. We challenged Barbara and the Dawsons and others to energetic deck-quoits, watched by onlookers who rewarded us with cheers for the entertainment we provided, and jeers when a rope quoit sailed off into the sea.

We missionaries met to pray together and study the Acts of the Apostles while we sailed through the Mediterranean. This put us in mind of our predecessors, the earliest Christian missionaries, who had sailed these waters many centuries before us. Near Malta John, as ship's chaplain, conducted the Sunday service in the face of a fierce storm. As he struggled to keep his balance, and hold onto the Communion chalice, he lurched about watched by his concerned congregation, who themselves were saved from toppling by having their chairs tethered to the floor. St. Paul experienced a much worse storm also near Malta, as described in remarkable detail in Acts Chapter 27. With 276 on board, his frail vessel was shipwrecked after 14 days of strong winds. For us just 3 days of being tossed about on the raging sea was quite long enough. Even though we avoided looking through the portholes at the swinging horizon, John and I felt sick enough to lie down and groan but the children were not put out in the slightest. They escaped as often as they could along the narrow dark corridors, a great game for them when again and again they were returned to us by their Burmese sailor friends.

Quite abruptly overnight the sea calmed down. After ten days on board we were at Port Said, the tip of the African continent, nearer Sudan! All around us was the spectacular harbour, its main waterfront lined with a variety of buildings including a low eastern-looking Woolworths I would have loved to visit! The Salween was tied up to buoys in mid-stream, surrounded by other vessels and numerous small boats, and already the air was filled with the voices of eager salesmen. They were leaping from small boat to small boat to get nearer. "Goods for sale - leather and copper, dates and fresh fruit. Good price, good price," they yelled! We bought straw hats and, for the children, two toy camels made of leather with brightly coloured saddles and gear.

After breakfast the 'gully-gully' man gave his display in the lounge, marvellous tricks with chickens and coins. Michael and Katherine, completely mystified by the chickens, ran around trying to see where they were coming from. We were mystified too!

Port Said

This was all light-hearted and fun but a couple of Egyptian police with revolvers and a rifle reminded us that this place was the scene of war only two years before.

2 Through the Suez Canal

The Salween shunted around in the harbour and manoeuvred to be the first in a convoy of 12 vessels lined up to pass through the Suez canal. I liked being first and seeing the canal for myself, this amazing achievement which has had such immense political and commercial significance.

Directed by De Lesseps a Frenchman who became the president of the Suez Canal Company, and designed by two Italian engineers, the canal was constructed by a workforce of 10,000 Egyptians and 1,000 Europeans, mostly Italian. Just imagine all that digging with spades to make it the required 100 miles long, an average of 100 yards across and 50 feet deep! It was completed and opened in 1869. In a lesser form, a canal to join the Mediterranean Sea and the Red Sea - both seas share the same level - had first been a project as long as two thousand years before Christ, and was known to Darius, King of Persia, and to the Emperor Trajan! It had silted up and was finally closed by newly Muslim Egypt in AD 776. Flat muddy sand and a few palm trees were all we had around us now, and in the distance a railway and two roads on the western side carrying very little traffic. Work was going on at several places to widen the canal. There were swarms of Egyptians working by hand, carrying heavy stones on their shoulders, while side by side with them a single driver on his own controlled up-to-date American dredging and hauling equipment. Maintenance work too was continuously carried out to prevent the canal silting up. In places the work-force looked like distant busy ants, as endlessly they carried sand in baskets back up the steep canal banks while relentlessly it continued to slip back down to the water's edge.

Suez Canal

The sand was lighter and cleaner further south, and here and there we passed small villages each with its mosque. Where the canal was double, ships sailing in the opposite direction appeared to us to be sailing through the sand. When it was single and we met a convoy made up of 25 ships sailing north, about half of them tankers and the rest carrying cargo, we had to tie up for them to pass. After dinner, when the children were asleep in the cabin, John and I wandered out and stood on deck together, our arms wrapped around each other. With the twinkling lights of Ismailia in the distance on that dark balmy night, we were madly in love with each other and delighted to be on this exciting journey together. We were totally confident of God's place and work for us.

The Salween was well into the Gulf of Suez when the next day began, and had reached the Red Sea - which wasn't red at all. The coast of Egypt was to the west and to the east was the Sinai peninsula, edged with impressive mountains, which kept John well occupied in trying to identify Mount Sinai. In bright and warm sunshine, Michael sat beside us on a deck-chair wearing his big straw hat and looking out to sea while, like his parents, he held a book in his hands! Later we saw him playing with Katherine, both of them arranging loads for their camels, and moving them along one after the other just as they had seen real camel caravans pass in the distance. John still had a full head of hair and took the chance of being sheared by the ship's Indian barber; ever since then he has taken his chances with me instead. At dinner there was a stir in our group when John received a 'wireless' message from the Captain with greetings from the Rev. J. J. Armstrong, the Missions to Seamen chaplain at Port Sudan. He was an Irishman known to us and would be meeting us when we docked. We teased Barbara by telling her that it was a telegram from CMS Headquarters advising us to take special care of her relations with the attractive young ship's officers.

First glimpse of Sudan

We had been on board the Salween for 16 days when we had our first glimpse of Sudan, the distant land lit up by the sun sinking behind dim hills to the west. This would be our last night on board. Soon the Salween would sail on without us. Miss Sandles returning to her work in Burma could hardly wait to get to Rangoon, the Dawsons were eager to be back again in Ceylon and the Burmese crew were longing for home and their families. We would miss them all, even the stalwart purser who was known to us by his title and never by his name. He took his duties seriously and looked after his passengers even when he clearly disapproved of them. He was a bit fed up that so many of us had not made much use of the bar, and in particular he thought John and I were mad and irresponsible to be taking ourselves and two small children to a remote part of Southern Sudan. He pressed us to accept several cartons of tinned foods when we disembarked so that at least, he said, we wouldn't perish until we were well out of his sight. For Ellsworth Balzer the purser had much less compassion; he was the passenger who had dared to put a label 'Not wanted on the voyage' on the rolls of barbed wire he took as his personal luggage and it had been a frightful nuisance stored with the trunks in the passengers' baggage room. It would be good to see that assortment of unconventional luggage unloaded.

Next morning with a bright blue sky above us, a gentle wind blowing, and the air not yet too hot, the Salween docked. She was tied up to the quay in Port Sudan, where all around us was the flurry of activity our arrival had caused. Unloading began without delay - metal barrels, girders, crates and trunks, the tankers for Sudan railways, Ellsworth's barbed wire bales and assorted packages, items of our baggage. We were told that most of the dockers were Fuzzy-Wuzzies (men of the Hadendowa tribe of the Red Sea Hills), given this name because of their abundant long matted hair and splendid physique, but to us it implied a lack of respect which made us feel uncomfortable. From high up on the deck we had a great view of the quay. "Look," said John in astonishment, "there's the 'ark'." And right enough a large crate was moving along carried on the back of one man. While in Liverpool at my parents' vicarage, I had watched

John making this large wooden crate and packing it with his bicycle taken to bits, a tricycle for Michael, a doll's pram for Katherine, spares and tools and other essentials. Two teams of men, our Liverpool movers declared, were needed to lift it onto their lorry to take it to the docks for shipping. Now one strong man was carrying it on his own beneath the hot African sun.

Soon we were hailed by Jack Armstrong, the Missions to Seamen chaplain, who guided us through customs regulations, and then took us to the Mission house. This was a spectacular white building set beside the sparkling turquoise water of the Red Sea, with fine sand in front of it and palm trees rustling in the breeze. The Mission provided games facilities for visiting seamen who were given a welcome and friendship when their ships were in port, and a swimming pool, which we were disappointed to find closed for the winter in weather which was much hotter than any summers we had known in Ireland. There was also a beautiful chapel built of coral slabs where I sat as often as I could, quiet and peaceful with always the sound of the sea and the wind in the palm trees surrounding it. In Port Sudan too there was a parish church where services in English were attended by about 20 expatriates and 30 Southern Sudanese worshippers and that was where John preached for the first time in Africa.

We had three days at the Mission between our arrival and the departure of the next train for Khartoum, most of the time taken up with the formalities of our entry to the country and our payment of import duty on our luggage. The Sudanese Pound was roughly equivalent to the Pound Sterling at that time and there were 100 *piastres* to the pound. This was the currency we would use from now on and we made a start by paying £S14 on Import Duty! Our 24 pieces of baggage, our hand luggage and the twin pushchair had all to be checked, roped and redirected for the next stage of our journey.

Port Sudan is the only sea port for Sudan, the largest country in Africa. The port was constructed in 1904 to replace Suakin which, because of its coral reef, could not be enlarged sufficiently to take the ocean-going ships needed for modern import and export trading. Suakin was 40 miles further south and had been the port for more than 3,000 years, the port through which in earlier centuries slaves from the west and south of Sudan had been exported to Arabia. We were told that its beautiful Arab-style buildings with their dazzling white and pink coral walls were now abandoned and gradually being covered with sand. They had been built by rich merchants and Turkish officials in their years of prosperity when great wealth had come from trading in ivory and slaves, gum Arabic for use on stamps by the British Royal Mail, and ostrich feathers when these were the height of fashion. We knew that officially the slave trade had ended more than half a century ago, but it was certainly not forgotten.

We looked at Michael and Katherine playing in the bright sunshine on the white sandy shore, making roads for their camels and arranging fronds of palm trees to shade them. In contrast with many children in Sudan they were children of privilege and opportunity but I couldn't help wondering how life in Africa would affect them. I wondered too what part John and I would have in the story of the Christian Church in Sudan and what effect this would have on him and on me.

3   Looking Back from Port Sudan

You will be wondering by now how it was that I came to be sitting under a palm tree in Port Sudan and waiting for a train? It began early for me, the idea of a purpose and vocation in life. The core of it was largely set by the time I was seven years old. My father, the Rev. Dr. Ivan William Stuart Jones, a Methodist minister in Ireland, worked under a system whereby he was moved from one church and part of the country to another at intervals of two to four years. When later he became a Church of Ireland rector he didn't stop the pattern of moving he had grown accustomed to, though he liked it better that he was the one choosing where he went and how long he stayed. He served a further three Church of Ireland parishes and two in England before, aged 76, he and my mother retired to live in Craigavad in Northern Ireland; that was at the end of a long ministry during which both of them were greatly loved and appreciated. When I was seven I lived in the Methodist manse in Longford with my parents, Stuart a year older, Audrey a year younger, Kenneth the baby of the family, Bridie our maid, a dog and a cat or two. Reading, school, fun and games and the usual life of the family were set beside saying my prayers, going to church and Sunday-school and life in a church house where helping others in the community was the way we lived. But our interests went wider to far away places.

Three members of my mother's Ludlow family were missionaries in West Africa and we were always very interested in them. Their letters arrived with unusual Nigerian stamps, and sometimes Auntie Elsie stayed with us when she was on furlough as 'home leave' was then called. She was a nurse, and very good at describing her patients and her work as the Matron of a growing hospital at Ilesha, where she made sure she trained her Nigerian nurses to do everything absolutely correctly, just as she herself had been trained at the Adelaide Hospital in Dublin. We liked those stories, but better still were tales she made up for us; there was one about an ostrich looking down from his great height to read our letters to her over her shoulder, perhaps a story to encourage us to write to her more often. She worked at Ilesha for 32 years and towards the end of that time had the courage to travel to Sudan to spend Christmas with us the first year we were there. You will find more about that in a later chapter.

Uncle Nelson and Auntie Joyce used to stay with us too, both of them also missionaries in Nigeria. Uncle Nelson, ordained and a preacher and teacher, was often busy too with building churches and schools and being inventive in making and fixing things. He particularly liked it when he came across spare harmoniums and organs in Ireland and succeeded in persuading their owners to part with them; after each furlough he would return to Nigeria with a collection of these instruments which he then repaired for use in the Mission churches. I have an old letter which he wrote to his parents in Dublin in 1930 in which he describes how he used forest trees, pit sawn to make planks, to construct the complicated roof timbers and ventilation of a church with a span of thirty-six feet. He made a collection of slides to illustrate his work in Nigeria and showed these to his supporters in Ireland using a 'magic lantern.' On condition that we were quiet and went straight off to bed afterwards, we children were sometimes allowed to stay up for these slide shows. I remember brimming over with excitement in the darkened room and I smell again the carbide which produced the fierce light for the projection. Auntie Joyce was a doctor and surgeon, and Uncle Nelson made a mobile clinic for her, by adapting a truck which he fitted out with an operating table and space for drug supplies. We could picture it parked under a tree with Auntie Joyce operating and treating sick people in it while Uncle Nelson preached to the waiting patients, their relations and bystanders, and amazed them with his magic lantern slides of Bible stories. We were sad when we were told that many babies and small children became ill and died while they were still only tiny and glad to hear how Auntie Joyce did all she could to keep those babies alive. She was, in fact, involved in early attempts to reduce child mortality by starting up 'Under Five' clinics. Such clinics, now accepted worldwide, have reduced the grief and waste of infant mortality, but without effective contraception have also contributed to population growth out of step with food and other resources. I was particularly attracted to Auntie Joyce because of her warmth and professional confidence and the way she sparkled when she saw the funny side of things; I longed to be like her. Into their nineties these three retained their interest in all of us, and their concern for others.

Under a palm tree in Port Sudan

So perhaps it was not surprising that at seven I had my mind made up - I was going to be a missionary doctor like Auntie Joyce. I wanted to help other people and that seemed the best way to do it. I don't remember at that time any sense of awe or humility, just certainty, a certainty that God would make it possible. I didn't know how difficult it might be for my parents to finance a medical education in Ireland where there were no supporting grants, or if I would be able for it. I just knew what I had to do and at seven that was enough. Little did I know how different the work of a missionary would be by the time I set foot on African soil.

Years later I read Viktor Frankl's book 'Man's search for meaning' where he expounds his theory of Logotherapy, that is if a person has a 'why' for living he can put up with any 'how'. Frankl was a psychiatrist in Vienna, and as an Austrian Jew was hauled off to Auschwitz in the holocaust. A captive himself, he observed other men and women as they arrived and he tried to predict who would survive and who would not. He noted that those who had ideas of some future goal for themselves, as he himself had, coped better and more of them lived through their terrible experiences. After the war was over and he had emerged alive from Auschwitz, he applied this insight and approach within his psychiatric work and wrote and taught about it. A goal, a meaning in life, is very powerful. My vocation to be a missionary doctor was my goal, my meaning, and with that fixed the difficulties and challenges of achieving it didn't seem impossible at all. (Viktor Frankl's teaching was to serve me well in all of my professional life.)

The education of four children was a huge undertaking for my parents living on a clergyman's stipend in the country, far from any secondary schools. Compulsory free national schooling ended at 14 and after that if we were to have further education we had to go to boarding schools in Dublin and that cost money. The solution was that we took it in turns to be away at school, for there was never enough money for fees for all four of us at the same time. When we were at school, for me a total of three years secondary education at Alexandra School in Dublin ending with examinations at 16, we were hard working and probably easy students for our teachers. In contrast when we were at home we had a varied life. Studies with my father in History and Latin and Scripture were usually followed by quite open discussion, an unusual approach between a father and his children at that time. In helping us with English my mother was very keen on correct spelling and good hand-writing, but what I remember most is the way we laughed over funny parts in some classic novels, especially Mrs. Bennet and her efforts to get her daughters married in Jane Austen's *Pride and Prejudice.* I remember too the hours we spent playing board games with her, games which were fun but also developed skills in how to cope with winning and losing and how to make 'fair' allowances for our different ages. Somewhat isolated by living in country places, my mother did not forget her own former musical successes when she lived in Dublin. Singing, and sitting at the piano practising scales, were encouraged, for surely she was not wrong to hope that at least one of us might take after her with her Dublin *Feis* (Music Festival) awards in singing and in playing the organ! Indeed she wasn't wrong in her hopes with her two younger children, Audrey competent on the piano and Kenneth organ-builder with a world-wide reputation. Various clerical and teacher friends took us on for other subjects and some time too had to be found to fit in housework, gardening and baking cakes for Mothers' Union meetings.

We needed money and the rectory land needed attention so my father developed it as a small holding to help support us. A horse for farm work and pulling the trap was also fun to ride to French and music lessons, but what were we to do for proper riding clothes? Make them of course, as we made most of our clothes anyway. Nothing daunted, Audrey and I set about manufacturing jodhpurs in our bedroom (not the easiest of garments but that was before there were jeans) and then caught our mother with a smile on her face putting her notice on the door -

' D. & A. Jones, Expert Tailors. All garments undertaken.

Reasonable prices. Jodhpurs a speciality.'

The cow had to be milked and the chickens and rabbits fed, the hay made and clamps dug and lined with straw to store potatoes and root vegetables for the winter. The turkeys kept by my sister Audrey were sold at Christmas and she became the wealthy and generous one with her presents. Our County Monaghan rectory was built on a ridge and below it to the front was a lake with a small central island which provided us with endless opportunities for imaginative games. We rowed out to Pirate's Island, as we called it, to plant a black flag complete with skull and crossbones; we caught eels and pike and roach, and then fried them for dinner. We swam across the lake, and we assisted my elder brother Stuart, aged 14, with his ambitious project of building our own boat to improve on the flat-bottomed one we already had. That clinker-built boat with its expensive copper nails and rivets, our presents to each other at Christmas and birthdays, survived on other lakes and even on the sea for many years until finally it disintegrated on the shores of Yeats's *'Lake Isle of Innisfree'* in County Sligo.

Outside the family our social life revolved around the church, Sunday services and choir. My father set up table tennis (Ping Pong) and various groups so we could have competitions among ourselves and also exchange visits with similar clubs in other parishes; these were good fun and were a way of introducing young people to those from a bit further away, perhaps providing a wider choice for future marriages. In the summer we had Church garden fçtes to organise. And then there were the socials! It was almost impossible for us to refuse to go. The party games were often crude and both Audrey and I spent our time escaping from one unsuitable and sweaty swain after another.

When it was Audrey and Kenneth's turn to have the available school fees I left school at sixteen and did my best to study again at home, but there were times when I was in the depth of despair and crying myself to sleep at night. "How will I ever get to medical school?" I used to ask my mother. Though she hadn't a clue about how it would happen, she was a great encourager and a great believer in the power of prayer; she would hug me and assure me that with God all things are possible. The next move looked as if it was in the right direction. An advertisement in the Church of Ireland Gazette stated that a girls' boarding school in Dublin required a house-mistress and teacher for its junior section and would pay the travel expenses for applicants attending for interview. A free trip by train to the Capital excited me and my interview was only, it seemed, to reassure the Headmistress that I could look adult enough beside some of the senior girls who were a year older than I was. I took up the post and no doubt those senior girls have been better off for the rest of their lives as a result of the diligent house-mistress who supervised their table manners! I too was very much better off. Not only did I have a small salary and acquire some teaching experience but a year on the staff of that school brought me nearer my medical school goal.

Perhaps these unusual childhood experiences made us confident we could face anything, for in time all four of us were to graduate from Trinity College, Dublin, and work in Africa. Stuart spent some years in the Colonial Service in Nigeria where, with his camping equipment and baggage carried in head-loads by a line of porters, he went on trek to remote places to administer justice in village disputes. Sometimes as an engineer he was seconded for work in designing bridges. Kenneth, also an engineer, was recruited for work with Nigerian Railways and, like his Uncle Nelson Ludlow before him, gave any spare time he had to the musical needs of West Africa where he made a start on his organ-builder career. Audrey and I organised our lives in remarkably similar ways. Both of us met our husbands while all of us were students in Trinity. I married John Lowe, she a teacher married Raymond Smith. When our two men were curates we gained experience in the churches in Belfast and then were together in CMS missionary training in Kent. After that our ways parted, the Smiths going to St. Paul's Theological College in Kenya and the Lowes to Sudan, yet all of us engaged in training African clergy.

In 1948 I was 17. It was time to press on with my plans. I wrote to the Dublin Secretary of the Church Missionary Society for an application form and, after I had struggled to fill that in, I was called for an interview. In a big formal boardroom, lined with beautiful old bookcases and with portraits of eminent missionary forebears on the walls, I faced the members of the Committee sitting all around a very large mahogany table at 35, Molesworth Street, Dublin. I could feel the serious atmosphere in that sombre room and knew the matter to be decided would have its effect on the rest of my life. These kindly and responsible committee members recognised my vocation alright, but they also recognised my limited finances and were realistic when they suggested I do a free nursing training rather than an expensive medical course. (There were no State university grants at that time.) Reluctantly I agreed but I had the nerve to say I believed that for me it would always be second best. My certainty of my missionary doctor vocation was as strong as ever. The Committee asked me to wait in the front office while they took time to confer among themselves. When I returned they offered me £50 annually provided I started my medical course at the beginning of the next academic year. (That £50 was a significant sum: full board and lodging in a Dublin student hostel cost just under £2 a week at that time.)

My State Intermediate examination results were sufficient for me to be granted Matriculation and entrance to Trinity College, University of Dublin, a place in the medical school was available, and in September 1949 I arrived in great excitement and trepidation to take up my course. It was hard work for me with such a scant background in school sciences, but my chemistry lab partner, an English girl with a science degree, often rescued me. Somehow I passed my vivas and exams, mainly I think by being calm after doing all the work I could. Perhaps the remarks of an earlier primary-school teacher were still true. "You have a very good shop window," he used to say, "but your stores are rather empty." To help with the finances, the Dean of the Medical School (Professor David Torrens who was a supporter of the Christian Union) gave me a small income in return for demonstrating physiology experiments to the years below me, and I had a variety of holiday jobs working as a waitress, in a tax office, in child care and housework, all useful experiences which helped me to understand the life and work of others and perhaps especially of my patients.

Of the societies in College for me the most important and interesting was the Christian Union with its busy programme of Christian and social activities. Through it I met many lifelong friends, several of them later married to each other. Early in my third year in College there was to be a University Mission with Bishop Stephen Neill as the special speaker. One evening I went to a committee meeting called to make the arrangements, and so did a Classics Scholar John Lowe who cannot have been concentrating on the business in hand for, he says, he fell in love with me on first sight! He was quite sure he wanted to marry me and that by going abroad together we could each follow our missionary vocations. My missionary vocation had been central to my life so far, thoughts of a husband had not. What was I to do about this wonderful man's proposal? Keep him waiting for a bit while I worked it all out and then delight in the passionate love we have had for each other ever since. He was a shy and kindly person and, of course, tall dark and handsome! I often saw him striding around College in his Scholar's full-sleeved gown and, when I cycled across the cobbled squares, we sometimes passed each other at speed in our rush to get to a lecture on time. The four years of our engagement, which we thought of as a thousand days and nights, were very, very long but at last the great day came when we married each other in August 1956 at Nohoval Parish Church in Co. Cork. With our families and friends present (including 17 clergy and the bishop!) my father and John's father solemnized the best decision and the most important promises we have ever made. By then John was a curate at St. Mary Magdalene Church in Belfast and I had completed my resident Junior Doctor year at the Lagan Valley Hospital in Lisburn.

Many years later Bishop Stephen Neill stayed with us in Uganda in Holy Week and we reminded him of the planned Mission to Dublin University when we were students there. Although he had been ill and unable to be the Missioner we told him that was how John aged twenty one and I aged twenty had met. "I am relieved," he said, "that it doesn't seem to have done you any harm!"

Medical housejobs, John's ordination and curacy, our marriage, the birth of our twin babies and a year of CMS missionary training in Kent were steps on our way to Africa. No wonder as we set off we were so enthusiastic. We were young and we were confident that we had made the right decision. Others could be apprehensive and afraid for us but we weren't hesitant in the least.

4 Rattling on the Train to Khartoum

It was time to leave the turquoise sea and the palm trees. We kept close together to make a way for ourselves through the surging crowd of noisy people and their mountains of baggage at the station in Port Sudan, and found a compartment with our names on the label stuck to the door. This train would take two days and a night to travel the 600 miles to Khartoum. Specially adapted for the journey, its windows had mosquito wire screens, glass and shutters for the coldness of the desert at night, and blinds for the scorching sun at midday. Our compartment was well designed and had a wash basin and upper and lower bunks which at night were made into beds by the attendant. With only a bag of toys and story books, John and I did our best to keep Michael and Katherine happy in the limited space, and were relieved when meal times came and we could carry them along the corridors of the swaying train to join our fellow travellers in the dining car. It was all really rather luxurious, like being on the Orient Express! The tables were set with the crested crockery and polished silver cutlery of Sudan Railways and Steamers; the food was delicious and all the better for being served by tall men in long maroon robes with matching fezzes and woven cummerbunds. They spoke only a little English but were friendly and eager to talk, and to joke and play with Michael and Katherine who showed them their toy camels and greeted them with *Salaams* and their best attempts at *shukran*, thank you.

The first day we could look back when the train was rounding a curve, and see the coastline receding further until it was a distant haze far behind; meanwhile the train was straining on its long climb to the summit in the Red Sea Hills where the second engine was left behind. By then the air was cooler and all around us the sky was lit up in a glorious sunset, reds and pinks, then pale yellow and grey and it was night. It was really happening, we were on our way to the interior of the great African continent.

Station in the Red Sea hills

Next day we passed small railway stations, each with a circle of round houses with white cone-shaped roofs of painted metal, and at some of them we stopped to take on coal and water for our steam engine. At several of them a white-washed mosque with its minaret looked dramatic against the blue of mountains behind, and once we saw a group of white robed men prostrated in prayer as they faced in the direction of Mecca. We were travelling First Class and were very conscious of our comfort in comparison with those travelling on the same train Second, Third, and Fourth Class. An old concession dating back to the years of the Anglo-Egyptian Condominium, which allowed missionaries to travel at 'Quarter Fare' by Sudan Railways and Steamers, had never been discontinued so for our travel we were only charged a quarter of the actual rate. We had the restaurant car and facilities while others bought what food they could at the stations as we passed. As soon as the train stopped hordes of children and adults, shouting in Arabic, came running along with bread and eggs and fruit for sale, appearing even where there was very little sign of habitation and the sandy soil made me wonder how anything was grown in it. Passengers also got out for toilet purposes and then had to run and jump on if the train started suddenly.

We travelled due west from Port Sudan until we reached Atbara on the Nile where, with all the noise and bustle of an important railway junction and sidings, we had a fairly long stop. Over three hundred miles due north from here across the sand was Egypt while for us the direction was two hundred miles south to Khartoum. We delighted to see glimpses of the great river Nile at last and to observe some of the ways its waters were used to irrigate the land. Once I noticed a young boy sitting on the drive shaft as he drove a pair of blindfolded oxen round and round in a circle, turning a large *saqiya* water-wheel geared to another wooden wheel with vessels attached to it. These dipped into the river, filled, and as the wheel turned were spilled into the small irrigation channels which took the water to the growing crops, just as it had been done since the days of the Pharaohs. The land was a brilliant green in the fertile and irrigated areas on the banks of the river, while not far off it was mostly arid desert. Small groups of rather thin and scrawny camels and goats nibbled on the scrub and thorn of the desert, the colour of their hides an almost perfect camouflage. I was amazed they were able to survive, and even more amazed when I read that cattle could survive for a time in the desert on a diet of cut up water-melons alone.

During the journey a minor disaster happened to our American friend 'Ebenezer', for at a sudden jerk of the train his wooden Scrabble letters were jolted off the rack and out of his open window. John and I had to laugh when we imagined what a puzzle these would be to the nomadic tribesmen who were likely to pick them up! Poor Ebenezer would continue his journey to his remote mission house with his barbed wire to protect his garden vegetables and with a Scrabble board but no letters. We never heard of him again.

We arrived in Khartoum in the late afternoon. The open-air station was hot and dusty and full of people, all shouting out on meeting others or just seeing what was going on. Expatriates and some Sudanese officials and men from the South wore khaki bush shirts and shorts, but most other men were dressed in the traditional long white robe called a *jallabiyah* and wore bulky well arranged turbans. Muslim women were enveloped in white or black cloth, and only their eyes were visible through their heavy veils, while alongside them Southern Sudanese, expatriate, and Coptic women wore bright cotton dresses and sandals. We didn't have long to wait before a friendly man in a white shirt and shorts rushed up to us; he was Ken McDouall who had been a teacher in the Nuba Mountains and now was the CMS Mission Secretary in Omdurman. He was full of enthusiasm as he welcomed Mary and Barbara and us. He had a car and the hospital ambulance with its driver ready to take us and our luggage to Omdurman, and soon we were all packed in. We drove through the wide impressive streets of Khartoum, with their shady trees and fountains and large Government buildings set well back. Michael was delighted to see so much traffic, trucks and taxis with some buses and bicycles, and Katherine kept pointing at the donkeys. It looked to me as if the men riding them were much too big, and certainly the panniers were far too heavily loaded for the meek little animals but, like the taxis and trucks, they wove their way from side to side and all of us somehow crossed on the bridge over the White Nile at a point just upriver from where it is joined by the Blue Nile. This bridge, constructed in 1927 with enormous steel girders and a long span, is the vital link between Khartoum the administrative centre and modern capital on one side of the Nile, and Omdurman with its flat-roofed mud-block houses and narrow roads all over a wide area on the other. We had left behind us the regular streets of Khartoum, laid out in the pattern of a giant Union Jack, and were now in a very different city. The residential areas were made up of miles and miles of high boundary walls built of mud, with sheet-iron gates protecting small courtyards and the houses behind, and sometimes we could see a shady *neem* tree kept alive by regular watering. There were some large buildings too, mostly mosques, and the high dome of the tomb of the Mahdi.

Dr. May Bertram's house beside the CMS Hospital in Omdurman was available for us as she was in England on leave, and for Barbara and Mary there was a welcome in the house of some other missionaries. May's single storey house, like most others, had concrete outside stairs leading up to the flat roof where in the hottest months of the year she had her bed and slept out under the stars. These unprotected stairs were like a magnet to Michael and Katherine who took themselves off to climb to the roof whenever they could escape. Indoors they investigated May's attractive collection of books and ornaments, a problem we solved by turning the bookcases around so that they faced the wall while we were there.

With ten days to wait until the departure of the next train south to Kosti, we had time for some exploring in Khartoum and Omdurman.

Silver filigree spoons

Joan and Ken McDouall, whose house was near May's, provided us with a lot of information and encouragement as well as all the splendid meals we ate as their guests. In those waiting days we walked around in the huge market, the *souk*, in Omdurman, and in special streets we watched gold, silver, ivory and leather craftsmen as they worked and sold their goods. We couldn't resist buying some attractive silver spoons with elaborate filigree work in the handles, crafted, we were told, out of high quality silver Maria Theresa dollars originally from Ethiopia. We still enjoy using them.

A letter written to my parents at the time gives some detail but is at the same time an example of how we had to keep to 'safe' material and avoid anything which had a political or critical flavour; in this country expatriates were suspect and letters in both directions were subjected to censorship:

> "We are still in Omdurman and enjoying seeing something of the Capital of the country. We set off for Kosti tomorrow by train - at 5.30 p.m. - and travel overnight. We then embark on the Nile steamer on Wednesday (11th March) and should reach Juba in between a week and a fortnight from then - so our journey is not yet over!
>
> "It is getting hotter each day here - this is 'Spring' - 96° F. today but this is regarded as not hot by the locals, including missionaries! We find it is not cold! but as we can stay indoors in the afternoon, it isn't unbearable. Michael and Katherine manage quite well, though they are always going to the 'Kig' for drinks of water.
>
> "There is a small garden in front of the house with quite a few flowers. It is flooded with water every second day early in the morning - there are irrigation channels which take all our waste water - bathroom and sink - to the parched ground, and taps also feed these channels which go to each tree and shrub and the small lawn. Everywhere else is just dry sand - reddish and blown into everything. The water is paid for by the amount used, as shown on a meter.
>
> "On Sunday I went to Holy Communion in Khartoum Cathedral at 7.15 a.m. - in English. John went to the only Morning Prayer service in the Cathedral in Arabic at 10.30 a.m. In the evening he went to the church in Omdurman to another service in Arabic while I put Michael and Katherine to bed. There is a Sudanese Pastor in charge - Pastor Philip Abbas - who was trained at

Mundri. He is very nice with a mastery of English, Arabic and several other languages. He has a little son 10 months old - he came with the baby to meet me this morning.

"So far we have eaten food not unlike English food - the bread is darker and the butter quite different but otherwise no new tastes except millet porridge which tastes rather like our wheaten porridge.

"Yesterday we found the twins up on the roof of the house! They thought it was great fun - but we couldn't agree as the roof has no walls, though it is quite flat of course. What a lot we thank God for in the safety and health we have all enjoyed.

"Did you ever put a camel to bed? Katherine and Michael are experts! They now say much more and string three or four words together without any verbs but otherwise a sentence. They both count to 'two' and Katherine to 'twee.' Michael knows his book off by heart - says what is on the next page before it is turned."

In Dr. Bertram's nice hospital house we were comfortable enough although we found the heat hard to bear. We even had a night-watchman to keep an eye on us, though, to our surprise, we saw he was equipped with his bed beside the closed gate so he was mostly not keeping an eye on our security but sleeping and snoring quite undisturbed. But not far away at the back of the Hospital was the *Hoosh*, an area set aside for people suffering from and disfigured by leprosy, mixed up with groups of elderly homeless and derelict men and women dressed in tattered rags; all were living in awful conditions. *Kisra*, the flat pancake made of millet and folded into quarters ready to dip in an enamel bowl of thin stew, was cooked for them in smoke, dirt, and heat with the irritation of persistent flies. It was terrible to see them as they sat around, scrappy bandages covering their moist sores, finding whatever shade they could, one day as miserable as the one before and the one to come. However, it was difficult to see what could be done, for the official line was that there was no leprosy in Sudan and so no need for money for these people's support. The little that was provided by the Mission was all they had. I began to realise that denying the existence of a problem, here as elsewhere, was one way of having to do nothing about it. *Maaleish*, never mind, was a handy comment.

I was itching to get on with doing something to help suffering people after all the years I had been preparing, and desperate to get a permit to work as a doctor. I couldn't bear to think that this might not be granted. One morning I set out with Dr. Trub, a Swiss Mission doctor working in Omdurman, to see Dr. Zaki, the Sudanese Director of Medical Services, in his office in Khartoum. This was 'just to meet him' but I had high hopes that I would come away complete with a medical licence. Dr. Zaki, in his high-ceilinged office with the overhead fan whirring, was very pleasant and I began my cautious negotiations by just asking about my position regarding medical treatment for other missionaries. "But of course," he said, "that would be very good, but you will understand that a licence will be necessary first and for that you will need to apply through the Provincial Director." The journey up and down the line of officials, none apparently being in a position to give a firm answer, had begun. In this newly independent country, despite the real situation, the official statement was that there were already plenty of Sudanese doctors and no need for expatriate doctors like me. Besides which there was less enthusiasm in the North for providing medical services in the South of the country where we were to be living. In fact in the years we lived in Mundri our nearest doctor was in Juba, a lorry journey of 180 miles of difficult road from us. The officials were affable and polite but I couldn't help hearing the dreaded phrases *lissa* meaning later, *bukra* meaning tomorrow or later still, and worst of all *insha'allah* if God wills rather suggesting that He wouldn't.

How would I be able to bear it if I never got a licence, if I couldn't be a missionary doctor in Sudan after all? It would be less than a year later that I faced the pain of just this when two-year-old Lusi died.

5   The Tomb of the Mahdi in Omdurman

On our way from the Railway Station we had seen the Tomb of the Mahdi in the distance. Since it wasn't far from where we were staying in Omdurman, John and I put the children in their pushchair one day and set off to have a closer look. There it was, bulky and prominent, with its 80 foot dome visible from miles away across the flatness of the desert. It was a reminder of past times.

The Ottoman (Turkish) Empire had originated in the thirteenth century following the invasions of the Mongols from further east and, with its centre in Constantinople (Istanbul), had grown in size and power until most of the countries surrounding the Black Sea and the Mediterranean came under Ottoman rule. These countries included Egypt and Sudan. By the mid nineteenth century Egypt under its powerful ruler, Mohammed Ali, became virtually independent of the Ottoman Empire and consequently Sudan came under direct rule from Cairo instead of Constantinople. Egyptian rule in Sudan was harsh, oppressive and corrupt. The Khedive in Cairo required the officials he had appointed and employed in outposts in Sudan to exact taxes and ivory by any method they devised so long as they forwarded these to him with a continuous supply of slaves. In time the extravagances and poor government of Mohammed Ali's successor plunged him into enormous debts in Europe, debts which he couldn't meet even by selling off his shares in the Suez Canal to Britain. A powerful anti-slavery movement in England, backed up by the countries in Europe to which the Khedive was in debt, required him to end slavery. This pressure was a real dilemma for the Khedive. His army depended utterly on a force of slaves from Sudan as its soldiers, so he must have hated to have to concur. But concur he did by appointing an Englishman, Charles

Gordon, to enforce the decree to end slavery and set up a reasonable government in the far south. Gordon was Governor of Sudan from 1874 to 1879. After his departure further turmoil erupted. By 1881 the oppression and suffering of the people had become too much for a Sudanese religious leader, Mohammed Ahmed: he believed he had a divine call as the Mahdi, the one set apart to promote Islam and rid the Sudan of Egyptian rule. Convinced of his special calling to lead a *jihad*, a Holy War, the Mahdi gathered a multitude of followers and rampaged throughout the country, waging fierce and bloody battles to destroy and end all foreign rule and presence in his country. But rather than liberation, the Mahdi's rule meant even greater harshness and suffering for the Sudanese people. The British, in control of Egypt since winning the battle of Tel-el-Kebir in defence of the Suez Canal in 1882, decided sorting out the Sudan situation was hopeless and much the best thing to do was to abandon the country to the Mahdi and so avoid further involvement and expense. Even to do this was an exacting project and it seemed that Charles Gordon was the only man for the job. He was persuaded to return to Khartoum in 1884 to undertake the task of evacuation and withdrawal, which included extricating 30,000 Egyptian soldiers from remote Sudan garrisons as well as various Europeans engaged in trade and diplomacy. Only a month after Gordon's arrival, Khartoum and Omdurman were surrounded by the forces of the Mahdi. A terrible siege lasted ten months and ended with General Gordon's death at the hands of the dervishes in 1885. In the years of the rule of the Mahdi and his successor the Khalifa, out of the 30,000 Egyptian soldiers in those Sudan garrisons only 1,000 managed to escape and return to Egypt; foreigners were killed or imprisoned; there was widespread destruction and cruelty with slave markets, beheadings, and starvation, and the population went down from nine million to just over two million. All this and the breakdown of any form of peaceful government outraged and horrified Victorian England. Besides which there was a wish for revenge for the death of General Gordon. In response to public outcry, an army of Anglo-Egyptian forces led by Sir Herbert Kitchener made their difficult way to Sudan where they defeated the Mahdists at the Battle of Omdurman in 1898, twelve years after Gordon's death. And that victory of Anglo-Egyptian forces was how Sudan came to be governed by an Anglo-Egyptian Condominium until Independence in 1956, just three years before John and I and our children found ourselves standing in the dust and sand beside the Mahdi's tomb in Omdurman.

But we didn't only stand in the dust, we learned a little of the places and people where we were. The 'Three Towns,' as they are called, Khartoum the capital, Omdurman the older traditional city, and Khartoum North the industrial area, are all built where the White and Blue Nile join. Living in the Three Towns were separate groups of inhabitants. The majority, Muslim, Arab by birth, light skinned and fine boned, proud intelligent people with an advanced civilization and a long history, identified more with the Middle East than with Africa. Another large group was dark skinned and African, mainly from the south of the country but living in the capital because of work or education, many of them Christian and the rest following African traditional beliefs. There were some also of part Arab and part African descent, their forebears probably brought to the North as slaves even in recent years. Added to these were the light skinned Christian Copts, originally from Egypt, who were well educated and trusted to take charge of financial matters by both businesses and the Muslim Government, and an assortment of more than a thousand expatriates who formed a considerable commercial and professional community.

This was our first experience of a mainly Muslim city dominated by mosques not churches, and where the voice of the Muezzin rang out calling the faithful to prayer. People in the streets stopped whatever they were doing and unrolled their prayer mats, washed, and prostrated themselves facing in the direction of Mecca. This was impressive, all those men in their long white *jallabiyas* and turbans attending to their prayers. So was the beauty of the architecture and art of Islam. Not so easy to take were the high walls and gates behind which the women were kept in seclusion and where the male head of the household was all powerful. When out on the streets, many of the women were so shrouded in clothing that only their eyes were visible through their coverings. I looked into those eyes - the mirror of the soul - and tried to imagine the life within. I saw some younger women whose eyes were decorated and outlined with kohl, their hands painted intricately with designs in henna, the outward sign of recent marriage. Older women too, bulky in their dark *tobes*, looked weary and sad as they shuffled along, while others with small grandchildren in tow were patient and very proud. In time I hoped I would know more and be a privileged guest of some home where a foreign woman visitor could be admitted. In the meantime I just went on wondering at their view of the world and how they coped with such heat and restricted liberty.

We found it significant and surprising that a central position had been granted for the Unity Christian Church, later known as the Church of the Saviour, near the Tomb of the Mahdi in the great Muslim city of Omdurman. This Church was built in 1949 by CMS and the American Presbyterian Mission, both in Sudan since 1900. Clubs had been in existence since 1942 to provide teaching and support for the Christian community made up of Southerners and people from the Nuba Mountains who had come to the North, and there were hostels too for men and for women. A literature and teaching centre, built around an open courtyard, had black-painted plaster blackboards on all four inner walls in full view of those being taught, and there were two houses for pastors, one of them occupied by Pastor Philip Abbas and his family whom we had already met. The Church building was used on Sunday mornings by the Presbyterian Mission, its Egyptian minister looking after a congregation of Egyptian origin whose background was the ancient Coptic Church. They spoke correct Arabic and were well settled in Sudan and prosperous. At the evening service Pastor Philip, an ordained priest of the Episcopal (Anglican) Church, used a simple Arabic service based on the Book of Common Prayer. This liturgy already familiar in many Southern languages made it easier for a very mixed Southern congregation to join together in worship. The two congregations were almost total strangers to each other. Although they were all Christians there were enormous racial, social and cultural differences between them, differences not yet bridged. I was struck by the open joy and exuberance of the large congregations at the services led by Pastor Philip and how they seemed to know each other and to help each other. The joy and caring among these Christians, though many were poor and in menial jobs, and their sense of community delighted John and me and made us happy that we were to have a part in training leaders to help in the growth of the Kingdom of God in Sudan.

6 The Next Train to Kosti

We didn't travel light. In addition to the crate made by John and called the ark, we had 23 items of baggage, a twin pushchair and hand luggage. We were setting off to live in a remote corner of Sudan and we had to take what we were advised we would need. During the final months of preparation we were given long lists of essential items, some of which like cummerbunds for evening wear for John we went without. We visited an export firm, Allinsons, in London and selected goods which were packed and forwarded direct to our ship, free of tax. A grain mill, a Tilley pressure lamp, an oil stove with two burners and a cube-shaped oven, all flat packed and a challenge to assemble when we reached our destination. Supplies of soap and candles and toilet rolls, toothpaste and talcum powder, cutlery and melamine cups and bowls, saucepans, plastic jugs and beakers, kitchen implements, as well as most of our wedding presents. Books and bedding, estimated sizes of sandals for Michael and Katherine's growing feet and enough sandals for John and me until we could shop again. Clothes were easier for I had my sewing machine and lots of cotton materials to sew. Then there were the toys for the children for the coming birthdays and Christmas presents, a doll's pram, a tricycle, books and art materials, games. Aware of the health risks, we also had various medicines and some medical equipment though, even while we were packing, there was doubt about whether or not I would get a licence to practise at this sensitive early stage of the country's independence.

Our baggage was an odd assortment. A big new tin trunk we had bought and 3 others given to us by retired missionaries and battered from previous journeys to foreign parts, one of Uncle Gilbert Lowe's formal uniform trunks complete with his number and rank as a World War II Army Chaplain, wooden crates from the export firm, and 3 forty gallon (200 litre) metal oil barrels, two black and one blue. The barrel lids were held in place by rings like meat paste jars and could be padlocked for security. An enterprising company had had a good idea in this recycling, for the barrels kept the contents dry and insects and raiders out and they could be moved easily by being rolled along the ground. Later they were very useful for collecting rain water.

All this baggage, its contents listed in detail, had been loaded at Birkenhead. At Port Sudan it took all morning and half the afternoon to have it checked and assessed for import duty. In Khartoum after a whole morning of negotiation John only got agreement for eight of our twenty three pieces to go with us by rail and steamer to Juba. It would be several months before the rest would catch up with us, and in the meantime it would be a headache for our CMS friends in Omdurman to see to it.

On the afternoon of Tuesday 10th March 1959 we boarded the overnight train which was to take us 200 miles south from Khartoum to Kosti with our permitted eight pieces of baggage. We passed through a great expanse of cultivated land where cotton, sugar cane and food crops grew on a highly fertile plain between the Blue and White Nile, an area known as the Gezira. Following someone's bright idea to build the Sennar dam on the Blue Nile in 1925 this land was irrigated by the converging waters to become a wonderful place for growing food in a semi-desert land where previously cultivation was only possible on the margins of the rivers. I was delighted to see this great development before the end of the daylight, and before the night we spent rattling along in the darkness, sleeping and waking and sleeping again.

By morning we had reached the port of Kosti. We could see steamers tied up by the banks of the White Nile which was calm and silky and more than a mile wide at this point; even more attractive were traditional feluccas sailing gently along, their brown sails filled in the light breeze. There was noise too, in languages we could not understand, as determined passengers jostled each other to board the paddle steamer bound for Juba and places on the way. These passengers also had their luggage, charcoal stoves, sacks of grain, a live goat or two, baskets with protesting chickens, basins for washing. There were excited children and anxious mothers everywhere and serious looking men seeing to the wellbeing of their families. The steamer was rather like a floating village made up of nine barges. At the back was the steamer itself with two large paddle wheels to its rear and an engine which ran on diesel, the helmsman's steering wheel and quarters to the front of it.

On the steamer, Kosti

Tied to its left was the First Class passenger barge made up of dining and sitting areas and the kitchen at water level, the cabins above and on the top a railed promenade deck. This was rather like a large aviary with wire mesh to keep the mosquitoes and flying insects out, especially at night. Its height above the water allowed a wide view of the river and all the activities going on around us, and sometimes it was a good place to find some cooler air after the sun had set.

Tied to the right of the steamer was a similar Second Class passenger barge. Leashed ahead of these three were six further barges, three for Third and Fourth Class passengers who marked out areas of the iron plated deck for themselves, set up their encampments, tied up their animals, and prepared to pass the next week or two afloat with very little shade; ahead of them were the three barges for cargo.

We were on the First Class barge travelling, as on the train, at the missionaries' Quarter Fare rate which made us feel uncomfortable again when we viewed the families on the barges in front sitting around in the heat, cooking on their charcoal stoves and fending for themselves.

Our cabin had two narrow berths and a wash-basin, with a mesh door out to the railed deck along the length of the boat. It was very cramped and uncomfortable. We chose to give the children an end each of one berth, and I had the other while John was provided with some extra bedding and slept on the steel floor. As he 'cooked' in the heat from the kitchen below us, his pale blue pyjamas turned navy blue with sweat. The same heat that 'cooked' John also cooked the food which we could smell at all hours of the day while special meals were prepared for the First Class passengers, even the ones like us who ate at 'Quarter Fare.' It was a great pity that meal times seemed to come round so frequently, long before we were hungry enough to enjoy vegetables, eggs, roast meat, fish, sweet potatoes, and puddings, especially the crème caramel, for it would be a year before we next had the chance of such a menu. We felt exhausted by the heat and, without any possibility of exercise, our appetites failed to the point where we had to take it in turn to miss one or two meals altogether. To miss more would have been unfair to the staff looking after us.

Among the First and Second Class passengers there were about fifteen Southern Sudanese teachers returning from a Headmasters Conference in Khartoum, and a number of Northern Sudanese business men and teachers, some with their quiet submissive-looking wives swathed in long white clothes and head coverings. I wondered again about what they were thinking as each day took them further away from their families and familiar places and into the unknown. It never looked as if they had any choice in what happened to them. The teachers sat around on the deck all day, talking and laughing together and wearing striped pyjamas, considered the height of fashion. They were friendly and ready to talk to us too, in fluent English, and answer some of our questions about their country. We shared books and we laughed with them over board games some hot evenings.

While the boat took us southwards by night and by day at about eight miles an hour, John and I kept an eye on the children and managed to read without being too disturbed by the chug of the engine. The river was very wide and glassy at this point, the land still pleasantly green and wooded. There were monkeys chattering in the trees, and the brief stops at riverside villages or to sort out problems on the boat were welcome diversions. On these stops the front barges were steered to the bank and one of the crew jumped off and tied a cable to a nearby tree. The bell clanged, the engine spluttered as it was turned off, and the paddlewheels, still dripping water, stopped churning. A gangplank was pushed over the side to the bank and passengers rushed with their baggage to get ashore while other passengers jostled and shouted to come on board. The arrival of the boat was a great event and the villages were full of people, everyone wanting to have the latest news and observe who came and who went. Sometimes maintenance work had to be done such as the day one of our front barges full of sacks of grain took on water; while repairs were carried out the crew received a lot of shouted advice from interested onlookers, none of whom seemed particularly knowledgeable! One evening just before dark we were entertained by a large herd of hippopotami. Almost submerged, their eyes at water level, with a mighty heave they would suddenly lift their huge heads, open their jaws wide and yawn before going under again. Some had old or healing scars from fights and could advance and retreat at surprising speeds. We were told hippos leave the water after dark to graze on the nearby land but we didn't see that. What we did see was how they lazed about in the water all day in family groups of twenty or thirty. Michael and Katherine laughed at their antics and tried to imitate them.

We were perhaps unfortunate that our journey on the Nile coincided with Ramadan, the annual month of fasting observed throughout the Muslim world. Each morning, for those observing Ramadan, a small breakfast was allowed before dawn and after that no food or drink was taken until the evening meal after dark. Nothing, not even saliva, was swallowed so we found it quite unpleasant to see and hear so much spitting going on around us all day. At the same time we felt very sorry for our Muslim fellow travellers, especially the working crew, who had to endure the heat and dreadful thirst and remain cheerful, and we were glad when we saw them sleeping whenever they had the chance. They waited all day for the evening when the 'steamer village' was filled with noise and the enjoyment of eating.

While we felt terribly thirsty all the time, we couldn't help but see that our water supply was hauled up in buckets from the Nile, habitat of the hippos and others. It was then poured into large earthenware pots called *zeers* for filtering and presented as ready for drinking. Despite our thirst, we knew we had to be very careful never to drink any of this unboiled water with our meals. A large Thermos flask was provided in our cabin which we used for treating water with Halogen tablets to make it safe for drinking. Sometimes we failed to keep pace but even when desperate with thirst we had to wait for the hour required for the Halogen tablets to work. In that terrible heat we drank over sixteen pints a day. Occasionally we could buy bottled mineral water but the children didn't like the fizz and in any case it was hard to be confident that it was as safe as our Halogen-treated water. Our precautions were worthwhile for we all stayed well.

Our journey south progressed, slowly and peacefully. Villages of round thatched houses passed by with all the signs of domestic living. Children played by the water side, women washed clothes, and men unclothed walked about carrying long spears, their heads held high. We saw an occasional crocodile in the less populated stretches of the river, another creature Michael and Katherine would have had a chance to imitate if only they had had more teeth. The flotilla of barges made four days good progress up river from Kosti to Malakal further south where we had a five hour stop, enough time for us to visit the American Presbyterian Mission there.

I'm glad I didn't know at the time that the stretch of the Nile we had just passed through was the scene of earlier tragedy. In March 1921 David Oyler, an American Presbyterian missionary in Sudan since 1909, and his family were travelling down the Nile to go on leave when their four-month-old baby died. They buried her at Renk, one of the small places we had seen from our boat. The following year, returning from America to their mission station in Sudan with their two young boys, they visited the grave at Renk. Next morning they were back on the steamer when five year old John became very sick. He died before the steamer could reach the small mission hospital at Melut, north of Malakal. No roads, no air transport, it makes me weep to picture the agonizingly slow progress of the steamer and then the quiet still body of that dead child. I wonder how the Oylers stayed on after such sorrow, continuing their evangelistic ministry and translation for five more years until 1927.

7   Through the Sudd by Paddle Steamer

At Malakal the Nile is joined by the Sobat, a large tributary draining the land south and east towards Ethiopia, a natural place for a river port. Crowds of people had gathered to watch the drama of the arrival of the steamer and John had to weave his way through when he set off to look for the American Mission half a mile away. He soon returned with two of the missionaries who welcomed us, packed us into their car and took us off for lunch. Barbara and Mary went to the Andersons and we to the Wilsons, very friendly and informal Americans. Alex Wilson was in charge of the Mission Spearhead Press which printed good reading primers in Anuak, Nuer and other Nilotic languages, and literature for use in churches and schools in other parts of Southern Sudan. It was good to see neat piles of books on the shelves and to be shown around by such an enthusiastic printer and to be introduced to the Sudanese members of his staff. And it was a great relief for all of us to be out of the confined space of the boat, for Michael and Katherine to have room to play and for us to enjoy talking with new friends. Although it was over 100°F (40°C) with almost saturation humidity, the Wilsons seemed to live quite comfortably here in Malakal with fridges and electric light, and locally produced food supplemented with imported tinned supplies. I still remember the taste and sensation of the iced fruit drinks they gave us, and remember that it was in hot Malakal we had our first introduction to iced tea!

When it was time to return to the boat we drove for a short distance through the town, the central part lined with Greek and Arab shops. Behind them were rows of mud and thatch houses, separated from each other by woven mat screens, where most of the town population lived. There seemed to be people everywhere, talking in low voices with occasional outbursts of shouting, carrying loads on their heads, tending children, chasing goats and chickens, milking cows, brewing beer. It was clear that we were now in the South of the country, and that the people around us were African belonging to a number of tribes which in time we would learn to identify by their differences in height, skin colour, and distinctive scar decorations. Along the river bank there were more permanent houses for Government officials and the wealthier merchants, with bougainvillea in orange, red, and purple scrambling all over them. Alongside was a compound of red brick buildings left behind by the Egyptian Irrigation Department where the barbed wire fences were now rusting away. I could imagine British administrators living there before Sudan's Independence, making the most of sailing on the Nile and enjoying the splendid gardens they had planted. Pale yellow trumpets of allamanda still survived, so did scarlet poinsettia bushes the size of small trees, and the air was filled with the sweet smell of frangipani flowers. If you could be protected from mosquitoes by wire mesh in your windows, this was a place to enjoy while at the same time you avoided the noise and disease of the town.

After Malakal the river became narrower, and tall papyrus banks soared above us. We had reached the Sudd. This was the Arabic word for 'obstruction', the impenetrable floating vegetable matter which made navigation on the White Nile so difficult for the next 300 miles. It was an area which had challenged explorers for centuries, many of whom guessed that the mystery of the source of the Nile was somewhere to the south of it. Day after day the brilliant blue of the sky was obscured as it became hotter and more humid, so that by the afternoon we could not see the sun in the still watery air. It was like breathing steam. The sweat poured off us. Michael and Katherine wore the scantiest of bright cotton clothes but their little bodies were wet and slippery and they became quiet and limp. In my letter to my parents on 17th March 1959 I wrote:

"I am writing this while John, Michael and Katherine are asleep. We have been hotter today than I think ever before. It is 108°F in the shade.

"We were delighted to get your letter at Malakal and also one from Papa. Dinner is at 8.0 p.m. after the twins are in bed so we have been able to let them enjoy tinned rice pudding on their own before that. They wear only towelling pants by day and night - no pyjamas even - and they spend a good part of each day playing in a cold bath of water. Katherine gets lots of 'pouring' practice and they both pour water over each other and squeal with delight. Katherine washes her hair standing at the cabin sink on a chair each day - also washes mine, John's and Michael's if she gets the chance! Michael and Katherine seem to manage fine and adapt themselves to all the many changes they have had."

The flow of the Nile at this point was very sluggish, the fall of the land so gradual that water oozed out over an area of 35,000 square miles. For long stretches there was a haze of pale purple from the flowers of water hyacinths, a pretty sight but also a menace because they were out of control and blocked the channels. A boat with the hyacinth tangled in its propellers and paddles could go no further until one of the crew waded in the water with a long knife to cut it free. We stood or sat on the deck for hours just looking at the water and lumps of papyrus floating by. We caught sight of kingfishers making sudden dives and an occasional one emerging from the water with a shiny wet fish in its beak. Great numbers of flashy yellow and black weaver birds were ceaselessly chattering away as they wove their complicated nests in the shape of laboratory retorts upside down with the 'funnel' forming the long entrance from below; they wove many more nests than they needed, perhaps, some said, to confuse snakes raiding their eggs and fledglings, but maybe it was just because they enjoyed weaving. Flights of white egrets passed over and grey herons stood motionless while they fished. It was a feast of a place for watching birds, more plentiful here than elsewhere because the Nuer people of the area protect and never harm them. But I was not specially interested in birds. I just wanted to be out of the Sudd.

The 20 feet tall papyrus surrounding us prevented us from seeing any distance as we went through this huge area of swamp. Alan Moorhead in his book *'The White Nile'*, published in 1960 after we had completed our journey, wrote:

"The papyrus reed when seen for the first time, or carved in stone upon some Egyptian monument, is a beautiful plant with delicate arching fronds making an hieratic pattern against the sky. But when it is multiplied to madness, hundreds of square miles of it spreading away like a green sea on every side, the effect is claustrophobic and sinister. The channels through which the steamer passes are often only forty or fifty yards wide, and so the passenger looks out upon interminable walls of interlacing stalks and they press upon him in imagination like the walls of a prison or a maze."

So others hadn't much liked the Sudd either.

To manoeuvre our flotilla of eight barges and the engine boat round many of the bends of the narrow navigable channel was no easy task. If he couldn't get round in one go, the helmsman crashed the front barges into the bank with an almighty bang, then revving the engine at top speed reversed off it, and slightly further on crashed and reversed again and again until we were through the curve and were back on a straight. This went on by day disturbing our reading, and woke us at night as the barges shuddered at yet another bend. Sometimes Michael and Katherine woke and feeling cooler and more energetic had to be persuaded it wasn't yet 'up-time'.

The crew were good at their jobs. The Commissary was able to manage all the affairs of the boat and we were astonished that the helmsman could steer so well, even without lights at night, and indeed that he could find the channel at all. In some places this looked a total puzzle to us, for where large islands of Sudd had broken away in currents and strong winds the channel had to take a new course, and sometimes we were upset to find we were facing due north for some distance when our destination lay to the south. We had read how Sir Samuel and Lady Baker were blocked while making their way through the Sudd in 1870 and how in 1881 one of General Gordon's steamers, on administrative duties to stop and arrest boats carrying slaves, was held up for three months, most of the 400 men in its escort dying of starvation before they could be rescued. The administration of Sudan as one country remained very difficult all these years later, because surface transport between north and south was only possible by slow boats on the river.

At night we walked about on the screened top deck spotting the glow of distant small fires where there were villages, inaccessible because separated from us by a quagmire of swamp. Some nights the whole sky was glorious. Velvet black with bright stars in one direction and red in another from huge grass fires lit to provide new growth and grazing for the cattle. The abundant water, heat and humidity was a splendid breeding ground for ferocious mosquitoes which attacked us if we ventured outside the screened areas at night. They were wily operators whose whining ceased when they landed to gorge on our blood, more often mine than John's, and made us hope the one which attacked wasn't carrying malaria and that our prophylactic pills would be effective. Each night we scanned the even horizon all around us. In this flat world we always seemed to be at the centre, and it was hard to know if we had made any progress between one dawn and the next. It was a strange and isolated existence, hemmed in by the tall papyrus with only swamp to each side, nothing to land on and no communication with the rest of the country, the rest of the world. John was reading '*The River War*' by W.S. Churchill, 1899, full of slaughter and soldiers marching and fighting in the difficult and uncomfortable conditions which we now could see for ourselves. Prickly heat, a red rash in the skin folds caused by constant sweating, must have been even more awful for those soldiers than it was for us. In such humidity it was impossible ever to be dry.

While supposing that somehow we must be getting there, we talked with the rest of the passengers, all of us in the same boat! The Commissary, a Northerner, was a well-built gracious man who spoke English. He must have been an even better linguist than I remember, for one evening he and Barbara joined John and me for a game of Scrabble which ended when he and John tied for first place! This game, so popular with missionaries at that time, was a good way to mix with the other passengers. We thought of poor 'Ebenezer' in his remote location without his letters, and were sad he wouldn't be able to play. We liked the Commissary, and he seemed to like us too for after our Scrabble game he said to John, "You know, your wife is very sweet!" I think now that this may have been why he liked to take me to the kitchen in the morning to make semolina for the children! Breakfast of eggs and milk and bread in the dining-room in the cooler time of the day was fine but otherwise we fed Michael and Katherine in our cabin on tinned food, some of which had been given to us by the Salween purser. We all had peeled fresh fruit whenever it was available. It was an odd life for little children. Although they were not sick I worried that they had grown rather listless in the heat. They were just a bit too easy to look after, too quiet, too co-operative. Of course John and I too were limp and enervated by the high temperature and humidity and the seeming endlessness of the journey through the Sudd. I think we would have been described as four rather limp Lowes.

We had the company of Canon Andarea Apaya from Malakal to Juba. He was a Moru from Equatoria Province to the south west, the part of the country where we were to live. Baptized in 1926, he was one of the first two Sudanese to be ordained and, trained by Dr. and Mrs. Fraser who started the hospital at Lui, he had earlier been a teacher and medical dresser. He had the growth of the Kingdom of

God at heart and it was good to have time to talk and learn from him. He was well known to many of the teachers travelling with us and when he asked for permission to hold a service on board the next day, a Sunday, this was welcomed. About 20 people assembled and we sang a few hymns, read the Bible, and prayed. The Canon introduced and welcomed us and, since John was to teach at Mundri, he asked the teachers to be on the look out for men who might proceed to theological training and ordination. He also urged them to be wise in their leadership in the new independent Sudan. Besides being a good and faithful pastor and preacher, Canon Andarea had worked alongside Mrs. Eileen Fraser years before in translating parts of the Bible and Prayer Book into Moru, essential for the growth of the Christian Church among his people. He was an athletic man and a good shot which earned him the unofficial title of Diocesan hunter. I remember hearing about a large fat hippo he shot, within the quota of his gun licence, to feed the multitude at the customary Christmas feast in his Parish at Lui. I have never tasted hippo but I'm told it is a coarse-grained meat rather like pork and is usually dried to remove the fat before being cooked. One of the Canon's sons, Alexander, started his medical studies in Khartoum, then completed his degree at the College of Surgeons in Dublin and married an Irish wife. Some years later we met him in Dublin, a very charming and well educated doctor. He never returned to work in his own country.

The papyrus growth was thinning out and we felt liberated when we saw surrounding countryside at last. We were out of the Sudd. One morning we woke to find our flotilla alongside a huge herd of over a hundred elephants, all in full voice and very noisy as they bathed near the banks of the river. We also saw many hippos as we came into semi-grass land with more frequent villages along the river banks.

We were now passing through the country of the Dinka, more correctly Jieng. At two million they are the largest tribe in the Southern Sudan. Very tall, very black, these handsome Nilotic people live for their cows and by fishing. Later we learned more about their way of life but from the boat all we could see were groups of very tall young men, their bodies coated only in white ash, rising like ghosts to run along beside the boat for long distances. We were upset to see Northerners on board throwing bread and empty bottles to them in a disrespectful way. We were even more annoyed that a German American fellow passenger (he was not a missionary) insisted on photographing them, despite being reprimanded several times by the Commissary. This man seemed to have no sensitivity to the feelings of the Sudanese at this early stage of the country's independence. For the Northern Muslims the nakedness of the Dinka was an embarrassment.

Next day we had rain, the first for five months. The parched land sucked it in and gave off a delicious fresh scent, and the air was cooler. Soon Katherine was looking for puddles to jump in and Michael was splashing about along the narrow deck between the cabin doors and the outside rail. A canoe made of woven rushes slid silently out of the reeds with two Dinka youths on board, one paddling, the other standing with a barbed fishing spear in his hand; he suddenly threw this into the muddy water and astonished us when he caught his fish. We passed more villages and herds of sleek light-coloured cattle with long curved horns and extraordinary humps above their bulky shoulders. We could see their herdsman standing like a stork for hour after hour on one leg, propped up by his long spear stuck in the ground.

We had plenty of time to view all these things when our steamer 'Marra' stuck on a sandbank near Mongalla the following day. We were stranded about 1,100 miles south of Khartoum and 30 miles north of Juba.

8   Juba Shopping

So near, but not yet there. Our engine boat, stuck on that sandbank, left our whole flotilla helpless. We felt mad with frustration and very hot. The engines revved as the helmsman attempted to manoeuvre but all his efforts came to nothing. We could only wait to be rescued. Later in the day a launch and then another with a winch arrived. The barges were disconnected and towed off but even with much tugging and pushing the engine boat remained firmly bedded down in the sand, its paddles churning uselessly. After having been tied up at various angles during the day we were shunted back and tied up for the night to the engine boat, so we could have our dim electric light from its generator. Next day a small launch came from Juba and the First Class passengers were transferred to it. Leaving Canon Andarea and most of the rest of the passengers behind we set off and by late afternoon had covered our last 30 miles on the river. We had reached Juba, the 'Capital' of the Southern Sudan. Normally on its arrival there the steamer blasted its hooter repeatedly in triumph, as well it might, drawing crowds of people, some to meet friends and relatives, some to get ready to travel north themselves, some just to catch up on news and be part of the excitement and bustle. For us it wasn't like that. Unlike the proper steamer our smaller launch did not hoot to announce itself. Our Mission Secretary, Brian de Saram, who was expecting us did not know we had already arrived and neither did the local population. Holding Michael and Katherine by the hand we walked down the gangway and onto the concrete quay. After 11 days on the boat we were now on dry land, the land of the Southern Sudan.

With none of our baggage, John and I and the children stood with Mary and Barbara on an almost empty wharf. It was as if we were all alone in the middle of 'darkest Africa'. I remember how weary and dazed I felt in the heat and humidity of that arrival. I had expected to be excited. Instead I looked around at the landing place where some barges were tied up, and at the basic goods sheds with their corrugated iron roofs, and there didn't seem to be much else except the smooth wide river. It was hard to think that this was the main port for supplies between Khartoum and Juba, 1200 miles apart, and that there was no road but only the slow waterway joining them.

News travels fast by 'bush telegraph' and soon a small crowd gathered to look at us. "Mr. Lowe, I presume," said Mr. de Saram as he and his wife Eileen drove up in a truck and took us all to the Mission compound about a mile away. Mary and Barbara were to stay with Louise Ryder and we were to be looked after by Brian and Eileen. By then it was dark; night took over suddenly now we were so near the equator. Having a look at Juba would have to wait until another day.

Brian in white shirt and shorts was tall and athletic, a very handsome man with a deep tan and a twinkle in his eye. It was not hard to guess at his love of cricket and tennis and to credit that even in this heat he managed a set or two in Juba whenever he could. Brian was a teacher and he and Eileen had been CMS missionaries in various parts of the Southern Sudan mostly in remote Dinka areas. Since 1957 when the Mission Schools had been taken over by the Government at Independence, they lived in Juba where Brian was responsible for Mission administration. For Eileen, attractive in her pretty cotton dresses, that meant looking after a stream of missionaries as they came to Juba for supplies or passed through when they went on leave or returned. It could be a very exhausting business especially when food was hard to get and the heat and humidity relentless. Brian and Eileen helped us with residence documents, work permits, banking arrangements and advice on the provisions we needed to buy before setting off from Juba to live in a more isolated place. They knew all about what that would be like.

They lived in the Mission Secretary's house, a large bungalow with wire screening at the windows and a wide verandah to the front where we often sat at odd moments during the day. By evening the mosquitoes drove us indoors to the refuge of a large high-ceilinged sitting-room furnished with bulky 'steamer chairs' which had canvas seats and wide level wooden arms pierced by circular holes just the right size to grip a glass of water or fruit juice. We always had cold drinks to hand, for in this climate we dripped with perspiration even when cooler air blew through from one side of the house to the other. The floors were of grey polished cement, and there were small tables, a bookcase, the dining-room table and chairs made of solid hardwood from the tall mahogany trees of the area. Our bedroom, its two single iron beds only slightly wider than the bunks of the steamer, was sparsely furnished but had a welcoming bunch of flowers, and we had a separate room for the children.   At first Michael and Katherine were rather bewildered and a bit fretful, but playing in a bath of tepid water and eating a light supper helped, and soon they lay down one at each end of their single bed to sleep the night until the time would come for them to get up and explore the place in the morning.

We spent the hot evening under the light of a rather feeble electric bulb, relaxing with Brian and Eileen, talking about our travels and their Sudan experiences and leaving all serious discussion until we had rested. We had arrived safely and were almost at our destination though the actual day we would set off from Juba would depend on when a lorry could be hired. There was no way of predicting when that would be.

Morning began with a cup of tea in bed and later we sat down to a breakfast which started with slices of pawpaw, a tree-grown fruit which tasted rather like a slightly sweet limp pumpkin but was greatly improved by a squeeze of lemon juice. This was followed by pink-coloured porridge made from millet which was the staple grain crop, known in Ireland as bird seed.   It was quite coarse with an occasional small stone which gritted on the teeth and made us cautious of what we might find in each mouthful. We took the precaution of providing Michael and Katherine with their usual cereal while we still had a supply.

Shopping was the first thing we had to do and Brian exaggerated a little as he told us what Juba had to offer. He packed us all into the truck with a driver and sent us off with Danieli, a messenger in the Mission office, who knew some English. We found the 'city' was like an extensive village of mud and stone houses, most with corrugated iron roofs, others thatched. There were some more permanent buildings for Government offices and officials at the *Merkhaz*, and a large open square for public occasions. It didn't look as if the town planners had yet arrived in Juba for we could see no order in the clusters of dwelling places. The roads were dusty and unpaved serving the lines of Arab and Greek shops, the schools, the hospital and the port, as well as the sprawling areas where the population lived.

Danieli recommended us to place our order with the merchant who had the biggest shop. It was not hard to find or identify it, with its roof and doors of corrugated iron and the wide verandah all along the front. The owner, whose name I think was Ibrahim, sat inside in an area marked off like a little office. With his quick darting eyes he reminded me of a spider in the middle of his web of goods and employees. It wasn't long before he hauled himself out of his chair to welcome us and hope that we wanted to buy a lot of supplies. "Yes," he said, "many goods I have." He was a short portly middle aged Northerner who spoke some English and was particularly keen to make contact with Europeans and salaried officials in the hope of increasing his trade. He also dealt with orders by post for customers working up-country, sending supplies to them on the post lorry. Through our years in Mundri we would rely on him for whatever he could provide. That morning he invited us to sit down, then clapped his hands and when a young boy appeared he ordered him to bring coffee for us. This turned out to be Turkish coffee in a tall conical container set on a circular brass tray. It looked thick and dark as it was poured into small glasses. Several spoons of sugar helped but we found it bitter and muddy, and we weren't sure how safe it was to drink the tall glasses of water served at the same time. Though we appreciated it as a sign of customary hospitality it was not immediately refreshing for us. Michael had a quick taste and made a face which warned Katherine not to try it at all.

Then it was time to begin our strange shopping spree. On the verandah were sacks of millet and groundnuts, lentils, rice, and dried broad beans known as *ful misri*. We ordered quantities of all of these, which were immediately weighed and poured into bright cotton bags sewn up by the tailors from remnants of printed cloth and tied tightly at the top. Plastic carrier bags were still in the future and nothing came ready packed.

The wide doors of the shop opened outwards displaying bright beads, bangles, enamel ware and tools wired onto the doors, all safely on the inside when the shop was closed for the night. It was rather dark inside, but we could see a long counter, and behind it shelves holding an assortment of smaller items like matches, ballpoint pens, exercise books, batteries and razor blades. The tinned food we wanted was arranged high up, the tops thick with dust; sacks on the floor were filled with tea, coffee beans, salt, flour, onions, spices. Even if I were blindfolded I think I would know I was in that shop in Juba if I met all those smells together again and could feel the fine dust covering everything.

Rolls of brightly coloured cotton materials were stacked up against one wall, together with bales of cream coloured *damariya*, unbleached Sudanese cotton cloth made at Nzara near Yambio and used for sheets, curtains, mattress covers and basic clothing. More expensive cotton drill was made into shorts and 'bush' shirts and trousers by the tailors who sat at their Singer treadle sewing-machines on the verandahs. I loved watching them, so quick and skilled at their work. With the flick of a measuring tape they were ready to cut out a garment and sew it up while the customer waited an hour or so. Some tailors were even ready to copy a dress from a magazine picture and could produce some weird and wonderful fashions.

When it came to ordering shorts for John there was a choice. The shorts could be short and wide or long to below the knees and rather narrow, a style favoured by the more conservative men of the Mission. John considered the short wide variety not immodest and likely to be cooler so he had a supply of these in white and khaki expertly made for him. I have to laugh now when I look at some old photos; the shorts John and some of the other men wore look more like skirts!

Our bed was our next concern. After the narrow bunks on the Salween and the cramped berths on the trains and steamer, John and I were longing for a proper double bed. We had been told that in the Mission only single iron beds were supplied and indeed were the only kind considered suitable in the heat of Sudan. We had other ideas. We would have a mattress made in Juba to take with us for our new home and then we would have a big *angareeb* bed made locally with turned wooden legs and a mesh of leather thongs woven to the frame. The tailor took down the measurements, 6ft. 6ins. by 5ft., and assured us that the mattress would be ready and delivered to the Mission house next day. As promised it came the next day alright, made of *damariya*, stuffed with cotton and tied through at intervals, but obviously the tailor couldn't believe that anyone would want a mattress as big as we had ordered so he had made it much smaller, for a human being perhaps, not an elephant! We had to send it back to be enlarged.

Next afternoon after tea Brian took John on a walk around Juba. Eileen and I laughed about our mattress as we sat on the verandah with Michael and Katherine playing in the sand near us. The sight of our children, of course, reminded Eileen that their Hugh and Rosemary were far away at boarding school in England. "You must value these years, Dorothy," she said, "you know you will only have the children with you for such a short time." She told me about when she and Brian with their two-year-old Hugh were living and working in Akot, a remote place in Dinka country on the edge of the Sudd, 380 miles north-west of Juba. Some weeks before their new baby was due, they had set out to drive 900 miles on very poor tracks and roads, crossing rivers by rickety bridges or pole ferries, putting up with the heat and dust until they eventually reached Kampala in Uganda. There their baby Rosemary was born safely at Mengo, the CMS hospital founded by Dr. Albert Cook in 1897. After that they returned the 900 miles stopping at intervals to feed the baby by the roadside. Eileen's face glowed with thankfulness to God as she recalled how it had all gone so well and especially the great welcome the local Dinka people at Akot gave them when they got back to what was their home at the time.

It was never far from Brian and Eileen's minds however that there was a limit to how long they could be together in Akot as a complete family. It was not considered wise to keep children above the age of five years in Sudan because of the climate, limited food supplies, and disease, quite apart from the isolation and the absence of schooling. Missionary couples, like all expatriates with children, whether in administration, medicine, education, the army or commerce, knew well the heartache of having to decide what to do for the best. We already knew the Sudan missionary pattern. Mothers stayed with the children in England or Ireland while their husbands remained overseas to continue with their work in Sudan. Later the children went to boarding schools, often to one of several Christian schools which catered for missionary children aged 5 - 18 and included provision of care in the school holidays for children without grandparents or aunts and uncles to look after them then. Parents tried to be on 'home' leave for the longer summer holidays every second year, but for the rest of the time mothers divided themselves between being near their children at school or in Sudan with their husbands.

It was no wonder people like Eileen felt torn by their longing to be in both places at once; the cost for all of them was great whether the priority was given to the work in Sudan or to the children. I felt sad for Eileen and Brian living in hot uncomfortable Juba and separated from Hugh and Rosemary, and happy for them when a year later Brian, after twenty years in Sudan, was appointed Africa Secretary at CMS Headquarters in London. He and Eileen left to live and work there, no longer separated from each other or their children, but eleven years later they were ready to be back in Africa when Brian responded to a request to be the Provost of the Cathedral in Cairo from 1972 to 1977.

Eileen's words were to return to me again and again. "You must value these years, Dorothy," she had said. "You know you will only have the children with you for such a short time." Michael and Katherine had no concerns for the future to trouble them just then as they played in the sand, but the painful questions were already there for John and me. How long would it be possible for us to follow our missionary vocation in Sudan? How long would it be possible for us to be together as a family even if the Government allowed us to stay on?

9   Don't Send any Lukewarms

Port Sudan, Khartoum, Omdurman, Malakal, Juba. It seemed extraordinary that these places were all within the boundaries of Sudan, an enormous country ten times the size of the United Kingdom and the largest in Africa. Because of how we had travelled we could never forget the vast distances separating these places and the differences in appearance and languages of the people. Swathed in clothes or wearing none at all, wealth and poverty, Muslim mosques, Christian churches, traditional beliefs - such diversity. Our journeying was well worth the time it had taken for we could not have imagined all this if we had dropped into Juba by air. You may be tired of reading page after page about our journey and be impatient for me to hurry on and get to our destination. I can say I was impatient too during the ten hot days in Juba when we prepared for the final 180 miles.

The advantage of those days was time to think over our new experiences and try to make some sense of them. We had seen a little of the North now inhabited by people of Arab stock originally from Egypt and Arabia. In the area around the Sudd we had entered the political Southern Sudan, passing through the lands of the Anuak, the Nuer, the Shilluk and the Dinka, all very tall Nilotic tribes with their very black smooth silky skin as described by the writer of the book of Isaiah in the Bible.

> "Woe to the land of whirring wings along the rivers of Cush
> which sends envoys by sea in papyrus boats over the water.
> Go, swift messengers, to a people tall and smooth-skinned,
> to a people feared far and wide,
> an aggressive nation of strange speech,
> whose land is divided by rivers."   *Isaiah* 18: 1-2 NIV

We had heard 'the whirring wings' of the birds and seen 'papyrus boats over the water'. These Nilotic people were probably the earliest inhabitants. Coming now to Juba and the extreme South of the country we were amongst people different again, of Nilo-Hamitic and Bantu stock, believed to have migrated from even further South. It did not surprise us that so many different peoples in such a terrain were often in conflict, difficult to manage and govern as one nation.

There had always been concern about the conditions for missionary work in Southern Sudan and we had read General Gordon's comments written in 1887. "There is no possible reason against a mission station but it is a most deadly country and few could possibly stand the climate - it is only fit for a man who is sick of life, has no ties, and longs for death. Now these men are not common." "Don't send any lukewarms," he warned. What a place to come to live! Still we were confident that there was worthwhile work for us to do here, and we had no feeling of being lukewarms. Perhaps we could even say we were quite hot!

The climate and insects had not changed for the better since General Gordon's time but the living conditions had, so that we had an easier and more comfortable time than he would have predicted. This was because over the intervening seventy years Westerners, many of them British administrators of the Anglo-Egyptian Political Service in Sudan, had devised ways of making their existence more comfortable, and had established a remarkably English upper middle class style of living with their large houses and plentiful staff. Traditional and arguably excessive domestic tasks were carried out for them by well trained Sudanese who instead of living 'downstairs' lived in small houses nearby.

In Juba the Mission houses were built of solid stone and orientated so that the arc of the equatorial sun moved along the line of the roof ridge, and never blazed directly into the house. Windows were large and without glass, designed to allow any slight breeze to pass through the high-ceilinged rooms from one side to the other, and fitted with wire mesh screens to keep mosquitoes out. Electricity from a town supply made it possible to have fans to move the air and give the impression of cooling it if you could stand the whirring noise. Food supplies were generally adequate in Juba even if the variety was limited. Treated water from the Nile was plentiful.

With an airport in Juba letters could now come by air rather than steamer, there were even some telephones, and if you had a radio you could keep in touch with news on the BBC World Service; knowing about the weather in England seemed to be a daily essential for one of our missionary friends. Missionaries resident in Juba had a constant trail of other missionaries and visitors using their guest-rooms as hotels, so all the latest stories kept circulating as if we were close relatives. There were some splendid accounts of how to escape snakes, especially if you saw one in the grass roof overhead when you were naked in your bath and your stick, or in earlier days your gun perhaps, was just out of reach! We were told of a missionary, John Parry, very fond of cake, who was cutting some on the verandah of his house in Maridi one day when he was struck by lightning. He landed kicking on the floor, with the cake knife still in his hand, and in his eighties told me what a good cake it was! We took these horror stories with a pinch of salt!

The missionary householders with their Sudanese helpers looked after us well, providing enjoyable meals, baths, and clean clothes. But even so conditions were a bit hard to get used to. One evening a scorpion stung Hezekiah, who worked for the de Sarams, and he was taken to the local hospital for his severe pain to be treated. Another day a snake was killed beside our verandah reminding us just how wary we needed to be, especially in watching the children. Everywhere there was dust and the buzzing and annoyance of persistent flies, as well as the high-pitched whining of mosquitoes after dark.

As in Khartoum, the sewage system was very unpleasant. Each house had a small building near the road boundary of the property. This was equipped with a lidded toilet seat on a wooden box with space for a heavy iron bucket beneath it, and a trap door behind.

Each night we heard the bucket men on the road outside as they slammed the trap doors when a used bucket was slid out and a clean one replaced it. In Khartoum the 'honey wagons' as the sewage carts were called were pulled by camels ambling along on their soft padded feet and looking disgusted, while in Juba mules and donkeys were used. The smell was awful if the men came late, but even more horrible and disturbing if the collection was earlier while we were still sitting around getting the best of the cooler air of evening. It was a terrible way for these men to have to earn their wages. Away from the cities and towns, there was no such provision of a sewage system. In Mundri we fared far better with our 'long drops', very deep pit latrines really like 'septic tanks' without the water element, relatively odourless and too deep for flies.

While we were staying with Eileen and Brian we heard how Juba had come to be the 'capital' of the South. In 1926 Arthur Riley, who had taken five months to travel from his home in Australia, arrived as a new missionary just in time to be present when the Provincial Governor and an official Government party were marking out Juba as a suitable place on the Nile for the capital of Mongalla Province. Archdeacon Shaw who had been in Sudan since 1900 was also present, and chose the site for the CMS Mission centre where we were now staying.

As we walked about in the heat and humidity, with our cotton clothes wet and flapping on our skin, it seemed to us that Juba was the most uncomfortable place imaginable. We were experiencing temperatures of more than 108°F (45°C) and were told that this was almost constant during the six months of the dry season. How on earth, I wondered, does the human body with a 'normal' temperature of 98.4°F (37°C) manage to adapt and survive under these conditions? The rest of the year wasn't any easier; high humidity and hot sunshine alternated with violent storms when dramatic flashes of lightning lit up the sky and the crash and crack of thunder was followed by pounding torrential rain. The smell of the moist refreshed earth was lovely if you were safe and dry indoors but the sudden contrast of colder air brought real discomfort and health risks to people whose only clothing was wet and inadequate.

I remember the climate of Juba as quite unbearable, but once the decision had been made in 1926 the administrators and missionaries got on with their tasks. The most urgent of these was language. What a challenge it must have been to listen carefully until words and sounds could be distinguished and the meaning grasped and then the Good News of the Gospel of Jesus Christ could be shared! And then to develop a written form! To ensure consistency, a language conference met at Rejaf near Juba in 1928 when the Roman script was adopted for the languages of Southern Sudan and the orthography agreed. This affected all those using the various Sudanese vernacular languages, whether missionaries or Government officials. Local Christian converts in teamwork with missionaries started the translation of parts of the Bible into their own languages, Mission schools were built, and school primers written and printed. And by the time John and I arrived thirty years later it was Sudanese Christians themselves, not the missionaries, who were the preachers and who were involved in direct evangelism. Our position by then was one of assisting but no longer leading.

We were glad one afternoon to be taken to see some of the Church developments. We had Michael and Katherine with us, sitting side by side in their twin pushchair and attracting a crowd of observers commenting out loud on this unusual sight. John and I were especially pleased to see that a tall wooden Celtic cross had been erected to mark the place where a cathedral was to be built in the future. We joked about the cross being an Irish one, and showed it to the children as the type associated with our 'tribe', though Jack Marden, the Mission builder, didn't think much of this association; he assured us that the style of cross was chosen because the circle of wood stopped the bars of the Cross from warping! The place was stony and barren but it was where a large number of people had gathered only a month before to see the Archbishop of Jerusalem lay the foundation stone for All Saints Cathedral, Juba.

Early mornings were the best time of the day in Juba. The air was cooler and, now that it was near the end of the dry season there was dew on the brown dried-up grass and on the buds of the hibiscus bushes. Each bloom opened up in its brilliant colour for one day of glory and by evening had faded to be replaced by new blooms the next day. It was in the early mornings too that we made our way to a small thatched house in the de Sarams' garden which was used for prayers, where we renewed our vision of why we were in Sudan at all. Like the hibiscus we needed to make the most of one day at a time for we didn't know how many days we would have here.

We met some of the Sudanese clergy who had been appointed to look after people of their own tribes living and working in Juba but the level of education of these men was not yet advanced and we were distressed to see their poverty and poor living conditions. They led services for their congregations in their own languages, the same church building used in turn by each group. In fact neither their people nor the clergy had an easy life in Juba. They had been used to growing their own food and collecting fire wood freely in the countryside; now in the town they had to have money to pay for these things, and for a constant stream of relatives arriving and needing to be fed or provided with school fees or taken for treatment at the Hospital. Their own poor health could be a constant drain too. The wife of one of the clergy had recently died and he had withdrawn his daughter from her school in Yei to stay at home to look after him and care for the younger children. Added to her sorrow at her mother's death she was very disappointed she would have no further chance of education, no hope of escaping to a more exciting future. I looked at her small frame, no longer in her smart school uniform but now poorly dressed, and felt her dejection and despair. "What can I do?" she asked, "I can do nothing."

10 Meeting the Missionaries

It was a tonic to the missionaries of what was known as the CMS 'Gordon Memorial Mission' in the Southern Sudan that Mary and Barbara and John and I had been granted visas and had actually arrived. Since Independence in 1956 the Government had been following a policy of 'Sudanisation' taking over schools and then medical work, and replacing missionaries and other expatriates in posts in the South with Sudanese staff. Whereas in 1950 there had been nine ordained men, including Bishop Oliver Allison, and thirty eight other missionaries - single men and women, and married couples some of them with children - now there were less than half that number. It had all happened at such speed. The strategy of CMS had always been one of proclamation of the Gospel through preaching, education, medical and other work side by side with training local Christians to take over and free the missionary for transfer elsewhere. The missionaries still in Southern Sudan agonised that the tasks they had set out to do could not be completed so soon; there were not enough trained Sudanese to do their work and they did not believe the interests and progress of Southerners and of the Christian Church within the South would be safe under Northern Muslim control.

Following the Education Act of 1957, the Government had taken over all the Church boys' schools except Loka, though for the time being the girls' schools remained under Church management. After all its years of pioneer medical work the Church hospital at Lui became a Government institution. A number of missionaries had been expelled or had been refused visas and now each missionary wondered if he would be the next one to be forced to leave the work that was his joy and his life.

Several of them thought it so unlikely that we would be allowed to stay that they advised us not to bother to unpack.

Despite their reduced numbers, however, at the time of our arrival missionaries were still very active in a range of projects, working as it were to make the most of every minute left. Bishop Gwynne College for training Sudanese clergy was actually expanding. Girls' schools - especially at Yei and Maridi and Yambio - and the Intermediate School for boys at Loka were still staffed by missionary teachers and their Sudanese Christian colleagues. Niall Watson had joined Stephen and Anne Carr in the agricultural work at Undukuri, and Jack Mardon, Ken Ogden and Lionel Brooker were busy with building and teaching at the Technical Training College in Lainya. Jean Drinkwater in Mothers' Union work, Philippa Guillebaud in translation, and George Bennett in literature projects were all in teams with local Sudanese Christians and making valuable contributions for both the present and the future. The Church Bookshop in Juba, staffed by Lucy Kedge with Oloni and others to assist her, provided access to Bibles, Prayer Books, school primers, literature and stationery. From his steamy office in Juba, Brian de Saram as Mission Secretary was responsible for the missionaries, their work permits, and negotiations with the Church leaders and the Government, assisted by Louise Ryder as his secretary and Ray Atkinson the mission accountant. In only a year or two all this would be very different.

Our arrival coincided with the time of year when missionaries returned from local leave in East Africa and stopped over as they passed through Juba; they were very keen to have a good look at us, for it could be that we would be the last recruits of their era. We too were keen to meet face to face with men and women who had only been names on lists. It was handy for us that we were staying with Brian and Eileen at the centre of the site chosen in 1926 by Archdeacon Shaw for the CMS mission station in Juba. It was large enough for several missionary houses set in spacious gardens of grass and shrubs and in most of these we, the new recruits, were on display at tea parties! Arthur and Grace Riley, Australians who after more than thirty years were coming to the end of their service in Sudan, were delighted to entertain us and talk of all that had been achieved. We were glad to be in time to eat their cakes and view Arthur in his bush-shirt over shorts barely covering his knobbly knees, and to laugh and joke with Grace who was friendly and warm-hearted. Their welcome to us was special and their support continued by letter and prayer and Grace's small water colour paintings long after they retired to Australia a year later. Another day Eileen invited Dr. Fahmi, the local Egyptian doctor, and his English wife to tea. Next day we went to Louise who had originally come to Juba from CMS Headquarters to help out in an emergency and then stayed on for years. She always looked deliciously cool and well-groomed as if she was still in London. None of us knew how she managed it. She returned with us to help me to bath Michael and Katherine; it was like a ballet, Louise gently sprinkling the water as if it was rain while the children responded by imitating her in the graceful way she moved her arms and hands, until they decided to giggle and slither and splash about instead.

Dominating the mission houses and a building not like any other in Juba was the Church Bookshop. Built on two floors with a deep verandah all along one side, the ground floor was a busy place where local schoolboys, teachers and clergy searched for the books and stationery they needed. Groups of people, especially schoolboys, often gathered outside to count their money and make hard decisions on what they could afford to buy. Brian's office where, following CMS rules, we were to have our formal official interview later in the week, was at one end beside an office for Louise and the office of the Archdeacon, Arthur Riley, though he and Grace were out on trek for three weeks of every month.

Lucy Kedge, dark and stocky and very direct, managed the bookshop and lived in the flat above it where there were several extra rooms for the many guests who climbed the concrete outside-steps to enjoy her hospitality. Ronald Gray, a tough looking veteran, arrived by lorry to collect supplies for the school where he and his wife taught, and Lionel Brooker stayed two nights in Lucy's flat on his way back to Lainya after leave. We met David and Mary Brown and their children Alan and Peter, on their way back to Mundri after local leave in Uganda. We would know them well when we joined the staff of Bishop Gwynne College where David was the Principal, and it was useful to have their immediate advice on the stores we still needed to buy.

After the six weeks of travelling together we said a fond farewell to Mary and Barbara when Brian drove them off to Yei, seventy miles away; he returned bringing Jean Barton with him later than expected because of a lot of breakdowns and car trouble, common on the rough stony roads as we would soon know.

All these missionaries were very strong-minded individuals with views on Sudan and everything else! Meeting them gave John and me a good introduction to life in Sudan, its politics and history, and we heard interesting discussions about whether they thought the future of Sudan would be full integration of North and South as truly one, or separation into two autonomous countries. In this huge country where we had travelled first through the North and seen Northerners, and then arrived in the South where we were surrounded by Southerners, we could see that the scattered population of about eleven million people in the North could hardly have differed more from the six million in the South.

North and South didn't seem to have much in common. The North was predominantly Muslim with an Arab culture, the South decidedly African with a growing Christian Church. Different languages didn't help. Arabic was the official language of the country as a whole but in the South English was spoken widely and was the language of education. Southern 'market' Arabic was the language of trade, in use by people from about 150 different birth languages and 600 dialects, but despised and discounted by Northerners. Difficult communication didn't help either. It was a great disadvantage that there was no road between North and South and that whole communities could be cut off in places where there were no roads at all or where, because of swamps and cracking black cotton soil, roads were only passable for a few months of the year. Telephones too were very rare instruments.

But the most insurmountable difficulty of all seemed to be the long-standing lack of trust and respect between Northerner and Southerner. Between them we did not see what Laurens van der Post called 'the right look in the eye.' Slavery had been widespread in most parts of the continent of Africa. Between 1874 and 1879 General Gordon had written of its awfulness in Sudan, of the cruelty of the slave traders and of how he despaired of it ever really ending. "When you have got the ink that has soaked into the blotting paper out of it, then slavery will cease in these lands," he wrote. At that time as many as 50,000 Southern Sudanese men and women each year, captured or handed over in trade, were taken shackled in boats down the Nile to be sold as slaves in Khartoum and Cairo, and the Egyptian army was made up mostly of slaves from Sudan. Later generations were filled with anger and mistrust of those whose forefathers had taken or bought theirs as slaves. How could these actions be forgiven or forgotten? The attitude of those in authority in the South, almost all from the North, did nothing in the way of healing.

The Sudan had been administered by the Anglo-Egyptian Condominium from the time of the defeat of the Mahdists at the Battle of Omdurman in 1898 until Sudan became an independent country on New Year's Day 1956, but the administration well knew that there would be difficulties. As a first step in preparation for self-government, elections were held in November 1948, resulting in Northerners holding 52 seats and Southerners just 13 in the Legislative Assembly which was set up. It should not have been surprising that this gave rise to unrest in the South; such a disproportion of seats only confirmed for Southerners that they would not have proper representation and equal terms in the new independent State but instead would find themselves dominated by the Northerners just as they had always been. This was made worse still after the 1953 elections when out of 800 Government posts only 4 at Assistant District Commissioner level and 2 local *Mamurs* had Southerners appointed to them. The seeds of the Torit Mutiny of 1955 and decades of war ahead had been sown. In the North and in Egypt, demands for Southern autonomy were unacceptable. An independent South, it was feared, could cut off the water supply of the Nile on which further down-river they were totally dependent, and besides, huge oil reserves were thought to exist in the South just waiting to be exploited.

Some within the group of missionaries in Juba were optimistic about unity North and South and believed the Christian faith would foster healing and tolerance. Others, John and I among them, thought that the long history of unhappy relationships and attitudes was still much too fresh for this outcome to be realistic for many years to come, if ever. Sudan looked to us as if it was really two countries. It seemed artificial and unfortunate that it had ever been thought of as one.

After a day or two of shopping, one by one our new friends went off to their distant places, while we still waited rather impatiently in Juba. Our ultimate location was to be Bishop Gwynne College in Mundri but first we were told we were to have some months of experience in Dinka country and become familiar with the Church and the Sudanese pastors there. Brian wasted no time in setting us down to work, and by our third day in Juba he had hired a Dinka schoolboy who came after school every afternoon to start us off on learning his language. Samwel Eli Deng was a true Dinka, very tall, very black with a broad smile which immediately showed us that his lower front incisor teeth were missing. With some hesitation we asked why he had no lower front teeth. Samwel, with pride, told us the reason. His people know a lot about cattle and prize them above all else. They also recognise the symptoms of the dreaded tetanus, a condition particularly prevalent in cattle areas, where contaminated wounds are followed by a locking of the jaw and death from starvation and spasms. I was very impressed by this custom of the

Dinka people who extracted the lower front teeth so that the sufferer in the spasms of tetanus could have some hope of nourishment and survival by being fed through a straw.

While I was a junior doctor in Ireland I had as a patient an adolescent boy from a local farm who was suffering from tetanus, now a rare condition in the West. With sedation, tube feeding, muscle relaxants and careful nursing in the dark, he only just survived the fierce spasms which convulsed him. I didn't see another case until I worked in Kenya in 1964 where tetanus in new-born babies was common, caught through an infected knife used to cut the umbilical cord. It tore me apart to see their terrible spasms and I grieved that they hardly ever survived.

The systematic removal of the lower incisor teeth was a good precaution in case of tetanus but, at the same time of course, affected the pronunciation of the Dinka language. Samwel or rather I should say '*Thamwell*' looked at us seriously. "If you are to pronounce Dinka properly," he said, "you will need to have your lower front teeth removed." Years before the same advice had been given to Arthur Riley by his old gardener who added that he knew of a man who would pull the teeth for nothing. We looked hard at our senior missionaries Brian and Arthur, both of whom had worked amongst the Dinka. Since they still had all their teeth we decided it must be possible to keep ours and still be good missionaries.

This was just as well for our plans were suddenly changed by instructions from CMS London. New missionaries with small children could not be posted to where they would be on their own in Dinka country. We were to go first to Mundri instead. This was great news. We would be leaving the oppressive heat and humidity of Juba for a slightly less hot and sticky place and there we would set up our own home. Michael and Katherine would have Alan and Peter Brown and some other children to play with and we would make a start on the work we had come to do. We were very excited at the prospect.

11   The Long Road to Mundri

The chickens squawked as every day Michael and Katherine chased them around the bare ground at the back of the de Sarams' house, but today was different. They rushed to climb into the truck shouting 'bye', and we were off. Such baggage as we had with us and the stores we had bought in Juba and the elephant-sized mattress were all lifted onto a hired truck which looked as if it was already full. John and I with a child each on our knees sat in the cab with the Sudanese driver, while his assistant perched in the open on top of the luggage and goods in the back. Mundri was 180 miles away and we were on the final bit of our journey through Equatoria.

We set off in the cool of early morning, the sun just coming into view and lighting up the sparse scrubland on each side of the stony unmade road. It didn't take long to leave the sprawl of Juba behind and after that for mile after mile there was no sign of habitation. The driver knew every bump and twist of these roads, and kept announcing that all was well: '*Kwayyis jiddan!*' he attempted in the few words of Arabic he considered all human beings would know and which we recognised. He avoided the worst of the huge potholes, sometimes with a sudden swerve which threw us and the children into a heap. '*Maaleish*', never mind, we'll get there '*insha'allah*', if God wills, he reassured us. Seat belts and child seats were unknown at that time. It was difficult to talk against the noise of the engine, and we had to keep the windows open to allow some air to circulate, and soon we were covered in a haze of reddish dust. We were hot from the sun, hot from the engine, hot from the iron floor beneath our feet - just desperately hot all over.

In and out of dozing, I thought over our eleven days in Juba, which ended when we sat with Eileen and Brian for an early breakfast. Staying with them had given us a glimpse of life for missionaries in

The Long Road to Mundri 73

Sudan, and the chance to meet the others passing, like us, through Juba. It was reassuring to know that the de Sarams in Juba understood remote places and would always be ready to help and support us. The sweet smell of the frangipani flowers on their breakfast table would always now remind me of them and how I could hardly wait to have our own table soon in Mundri.

It was a long and tiring journey. The distances had seemed endless on the trains and the steamer and now, nearer our destination, the distances still seemed endless and I felt irritable and impatient as well as hot. For long stretches we drove through uninhabited land, khaki-coloured for it was the dry season, and mostly flat and undeveloped. Occasional small stunted trees, damaged by previous fires, stood out above thin bleached grass which stretched in every direction as far as the eye could see. In some places dramatic black patches had been left behind after huge fires deliberately lit, and now, with the onset of the rains, startlingly green growth was just beginning to appear.

The children were floppy and hot on our laps, sometimes asleep sometimes restless and needing drinks of water, and often just wanting to get out. When our stops for getting out coincided with an occasional lovely clearing where fine short grass was like a carpet beneath tall trees, I felt refreshed by the beauty and mystery deep in the heart of this land. We only had glimpses of scurrying wild life which we failed to identify, but once in the distance we spotted a line of men out hunting with bows and arrows and spears as well as their pack of native hunting dogs. These dogs, light tan and smooth haired, were a local breed the size of large terriers, characterised by the way they carried their long tails tightly curled above their haunches.

We had been told that when we saw Gumbiri, a spectacular blue mountain with twin peaks, which rose abruptly from the plain to the west, we would be near Lainya, which was about seventy miles south-west of Juba and the first real village on our road. A Technical Department and Training School had been established there by CMS where young men were taught skills in building, motor mechanics and carpentry. For their practical training they built schools, staff houses and mission and church buildings, and all the mission furniture was made in their workshops out of the local solid hardwoods. At the time of our arrival in Lainya, Jack Mardon, who was in charge, was away with a team of students, and his wife Noreen was in England caring for their school-age children, a reminder of the cost for families of working in Sudan. Ken Ogden, Jack's colleague, heard our truck arriving and rushed out to give us a great welcome and take us into the cool of his house.

Ken setting to work

Ken, who was still a bachelor at that time, supervised the students in the workshops and took his turn to go out with them to the various places where they were building or doing other work. Ken had served in the Royal Air Force during the War before becoming a CMS missionary and joining the team at Lainya. We became close friends and when two years later he married Betty Ruth, who was an American missionary nurse in Kenya, we became lifelong friends and in time godparents to their two children. Ken was a gracious and godly man, a kind of saint and very good company. He worked 'hands on' with the men and made sure proper standards and skills were maintained. Once when a wall had been built off-plumb by his student, I saw him setting to work himself to take it down and help to build it up again correctly. In contrast, Jack enjoyed a good shout when things were not done the way he wanted, but that method seemed to work too because Jack was known and respected as a hard working and effective person. The Christian witness of both men was infectious.

We flopped into Ken's wooden 'steamer' armchairs, drank glasses of water and lime juice, and ate an early lunch. Ken's lorry was already loaded with building materials for a staff house at Mundri, but had enough room left to pack in a couple of workers and the four of us and our baggage. He drove the remaining 110 miles north-west on a road which was sometimes sandy but otherwise had the familiar hard stony surface. The monotony of the endless 'bush' was broken here and there by craggy outcrops of granite rocks and hints of distant hazy blue hills. We had to hold on tight when the truck swerved and dipped around water courses left behind by the rains, or when we bumped over deep ruts made in the mud by passing lorries and now dried as hard as concrete. It was no wonder lorries and trucks were shaken to bits on these journeys and were always in need of welding and repair, and no wonder the Government Works Department had a constant job with their road-grading machines, a job which it was impossible for them ever to complete.

We passed the village named Chief Jambo's, after its chief, where we stopped to drink hot sweet black tea served in glasses and bought at a wayside shelter. Some miles further on, Ken pointed out Lui Hospital, the group of large thatched buildings where Dr. Kenneth Fraser and his wife Eileen, CMS missionaries, had established their ministry of healing, education and Christian faith in 1920. Nearby was a large evergreen ficus tree. "That," said Ken, "is where men and women were rounded up and shackled in irons before being marched off and shipped north on the Nile to a life of slavery. The people have not forgotten." Dr. Fraser chose to hold the first Christian services in the shade of that tree, known as '*Laro*', turning a place of awful memories and associations into a centre of hope and joy and Good News. At intervals on our road we had noticed the dark evergreen leaves of mango trees which according to Ken marked the slave route to the Nile; elsewhere in Africa too, mango trees are believed to have been planted by Arab traders during the centuries of the slave trade.

Not too far to go now and as the tropical darkness fell we rattled across the long iron bridge spanning the wide river Yei, just before Mundri. So this was Mundri, this small cluster of basic shops and a police post was the town, so small so insignificant and only just visible by the light of a couple of oil lamps on verandahs where groups of men sat and talked. We had travelled a long way to reach such a destination! A sharp turn to the left and down the hill on a much narrower road, over a small bridge above the Mori river, a tributary of the Yei, and the dim lights of Bishop Gwynne College were there in front of us. The moment of our arrival had come.

The sound of a lorry in the stillness of the dark evening brought figures flickering through the shadows as we rounded the circle of low houses. Glimmers of feeble light showed that some students with their families had arrived early for the new term. We passed other buildings, their high thatched roofs outlined by our headlights, and at the far end of the circle came to the lit-up verandah of the Principal's house. Mary and David Brown, whom we had met in

Juba, were there to give us a warm welcome, Alan (3) and Peter (1), all ready for bed, peeping from behind them to see what was going on. Soon we were in the house, blinking in the sudden brightness of the hissing Tilley pressure lamp. We were covered in red dust, and longed to wash and longed to quench our thirst and probably most of all longed for it to be time for bed. Michael and Katherine, quiet and uncertain, held closely to us when Mary, carrying an oil lantern, led us to the guest room. She told us they would enjoy having us staying with them for some weeks until a house was ready for us. Meanwhile Ken would sleep in the College guest *tukl* but have his meals with the crowd of us in the Browns' house where each day we had regular reports on the progress of the house he was building.

I remember very little of the rest of that strange evening except baths and supper, the bliss of getting to bed, and the relief of finding that the air was cooler and less humid than in Juba.

John and I fell asleep thanking God that we had arrived safely and wondering if this was the place where our vocation would be fulfilled, if this was where we would be able to make a home for ourselves and our children.

12 Bishop Gwynne College

David and Mary Brown's house

Dawn, our first day in Mundri. A knock on our door at 6.00 a.m. and in came Micah carrying a tray with tea. He was tall, very dark and serious, but ready with a smile and a greeting in Moru. He had been up long enough to light a fire, boil the kettle and follow the pattern in giving Mary and David and the visitors their early morning tea. It was very refreshing though John and I felt rather embarrassed; being served tea early in the morning, and what was worse while still in bed, was certainly not an Irish custom. We could hear Michael and Katherine awake too, playing with Alan, and then a shout or two and the noise of a skirmish over toys. This was hard for Alan who had a lot of things to play with while our children, with none of theirs unpacked, had nothing to share and anyway did not acknowledge such a thing as ownership. That was not the last of these disputes!

Bishop Gwynne College 79

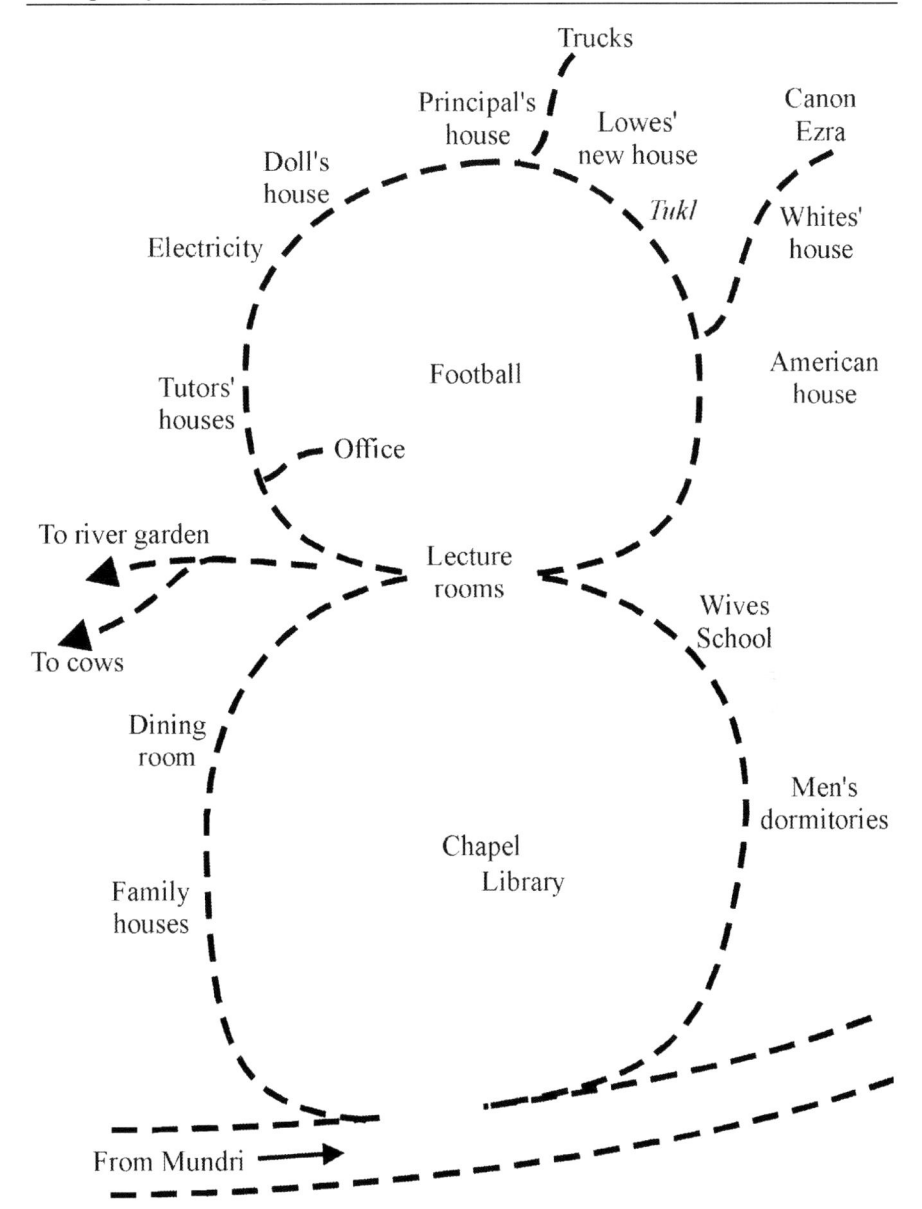

Trucks
Principal's house
Lowes' new house
Canon Ezra
Doll's house
Tukl
Whites' house
Electricity
Tutors' houses
Football
American house
Office
To river garden
Lecture rooms
Wives School
To cows
Dining room
Men's dormitories
Chapel Library
Family houses
From Mundri →

BISHOP GWYNNE COLLEGE
MUNDRI, SUDAN, IN 1961

After a breakfast of mango cut in cubes and millet porridge we could hardly wait to go out to see the College. It was still cool when we set off, David walking round with John and talking College matters, while Mary and I followed with the children just chatting as we went and enjoying getting to know each other. It was the end of the four month long dry season so the grass had been burnt to a frazzle, and apart from a few evergreen mango trees and an enormous ficus in front of the house, the trees were bare. I could see the attractive way the College had been laid out in two circles like a figure eight, and planted with flowering shrubs. I was particularly interested in the frangipani trees which I had never seen before coming to Sudan. Growing to eight or ten feet high they bore small star-like blooms, sometimes called Temple flowers, which were white and waxy and gave off a heavy sweet scent; they bloomed in the dry season on grey-ghost branches which if cut oozed sticky latex. The Temple name suggested India and, since it was almost invariable that these strange little trees were to be seen in the gardens of missionaries and expatriates, it seemed likely they were imported rather than native to Africa. The scarlet bracts of the shoulder-high poinsettia bush outside the *tukl* where Ken was staying, and the other shrubs flowering in brilliant colours, were a kind of promise that with the wet season life would return. The first of the rain had fallen as we arrived and it was nice for us that the people were shouting their thanks to us for bringing it!

We left the Browns' house behind us at the far end of the circle of staff houses surrounding the football pitch, and passed the lecture rooms and the office before walking into the much larger circle around which the students lived. Here were dormitory blocks for single men and a wide arc of thatched houses for married students and their families, students of the same language group being housed as neighbours and all having their own food gardens nearby. We cut across the grass to reach the chapel, beautifully set in the wide open space in the centre.

Canon Ezra Baya Lawiri

Going to the chapel first was special, and there standing at the door was Canon Ezra Baya Lawiri, Vice-Principal since 1956, his hands outstretched, his dark face radiant with a wide smile of welcome for us. Although he had called at the house the night before, it was good that our first proper meeting with him was in the chapel. He was a neat man of medium height with a calm and friendly nature and it wasn't long before we found in him a very special and wise friend. He was one of the first of the Moru people to accept the Christian faith as his own and was a teacher before his ordination. He established the new parish at Mundri before joining the staff of Bishop Gwynne College. His life-long work of translating the Bible was very important for the Moru people, but it was Ezra's understanding and wisdom that made the difference for us when the going was tough. "But God is not defeated," was what he loved to say whether the discussion was about the story of the Sudanese Church, its problems and failures, or the successes and triumphs of its growth. The chapel was the place where staff and students met regularly as a Christian community, the place where we would come when we were happy and when we were troubled or sad, where we would find the strength and vision to persevere. Ezra with his wife Hana were the core of the College; we do not forget them.

Library end of the Chapel building

Arthur Riley from Australia had designed and built this chapel when he was Principal between 1951 and 1956. By then he had developed considerable skills in the design and erection of school, Mission and Church buildings in various places. He wanted the College Chapel to be large but at the same time to reflect the local traditional buildings rather than look foreign; two very large round African huts joined by parallel walls for the nave was his brilliant solution. The walls were of ironstone neatly pointed and the high thatched roof was massive, supported on beams stained black with old engine oil. Inside the walls were plastered and painted white. One of the rounded ends was walled off to house the library which was named after the Rev. Charles Bertram. He had died of black-water fever in 1945 while working in the Nuer swamps. For some time after that, his doctor wife May stayed on in those swamps, going about her work riding on an ox, but later transferred North to be the doctor for many years at the CMS Hospital in Omdurman. It was her house we had stayed in on our way to Mundri. The other rounded end formed the chancel at the east end of the chapel where a special three-foot cross, made of cut and polished alabaster, was set in the wall as the central window. It had been made as a copy of a similar cross in a church in Old Cairo and brought from Egypt as a memorial to Eunice Kerr, a CMS missionary wife who died in Bari country in 1945. Below the cross was a framed map of the world, a daily witness that we in Sudan belonged to the great company of Christians in every country. The library at one end and the cross at the other were an inspiration but also reminded us that there was a cost to missionary service here. The cross with the sun shining through its translucent stone looked wonderful and must have delighted Brian de Saram at his ordination here in February 1959 a month before our arrival. It delighted us later when our baby Patrick was baptized by Canon Ezra with that same glorious light shining on him.

Dried up crinkled leaves crackled under our feet as we continued our walk, and funny little lizards scuttled off when we disturbed them. No danger or nuisance there but ants were a different matter as Mary told me when we passed what looked like a dark rope across our path. This was a marching column of safari ants with much larger 'soldier' ants stationed at regular intervals to govern the line on each side. Many of these busy regimented insects carried burdens almost as big as they were themselves, whether supplies or the cocoons they raided and enslaved from other colonies, and it was a puzzle that wherever they were off to some seemed to be going forwards and others back. They were quick to attack any obstacle in their way. In fact they were capable of cornering a small chicken or animal and eating it alive, leaving only the bones picked clean. If you were a child or an unsuspecting or dreamy person you could be surprised by a sharp and painful nip on some juicy part by a 'soldier ant'; it wasn't long before all of us knew what that felt like. The way to stop the safari ants was to put fire or a barrier of ashes down to divert them, something we rushed to do whenever we spotted a line heading in our direction. Ants were fascinating to Katherine and she would stand for ages watching them, though she took care to be far enough away not to be attacked herself. She had some questions when she was a little older. "Did God make everything?" she asked. When we agreed that was so she immediately had a second question. "Why then," she wanted to know, "did He make ants and flies?" But on our first day all this was new. It would take us some time to get used to our new surroundings, and learn how to stay safe from creatures such as snakes and scorpions and safari ants.

Hanging from a tree ahead was a piece of iron girder. Alan knew about it and ran to show our children how to bang it with a piece of metal. "You'll be hearing that every morning," David told us with a smile, "the loud clang is when the College workmen begin work at 6.00 in the morning and it clangs again when they stop and go home at 2.00. They have a break for breakfast from 8.00 to 9.00 and we're glad we have one then too!" The clanging of that iron bar would be the sound which regulated our days from now on.

The first group of students and their families had already arrived on a hired lorry, some of them at the College for the first time and others who had returned for another year. We could feel their enthusiasm

Student family houses

as they settled in, busy preparing their gardens and looking forward to their studies and preparation for ordination. It was exciting for us too to feel the hum of life as the houses filled up with students, and to know that soon the work we had come to do would begin.

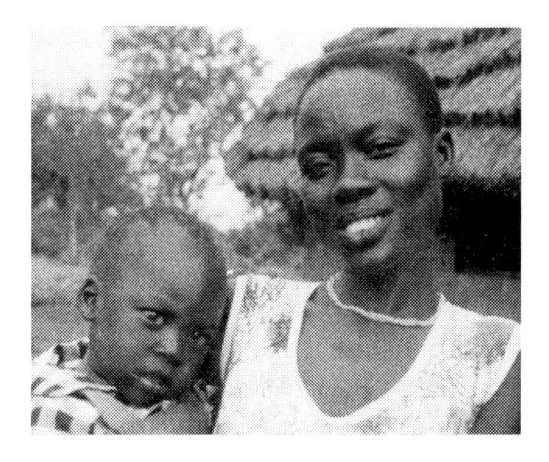

Our next call was on Richard Gill who was living temporarily in a small thatched house near the classrooms. More than lecturing, he loved to be with his students in their home areas. We often watched him when he packed up for these treks and tied tin *safias* to the back of the lorry for his hens, which made agonising noises with their claws scraping on the shiny tin surfaces but at least provided Richard with his breakfast egg. It wasn't long before Michael and Katherine discovered that Papa Fluff, as they called Richard because of his big beard, was always pleased to see them when he was at home. Perhaps his tin of sweets was another reason why his path was the one they always chose for their walks. At the end of the following year Richard became Principal when David and Mary transferred to work in Juba and later in the Middle East. By then bachelor Richard's days of going off on trek were at an end for, on local leave in Uganda, he fell in love with Elizabeth and brought her back to Mundri as his bride. That made us all happy, and most of all the two of them.

Richard Gill's temporary house

The sun was now higher and it was much hotter, time to retreat to the shade of the Browns' verandah. From there we could see Ken Ogden going about his work with the men constructing what looked like a very small house, a very small house indeed for such a hot climate. It was being built on a tight budget without a verandah and with neither electricity nor plumbing it wouldn't take long to finish. Although it had been planned with Richard in mind, when he walked about in the foundations he decided that it was going to be too small for him. I think he was quite right. In this climate it was mad to be building such a house. But if too small for one man how could it possibly be considered big enough for John and me and our two children? Still that was the decision made in our first week in Mundri. Barely able to keep my thoughts to myself I stayed quiet and didn't express them. My missionary training to be accepting and calm hadn't yet worn off.

While we waited for the completion of the 'Doll's house', as we had begun to call it, I had time to learn from Mary about living in Mundri. Missionaries provided hospitality for each other at a set payment and though it could be a chore when food and water were scarce, we all enjoyed having guests to stay. Looking after us and Ken as well as her own family, however, meant a lot of work for Mary. Before she married David, Mary was a teacher and here in Mundri she taught in the Wives School as well as devoting herself to caring for David and their children, not to mention guests like us. She began her long day by planning meals from scant ingredients, and seeing to the other household tasks which the various helpers would be doing. For Elia, the cook, she weighed out supplies of food and gave him money to pay for whatever meat, fruit or vegetables he could buy in Mundri market a mile away. More tricky was getting him to agree to cook what she wanted. For Micah and Elisa there was the endless sweeping of the dusty floors, putting local beeswax on the furniture to stop it drying out, making the beds and, using a large bar of coarse soap, washing clothes in the bath water of the night before. These clothes dried almost instantly and were then ironed with a box-iron filled with hot glowing charcoal.

Making tea, setting tables, serving food and washing-up were regular activities throughout the day, and at some time before dark at 6.00 the blackened glass globes of the oil lamps had to be cleaned, the paraffin replenished and the wicks trimmed. Every day too, Mary had to make sure wood and water were collected and brought to the house ready for use, and enough water boiled and cooled for drinking. I began to understand the need to employ so many people to give us time to do our work and keep reasonably comfortable and healthy in this hot humid climate without the machines and conveniences we had been used to.

David and John attended prayers in the College chapel every morning, and returned to join us for breakfast at 8.00. I used to look out for the two of them, both quite tall men and academic types, and chuckle to see the contrasting shape of their khaki shorts, John's wide and short and David's narrow and down to almost cover his knees! David was ten years older but had a boyish fresh-faced complexion while John, after our weeks of slow travel, had cooked to a deep tan as if he came from the Middle East. They worked well together, each respecting the other. It was under David's leadership that Bishop Gwynne College made great progress and began to attract more educated students including some who were able to study for the Certificate of Religious Knowledge of the University of London.

After breakfast, to our surprise, the six people employed by David and Mary joined us in the dining-room and without any sign of shyness or hesitation they led Christian prayers in Moru ending with the Lord's prayer which we said in English. It made a good start to the day when we all prayed together.

Our main meal consisted of one of the three staples, sweet potatoes, cassava, or rice, served with a stew of meat or tough chicken, or occasionally a pot roast. Vegetables were more difficult. In the wet season the garden produced green beans and spinach but otherwise we depended on dried broad beans (*ful misri*) and boiled onions. The children were particularly pleased when there was a pudding made of milk and cornflour and sugar which could turn out to be yellow and called custard, white and called blancmange or best of all with cocoa added to make it chocolate!

After lunch it was time for a *'raha'*, a siesta when we all lay on our beds for a brief rest to refresh ourselves before getting on with our work, and after tea on the verandah we often walked around the College with the children chatting with students and their families. Supper, bath, a story and bedtime prayers for the children came next, followed by our turn in the bathroom and a change into clean clothes and a simple evening meal often of groundnut or lentil soup.

It was relaxing and peaceful when we sat together in the lamplight after work, at the end of the day, the tropical night outside remote and quiet, cooler air blowing in. We were protected from whining mosquitoes by the wire-mesh windows, but moths often managed to be inside where they fluttered around the oil light, singed their wings and crashed to the ground. There were always lizards to watch; the sitting room was a special kind of hunting ground for them. Grey-green and about the length of my hand, their heads were triangular, their bodies and long tails almost transparent. They secured themselves by the suction pads at the ends of their little hand-like limbs, and could stay very still for ages at odd angles on the walls. I waited fascinated to see them move their heads up and down, and then, just as I was giving up, dart to capture and swallow their prey.

The evening ended when one of us read the Bible reading for the day and trusting in the love and care of God we took ourselves off to bed.

13   The Doll's House

The Doll's house was begun, built and finished before our very eyes. Before writing about the students and our purpose in being in Mundri I want to tell you about that house and our surroundings. Every day from the Brown's verandah we looked across at Ken and the Lainya men as they worked. Every afternoon when the men had gone home we walked about in the Doll's house with Michael and Katherine and longed for the day we would move into the first place on our own in Africa. Typical village houses were constructed with branches woven together and plastered with mud under a circular thatched roof. Schools and churches were bigger and oblong but constructed in much the same way. George Frangos, the Greek merchant in the village, had built his shop with bricks under corrugated iron, and the Intermediate School and several buildings in Bishop Gwynne College were of cut ironstone and hand-made fired brick. All of these were attractive but cost more than the greyish blocks being used for the Doll's house. Ken had brought his block-machine from Lainya, and set it up just beside where the house was to be built. The men used shovels to make a mixture of mud, sand, and cement and then packed this into the heavy metal block-mould, compacted it with a descending lever and one by one pressed each block out. They were then set in rows under grass shelters which slowed down the drying-out and prevented cracking before the blocks were ready for use.

Although it was not beautiful, the Doll's house was going up at great speed and was not expensive. By now the openings for windows were filled with frames of cut timber made in Lainya. Later each would have its screen of fine wire mosquito mesh nailed into place and supported on expanded metal bars in a diamond pattern. There was no need for glass for every whisper of wind was welcome and rain coming in could soon be mopped off the concrete floors. When

Michael, now adult, recalls these windows of his childhood and teases me that when I shut the door he remembers it was like being put in prison, I remind him that our own bedroom was much the same! Most unusually there was no plan or money for either a verandah or shutters, so the Lowes would live a hot life in public view for the first bit of their time in Mundri.

The Doll's house

The roof of the Doll's house was of corrugated iron supported on wooden poles; the walls were plastered with a mixture of mud and sand, and then painted with a yellow wash made from a deposit found in the forest, a colour we called 'CMS Custard!' The grey concrete floors were given a finer top screed. At first clouds of fine dust rose when these were swept but with old engine oil and wax from the local bees they improved and became shiny and easier to keep clean. In general dusting was a noisy job in Sudan carried out by banging cloths against surfaces so that the dust was redistributed rather than removed.

The Doll's house consisted of a small central sitting/dining room, to the left a tiny room intended as a study but just big enough for the children's cots, and to the right our bedroom with an alcove off it for a bathroom. In this a low concrete wall surrounded an area with two taps in the wall and a drain hole to the outside. There was no bath or basin but we managed well with a tin bath we bought from a retiring missionary and some plastic basins we had brought with us. What bliss it would have been had we been able to have a shower! Two 40 gallon (200 litre) barrels, set at the top of some steps outside and never more than partly filled, served as the water system, the gradient allowing the water to flow into the bathroom. To prevent either barrel being left with stagnant water long enough to become a breeding place for mosquitoes, the fire was lit below one or the other on alternate days. To find out which tap had warm water all we had to do was to glance through the window to see where the smoke was coming from.

Having enough water in Mundri was always difficult. In the wet season the College wells filled up and provided water for most of the time the students were in residence, but in the dry season our only source was the river Mori about a mile away. Then all our water had to be collected and carried in four-gallon paraffin tins called *safias*. With no rain the river Mori itself soon dried up, and Bunya, whom we employed to bring our water, would sit on the sandy river bed collecting water with a cup out of a hollow he had made in the sand. We had to be very careful with the limited supply he was able to get for us. Some was poured into tall fired-earthen pots called *zeers* and dripped as it filtered from these into a tin *safia* below; the house was never free day or night of the sound of the drip drip of this water echoing ceaselessly around our tin roof. It forms a background memory of Mundri for all of us. After being filtered and boiled the water was poured into smaller earthen pots called *gullahs* where, in the heat, condensation of the surface moisture cooled it for drinking. All this was essential. Many diseases were water-borne; to neglect extreme precautions with drinking water would have been foolhardy and dangerous.

Bath water was a luxury though it didn't always look great. I remember one visitor from CMS Headquarters in London declined to use it, saying he thought he would be cleaner before than after a bath in water like ours! That made me pretty annoyed at the time. We all bathed in turn in the same water, the children first, and next morning it was used for washing clothes and finally poured onto the few vegetables we were trying to grow. It was no wonder the rains were so welcome when they came.

The sanitation was an improvement on the bucket systems of Omdurman and Juba. We had our mud-walled thatched 'little house', a long-drop pit latrine twenty yards away outside with a *zareeba*, a grass screen, around it but no door. A red flag on a long bamboo pole was provided to warn others when the place was occupied! When one day we found a snake inside Katherine protested with a giggle: "But Mammy, it didn't put up the flag!" The main disadvantage was not the lack of a door but that it took some courage to cover those twenty yards outside if the need arose in the darkness of the night when a leopard could be on the prowl or a snake slithering along on the path.

A small store, a work table and cupboards standing with their legs inside tins of water as a barrier to ants, space for our oil cooker which we only used for occasional baking when we had enough paraffin, and space for the *zeers* for filtering our drinking water completed the Doll's house. The kitchen was a thatched building quite separate from the house, for there was always the danger of fire, besides which we didn't need extra heat any nearer to us. At first our cooking was done in the open on a fire on the ground, the pot supported on three large stones, but later we had a sort of cooker. This was built of ironstone with a space for a fire beneath a 'hot plate' made from corrugated iron hammered out so as to be almost, but not quite, flat. There was even an oven. A small oil drum was set on its side with a fitted door and a piece of metal for a shelf, and then another fire was lit beneath it. There were no controls and no thermometer and sometimes the place was thick with smoke, but Tito never complained and often amazed us with the dishes he managed to produce from limited ingredients and on such elementary equipment. Tito made a shoulder high drying rack outside the kitchen. Pots and pans once washed were put up on this to dry in the sun and be safe from chickens and animals though not from flies. After Bunya came back with the water, he went into the forest each day to cut firewood for us and we liked to astonish our supporters in Ireland by telling them that we cooked on fires of mahogany and lived on bird seed (millet) and monkey-nuts!

By the end of April the Doll's house was ready. The eight pieces of luggage we had with us were soon unpacked and the rest of our 23 items were expected any day now for we had heard they had reached Juba. But before we could move in properly Ken took us the fifteen miles to Lui. Dr. and Mrs. Fraser had started the Mission hospital there in 1921 but a year before we arrived it had been taken over by the Government, and now the furniture left behind when the missionaries departed was available for us. We drove past the oblong thatched wards, an operating room, dispensary, laboratory, the Chapel and staff houses, and then the houses built for the missionary nurses and doctor, and at the house where Joan Bradford had lived we collected a set of basic issue CMS house furniture. This consisted of two large steamer chairs, one dining room table, six dining chairs, one food safe, one washstand, one wardrobe, two single iron beds and a *zeer*-stand but no *zeers*. Really very basic! The steamer chairs didn't fit in our little Doll's house but we paid to have smaller armchairs and a settee made of hardwood by the carpenters at Lainya, and bought locally made cotton cushions for them. This furniture was screwed together and has been unscrewed and screwed up again in every house we have lived in since.

My hopes soared when, as a special concession for me as a doctor, we were provided with a small paraffin fridge, the only fridge in Mundri. Could it be that after all I really would have medicines and vaccines and patients needing them? Not that our small antique model fridge with Queen Anne legs would be much use for it only managed to make ice occasionally. It belched black smoke when the wind blew out the flame and made me furious when I found everything covered with a black soot deposit. It also belched black smoke on the day when Michael managed to open the enticing little screw-top and pour water into the paraffin container. "Poor fridge wanted a drink," he explained and then had a question for me. "But what I want to know, Mammy, is how can heat make things cold?" I advised him to ask his father instead!

Setting up our home and trying to make it as attractive as possible was fun. A packing case made a dressing table for our bedroom, with the Fablon we had brought with us on top, and a shelf inside, a mirror on the wall and deep pink curtains in front. And at last we had our double bed. With the 'elephant' mattress spread across the two single iron beds CMS provided, I stretched myself out on that nice wide space well pleased and happy to be sharing it with John. And stretched out on that bed every night for the next two years, we woke about 2.00 a.m. to the creaks and groans of the corrugated iron roof above us as it cooled down after the heat of the day and contracted. The house would be cooler from then until dawn and we needed to get up to put covers over the children.

It's a man's world!

It was only when we went on local leave to Uganda and Kenya that we found CMS missionaries there did not live in as Spartan conditions as we did in Sudan, though we accepted that it was right for us to be more in tune with the people around us who had a lot less than we had. A couple of years later a more adequate house was built specially for us and we were able to have a part in its design, and include an enclosed passage to the pit latrine. Amongst other things we bought brown powder cement colouring when we were in Kenya on local leave and, when this was added to the top screed and polished, our new house had a floor which looked like cork and was greatly admired. We have been told that that floor still survived 40 years later so that our house was known as the one with the beautiful floor in the main room.

Our barrels make good toys

Mary and I often had a good laugh together that first year, both of us the mothers of two small children and trying to support our husbands as we all lived in the isolation of Mundri. When everything in the garden near the house was shrivelled up by the sun and the roots could not survive the heat which radiated off the ironstone only a few inches below the surface, Mary taught me to have a dry-season garden by the river where Ro'ba, employed as our gardener, would have water to pour on the growing vegetables. We were successful in producing tomatoes, cucumbers, and beans as well as a local cress called *jir-jir*. New Zealand perpetual spinach was new to me and a most useful vegetable. It was strange to see Ro'ba standing a long way distant from the ground he was working on until I understood the reason. His hoe, in the shape of a seven-inch iron plate, was attached to a very long handle so that if there was a snake in the area he was hoeing he could deal with it without being in danger himself. He prepared seed beds and I placed the seeds, most often two beans, in holes after mixing in ashes as a deterrent to termites. In the fierce heat everything had to be watered twice a day. Ro'ba erected little eight-inch-high grass shelters to protect the seeds from being washed away by heavy rain and to keep the sun off the young plants. These efforts sometimes produced very quick results with beans, though on one occasion when Ro'ba followed the same method with carrot seed, just two tiny seeds deep in each hole, the result was not impressive!

In the rainy season we were able to produce good tomatoes in our garden near the house. Katherine and Michael enjoyed picking them and laying them out in boxes to ripen where the chickens couldn't eat them, and I bragged about them. I even bragged to my father, who knew what a reluctant gardener I had been, "of course the vast amount of gardening experience I have had as a 'bystander' and 'interested observer' is a great help so thank you for those years of big Rectory gardens. At least I have seen almost every species from seed to fruition at some time or other."

14 Diya's Village

"Don't unpack. The way things are going we really don't think you should bother to unpack for you won't be here long." That was the advice we were given all around. An American missionary family took it literally and for the couple of years before they left lived with their possessions still in their packing cases. But we couldn't wait to set up our own home. It was over a year since we had packed up our flat in Belfast to go for a year of missionary training and here we were in Mundri, all excited and ready to set ourselves up in the Doll's house at last.

Ready to move into the Doll's house

So we unpacked all those baggages, the familiar household things and the wedding presents, the things we had bought from the export firm and which we had hardly seen, the clothes, toys and sets of new sandals to fit Michael and Katherine over the next two years. John had done a good job with the packing and it was amazing that our goods had travelled all that way without breakages. "Where can we put this?" John asked, holding up a very tall cut-glass flower vase, a wedding present he considered only suitable for an arrangement of hollyhocks or rhubarb! We were enjoying ourselves and being 'helped' by the children who thought everything was a present for them. "How does this go together?" was what I wanted to know, my hands full of nuts and bolts and the flat-pack pieces of our oil stove and oven spread out and waiting to be assembled. It was a lovely feeling, John and me and our children at home in our tiny house.

Breakfast, fitted in after chapel at 7.00, was probably our favourite meal for we ate it when we were fresh and rested and it was not yet so hot. Fruit whenever we had some, millet porridge sprinkled with roasted *simsim* (sesame seeds) for John and me, and sometimes ground rice or *dukhn* (finger millet) for the children now that we had unpacked our small grinding mill. Michael, always mechanically minded, used to watch the grinding and help with turning the rather stiff handle; he kept telling us he was big now and able to do it himself.

Each day Tito and I organised the meals depending on what ingredients were available. In the wet season the local schools were open which made it worthwhile for the Greek merchant to butcher once a week. A rumour would reach us that there was meat, a rumour that would take Tito off at a run to the market in Mundri to buy what he could. Fillet or brisket or bone were all sold at the same price of four *piastres* a *rotl*, (about the same price for a pound of meat in Mundri as for a pound of sugar in Ireland). The meat was tender and good when Tito got over his fear of the hissing Pressure

Cooker which was a gift to us from the Mothers' Union in St. Mary Magdalene's, the Belfast church where John had been curate.

Some days I went to the river garden to see if there were vegetables ready to eat; at other times we relied on dried beans or onions sent on the post lorry, the *busta*, by the Arab merchant in Juba. Special items we had dreamed up and put on our lists sometimes turned up as a nice surprise though we really had very little choice in what Ibrahim sent. Neither had we any choice in the condition it arrived in. The main hazard was in the packing, for no attempt was made to protect food from the four-gallon tin *safias* of paraffin which were always part of the load, and which after lurching and banging on the lorry for 180 miles could arrive leaking or even completely empty. It was very frustrating when cotton bags of precious beans and lentils and coffee burst and got mixed up together or sugar and flour were saturated with paraffin, but we learned to sort and save and disguise as much as we could in those days before strict packaging and sell-by dates had been invented. We had grapefruit from the College trees, lovely in the dry season if there was the sugar or honey to sweeten them, and local people came to our door to sell mangoes and pineapple and sometimes a chicken or eggs, eggs which Katherine liked to help us to check for freshness. If they floated to the top when we lowered them gently into water we could tell they were bad and we didn't buy them, though we hated to disappoint the hopeful trader and we were sad too because eggs were a valuable source of protein which we would have been glad to pay a higher price for if we could have had more of them.

So far I was busy settling in to our new house and new life and, although I had no licence yet to do medical work, I was well occupied and happy preparing lessons to teach in the Wives School, helping John with the Library, typing notes for the students, and sneaking some time for my own reading as well as caring for Michael and Katherine and John.

I often sat on our small settee, a child cuddling up to me to the right and to the left while stories were told and stories were read and reread until we all knew every word by heart. At other times, in the shade outside, Michael never tired of playing with his trucks and making roads for them and Katherine kept herself busy looking after her family of dolls and teddies and teaching them good behaviour.

For our first year or so there were other missionary children around too, Alan and Peter Brown, Ian White, and Julie and Johnie Koehler, and while they all played together we four mothers, Mary, Violet, Mary Jewell and I, had only to watch them entertaining each other and sometimes intervene if there was a problem. Farms were laid out, mud or plasticine animals assembled, gardens decorated with flowers picked from the shrubs; sand for roads and mud pies, water to pour and pour and splash on each other; paints in bright colours and brushes to decorate pieces of paper and even their own little bodies. Two old 40 gallon oil drums, with too many holes to be any use for liquids, were now very useful as large exciting 'toys' for tumbling over as they rolled along. It was a safe and carefree world, their mothers always there, local people always friendly, and though it was very hot there was nothing at all except an odd expedition to disturb the simple routine.

I was to hurry, Katherine said, for she had buckled on her sandals and was ready for the visit to 'My Diya', as she called her, the young girl who looked after her and Michael while I was teaching. Diya had offered to come for us but we wanted to find her village for ourselves, so John and I and the children set off - turn here, take the second path there, look out for some trees - it was like exploring though I'm not sure we would have found the place at all only that Diya came to meet us.

Going to Diya's village

We walked in single file trying to keep in the shadow of the millet which, near harvest, was turning to gold and soared ten feet high on each side of the narrow path. It was quite an event for her family that white people from the College, and particularly the children, had come to where their skin, their hair, and their clothes could be examined and touched and commented on. All this scrutiny didn't suit Michael who wanted to chase the chickens or Katherine who was set on taking Diya by the hand to see where she had her bed.

Since I was the one learning Moru, I was the one to greet Diya's mother and the others of her family in the few sentences of their language I had so far learnt; I was not surprised that my faltering words brought the usual wide smiles and exclamations and then a torrent of Moru so fast I had no way of understanding it. The family were proud to show us their village. The round thatched houses over there were for family members and visiting relations. The brown earth they were set on was beaten down hard and always kept clean by someone, a granny or a child, sweeping it with a broom of small twigs. Those were the water pots used by Diya and the women to carry water from the river about half a mile away and that was the broken pot which used to be the one for brewing beer. Grain stores, in the shape of the houses but less than half the size, complete with layers of thatch, were raised on posts the height of a man's shoulder to protect the contents from bush rats and termites; high up under them was where the chickens roosted at night, the small ones helped up 'ladders' to keep them safe and not in the direct path of safari ants.

The grain, though there wasn't much left so near harvest time, was *dura*, the local millet. Hard and spherical the size of a peppercorn it was the staple food; in areas with good soil and rain, a crop could mature in three months making two crops a year possible, though that didn't happen often in the Mundri area. Even one crop here could be badly damaged by swooping flocks of red *dura* birds. Small boys spent all day on high platforms to frighten them away by shouting very loudly and aiming at them with their catapults, just as we could see they were doing now. Michael, who loved climbing ladders, fancied joining the small boys though he wasn't so keen to be up there with them for hours and hours. When ripe the seed heads were cut and stored on their stalks or as grain in large baskets in the grain stores.

We watched Diya's mother remove her dark blue cloth knotted over one shoulder like a toga and, in her old skirt and top, start to prepare millet for the family meal. She used a hollowed-out tree trunk as a mortar in which she pounded the grain with a heavy wooden pestle to separate it from the husks. This job made her very hot and sweaty. She got rid of the chaff by tossing and blowing at it in a specially woven flat basket, then she poured it in small amounts onto a worn rock on the ground, took her grinding stone in her hand and with her strength and weight crushed the millet to meal beneath her. This hard work was woman's work and was never done by a man. It had to be done every day for, because of weevils, grain was never stored in the form of flour.

Weevils were a great nuisance to us too for they got into everything except tinned food. To buy wheat flour for bread we had to apply for a Government permit which could take many weeks to come. The flour was often infested with weevils and although we did our best with sieving, these insects added their own distinctive and unattractive flavour which was hard to disguise. One day when I was particularly disgusted with the condition of the flour, I measured some for closer examination. I haven't forgotten that in two tablespoons of it I counted 64 whole weevils and several little writhing maggot offspring as well. Still we ate it!

Diya, her skin a deep ebony, was young and slim, her hair arranged in tight little plaits. She looked lovely standing very upright and poised in the turquoise dress I had made for her. You might think that, with the sun shining and the sky a bright blue, everywhere would have been colourful and sparkling in Mundri, but apart from our clothes and Diya's dress and flowering shrubs this is not how I remember the villages at all; vivid green only at the start of the rains, grass soon faded in that fierce heat and, like the leaves of the trees, looked dull and rank; the earth was sandy and tinged with the red of ironstone, not distinct at all as it merged with the houses of dried mud thatched with dried grass. Clothing worn in the villages was no particular colour; perhaps with poor washing conditions it merged to the darkish shade that was usual, though in the towns primary colours and patterns had come into fashion.

Diya changed into old clothes before she set about cooking a thick porridge called *asida*. She poured a thin stream of millet flour into a pot of boiling water set on three large stones over the fire and, to prevent lumps forming, stirred it vigorously with a long stick which she was constantly spinning between her hands. At first it was easy to stir but as the mixture thickened it became stiff, too stiff for Katherine to manage it when she wanted to help. Meanwhile Diya's mother had cooked a sauce of groundnuts and a green leafy vegetable. The old grandmother, wrinkled and with only a few teeth left in her sagging mouth, woke up where she was sitting propped against the wall of her house and, leaning on her long staff, hobbled over. An uncle and an older brother had been waiting for the meal to be ready, and Diya's father invited us to join them as one by one the family gathered. The men and John, and I as an 'honorary man', were given *gba'da*, small Moru stools to sit on, while further away the women and children with Diya and our two sat on woven mats on the ground. Before sitting down all of us held out our hands in the accustomed way while one of the family poured water over them. The *asida* was turned out like a moulded suet pudding onto a decorated enamel basin, and by turns we used a clean right hand to take a lump of it about the size of a small egg, dip it in the sauce and eat it. Perhaps not at first, but when its coarse texture and sour taste became more familiar to us we could enjoy it.

But neither at first nor later were we able to enjoy another local dish served if our visit turned out to be at the season when white ants in their winged stage fly. Rugged ant-hills, built of reddish earth enclosing a maze of tunnels, could be several metres high and were a feature of the countryside. We came across their occupants known as termites or white ants all too often when they raided our houses for the timber which was their main diet, or when they invaded the library to eat the books. A new patch of mud on a wall or door-post would indicate their overnight arrival and we would know that beneath the mud there was an invasion of termites destroying and consuming any wood they found there. Termite damage to wooden structures was the most usual cause of a building collapsing. However, each ant-hill was also valued and its ownership closely guarded in the villages. In the season, its owner prepared for the night the termites were expected to swarm. He made an exit hole in the side of the ant-hill and a deep hollow in the ground at the base and prepared tapers to burn. An excited crowd, who had some way of sensing when it was time for the swarming, gathered in the darkness when the ants began to emerge in vast numbers. As they flew upwards they met the flaming tapers, lost their scorched-off wings and fell into the prepared hollow. Quickly scooped up, their pale fat bodies were fried in their entirety. Fried ants tasted a bit like shrimps and were considered a delicacy by the Moru people though never by us!

We were learning all the time, learning how the Moru people around us coped. When Katherine noticed that children her own age cleaned their teeth by chewing on a stick while walking about, she had a go at copying them but not for long; she preferred the taste of her own toothpaste. We learned that narrow wooden cylinders about three feet long with pointed ends lying along branches high in the trees were local beehives and it was honey from hives like these that we bought at our door from local people, a full *safia* at a time. Just imagine when we had strained out the bits of wax and dead bees we could have four gallons of honey even if we had no sugar! Another local curiosity we spotted was the 'sausage tree.' The seed pods of this tall tree were a foot or more in length, and were the shape and colour of very large sausages hanging on thin fibres from high up. Though they were not edible.

At the end of our walks we nearly always went to see the College cows. They looked impressive and provided us with some fresh milk though, all costs considered, it was very expensive compared with tins of dried milk if these were available. The cows had been bought in Dinka country, and reminded us of our time on the Nile steamer when we saw great herds scattered over the open plain as they grazed, with always a lone herdsman standing on one leg keeping watch. White birds, egrets, lined up in groups of five or six along the backs of the grazing cattle and feasted on ticks and other insects before flying off for further supplies on other cattle; this was a mutual arrangement, good for both beasts and birds. Dinka cattle in shades of coffee and cream were splendid animals, large framed and sleek with huge horns arching out from their soft-eyed faces. Their ears were usually indented with decorative cuts which together with their individual features seemed enough for the pedigree and place of birth of each beast to be recognised by their Dinka admirers. Bukaru, the Dinka herdsman employed to look after the College cows, milked them in the mornings and evenings, and took them out for grazing during the day. Back in their *zareeba*, their enclosure for the night, he lit a smoky fire to give some relief from biting insects. Every morning we collected our ration of milk in a saucepan and boiled it using a glass 'milk-saver' to clonk on the bottom of the pan and prevent the milk from boiling over. When milk was plentiful we could buy more and we enjoyed the creamy top of it and even made butter occasionally.

Bukaru, like most of the men of the Dinka people, was used to a more nomadic life, living with his family in a permanent village on higher ground during the wet season, when grass for the cattle was plentiful and women could engage in some cultivation, and then migrating in the dry months to a 'cattle camp' in swampland where the cattle could find grazing not yet dried up. Bukaru liked to use the cow manure for his fire and used to shout and rage when it was collected for student and staff gardens instead.

Every evening in term-time we could see a line of Dinka students on their way to visit and admire the cattle, to take comfort that though they were so far from home they could be in touch again with the animals so central to their lives and affection, in fact almost like members of their family, for each one was known and recognised by them. John and I were amazed this was possible since the Dinka area is so large and its people and cattle so scattered. The only blemishes I suppose they disliked were the egg-sized lumps on the necks of the College cattle, each one representing the essential annual injection of a prophylactic compound. Without this the cows could not have survived disease carried by the tsetse fly prevalent in Moru country, the Dinka students would have been more homesick, and there would never have been fresh milk in Mundri. Dinka herdsmen were well known for their remarkable habit of standing on one leg while watching their herds. We often wondered how they sustained it, so one day we asked Bukaru to show us how it was done. With a laugh he stuck the shaft of a long Dinka spear firmly in the ground and took up his position. Holding onto the spear with one hand, he raised one foot and rested it on the knee of the other leg. Like this he could stand for hour after hour. Michael and Katherine tried to copy Bukaru but couldn't stay upright for more than a minute or two before tumbling over in a giggling heap.

These walks gave us some small contact with the people who lived around us, a contact we appreciated and so did they.

15   How it Began

You may think it was no small matter for John and me to set out as we did and travel so far to help in the training of Sudanese clergy in Mundri. Settled and unpacked now in our new house and surroundings I have to say it was no small matter either for a Sudanese Christian man to come to Bishop Gwynne College to be trained as a pastor of the Episcopal (Anglican) Church of Sudan (E.C.S.). This chapter is concerned with how that came about.

Each year thirty to fifty students, with their wives and children, many of whom had never been more than walking distance from where they had been born, passed the selection hurdle and prepared for the big adventure of travelling for hundreds of miles to the College. They brought their Bibles and Prayer books, small items of furniture, bedding, a hurricane oil lamp, pots for cooking and sacks of millet and groundnuts. Older children were left behind to continue at school in their own language area where relatives cared for them, while the youngest two or three were brought with their parents on the lorry and often joined by a new baby brother or sister during the College years.

Bishop Gwynne College, named after Llewellyn Gwynne the first bishop of the Episcopal Church of Sudan, had been founded in temporary buildings at Yei in 1946 and transferred in 1948 to Mundri in Moru country. Mundri was chosen as central to the areas of the four main tribes, Zande, Moru, Bari and Dinka, where the church was growing fast and in need of men and women who could teach the faith. It was also chosen at that time because the new joint Church and Government Teacher Training College was to be sited in Mundri, and a valuable link between the two Colleges could be forged. Mundri, however, was not the easiest place to establish a College. It was short of water in the dry season and, with ironstone just below the thin surface soil, growing food crops was difficult, besides which it was a very hot place to live in and not easy either for students and their families or for Sudanese and expatriate staff. But all of us wanted to help these students to become pastors, so we settled down and got on with the job.

But to understand how a man would go to Mundri to train as a Christian pastor you will need to learn about the coming of the Christian faith to Sudan, this part of the world which had been torn by war and where there had been little development for centuries. When I typed John's Church history notes I learned that there had been a strong Christian presence in Sudan more or less continuously for over a thousand years from Byzantine times until the sixteenth century. It was exciting to have this confirmed by archaeologists in the 1960s who were finding evidence of many ancient Christian churches in Nubia and on islands in the Nile. Those centuries of Christian civilization in Sudan had come to an end through isolation and advancing Islam.

For a short period in the nineteenth century the Christian Church was re-established by Roman Catholic missionaries but the deaths of many of them brought it to an end. The present era, our era, began with the arrival of CMS missionaries and missionaries of the American Presbyterian and Roman Catholic Churches around 1900, and all the signs were that this time the Christian Church saw itself as part of the worldwide fellowship of believers and was not isolated but in Sudan to stay.

During the Anglo-Egyptian Condominium, set up in 1898, the administration of Sudan was in the hands of British officials serving with the Sudan Political Service. Rather reluctantly they permitted some missionaries to develop schools and medical work in Khartoum and Omdurman but, dreading a resurgence of the Mahdi *jihad* of only a decade or two before, they forbade any direct Christian teaching or preaching among the Muslim population of Northern Sudan. For the Southern Provinces their policy was different. The British administrators declared the South a Closed

District to restrict the entry of the more educated and developed Northerners and prevent them from exploiting and dominating the South. Instead of Arabic they established English in the South as the official language and Sunday not Friday as the day of rest. Christian missionaries to the Southern provinces were welcomed and while pursuing pioneering efforts in the development of the undeveloped South were permitted to teach the Christian faith. The missionaries learned vernacular languages and produced written texts, using the set orthography. They set up the schools which, with Government subsidies, in time provided Southern Sudanese staff for administrative posts, and for hospital, school, commercial and agricultural development. In fact in the South medical services and education were largely provided by the missionaries rather than the Government. And missionaries too had a part to play in establishing stability in the South. Many of the administrators of the Anglo-Egyptian Condominium were former army officers whose way of dealing with rebellious peoples was a punitive show of strength. This only reminded the people of their previous bad experiences of cruelty under the Turks (Egyptian Government) and Mahdists and was not an effective method; the administrators soon recognised that it was much better to have the help of the missionaries who mediated peace and stability by friendship and persuasion instead.

Over the years, despite difficult living conditions, heat and isolation, illness and a number of deaths, Christian missionaries who made their way to Southern Sudan found satisfaction in the work they did and the Sudanese people they came to love and with whom they shared their Christian faith.

Some of these missionaries had dramatic ways of arrival. It's probably invidious to select them, but I'll pick out three who reached their destinations in Equatoria, the Province of the far south of Sudan, by boat, by bicycle and by motorbike.

Archibald Shaw (1879 - 1956), later Archdeacon, arrived well equipped. He bought a two masted sailing boat in Khartoum and had a superstructure looking rather like a two-storey house built on it to his own design. It must have been quite a spectacle for, referred to as 'Noah's Ark' and towed by a Government steamer, it had a P. & O. style saloon and accommodated himself and six missionaries, Sudanese helpers, building materials, food, two cows and a calf, an English cock and hens, and a pair of turkeys as they sailed south on the Nile in 1906. He was 27 at the time. He set up the first Mission station among the Dinka at Bor. Archdeacon Shaw is well remembered by the Dinka (Jieng) people of the past and even today to their third and fourth generation of descendents, for he (alone of those six with him) spent his entire life among the people whose language and customs he learned. It was he who translated the Bible into Dinka. Even after his retirement in 1940 he lived in Nairobi to be near enough to spend every dry season back in Dinka country with the people who had been his whole life concern. Although he saw very little response in his lifetime, that early teaching and example is now acknowledged as the seed of the present tremendous growth of the Christian Church among the Dinka people; an increase in the number of Christians in one area from 20% of the population to 80% in the past ten years according to Canon Diana Witts.
(*'God is not defeated'*- editors: Samuel E. Kayanga and Andrew C. Wheeler, 1999)

In 1920 **Dr. Kenneth Fraser (1877 - 1935)** and his Irish wife Eileen travelled by Nile steamer as far as the port at Tombe which is north of the present port at Terakeka; from there they astonished the local population as they cycled 120 miles on rough tracks in the heat, taking nine days to reach Lui, while on foot their luggage was carried in head-loads by fifty porters. At Lui they started medical work and set up a hospital, a church, and a school as they introduced the Moru people to the Christian faith. From these small beginnings young Christian converts were trained to be the medical dressers, the preachers and the teachers in a whole network of outreach

dispensaries, preaching centres and schools which they established in the area. It was a very effective strategy, the evangelisation of the Moru people being undertaken by the earliest Moru Christians themselves, with Dr. and Mrs Fraser there to encourage and help them. In Bishop Gwynne College we had particular reason to appreciate the mission and strategy of the Frasers for Canon Ezra, born in 1917, baptized in 1934 and ordained in 1946 was now Vice-Principal. He had been one of the boys to attend the very first school in the Moru area, and had been a teacher, Bible translator and pastor before joining the College staff. Dr. Fraser died in Lui in 1935 and was buried near the hospital he founded there.
(*'The Doctor comes to Lui'* - Eileen Fraser, 1941)

Arthur Riley (1901 - 1967) took five months in 1926 to reach Sudan. He sailed from Adelaide in Australia to Mombasa, made his way by train through Kenya, by steamer over Lake Victoria to Uganda and from Kampala northward on his overloaded two-stroke motor bike on unmade roads and tracks to Juba; 300 miles west took him to his location at Yambio in the Zande area almost on the Congo border. Safely there, he wrote a letter of proposal to Grace in Australia. That letter took 3 months to reach her and after deliberation her reply accepting him took another 3 months. It must have felt an eternity to both of them, that wait for the answer to such a portentous question, a wait which is hard to live through in imagination in these times when instant communication is possible even between the most remote of places. They were married in Australia on Arthur's first leave, and were amongst the missionaries still in Sudan when we arrived in 1959. To Michael and Katherine they were favourite 'Uncle Awful' and Auntie Grace; to me Grace was special and this must have been obvious to Elizala who helped us with the housework, for he used to be pleased for me when she was coming. "To-day you very happy," he would say, " because 'your mother' coming."
(*'No drums at dawn'* - Grace Riley, 1972)

These and many others have their part in the history of the growth of the Christian Church in Sudan but much more has resulted from the energy and initiative of Sudanese men and women who continue to spread the good news amongst their own families and communities. Followers of Jesus Christ live in a new way. They are transformed by the Holy Spirit and their changed lives attract others to believe and change. In time local Christians became the leaders, and it was at their request that missionaries like us arrived to help with specific tasks such as the training of the clergy at Bishop Gwynne College. The College did not work under CMS administration but under its own Council which was composed of Sudanese Church leaders, the Principal, a representative of the American Mission and the Bishop. Its members met regularly in the College to deal with serious business and to keep in touch with the students being trained.

John wrote:

"It is less than 40 years since the first missionaries came to this area, but now we have seen in the villages around that there are a great many Christians, and hundreds of new converts are baptized every year. Under Sudanese leadership, the Church is going forward at an amazing pace. Our Bishop confirms 5,000 new Christians annually. There is progress in other ways too, as the Sudanese Church takes over many things that used to be done by missionaries. All the pastors are Sudanese, Sudanese councils are in control, and now there are two Sudanese archdeacons, each supervising the Church in an area the size of Ireland.

"This story of rapid development will help you to understand the work of Bishop Gwynne College in its training men for the ministry of the Church, for its whole future depends on an adequate supply of pastors truly called and well equipped. The College still largely depends on missionary help from outside the Sudan for its teaching staff and funds, and in this the missionary societies are making an invaluable contribution. To see the Church flourishing here has been a tremendous spiritual encouragement to Dorothy and me."

While we were in Mundri, Bishop Oliver Allison provided inspiring and strong leadership. He had served as a CMS missionary teacher for ten years in the Bari area before he was consecrated Bishop in 1948. For the rest of his life he gave himself with utter devotion to Sudan. He never spared himself, even when he was in poor health, including through difficult years of conflict and right up to his retirement in 1974 and beyond.

When we first knew Oliver Allison he was Bishop not only of Sudan but also of the expatriate church congregations in Aden, Ethiopia, Somalia and Eritrea. He was a man of no fixed abode, staying in Clergy House in Khartoum when he was at the centre of his Diocese but otherwise constantly travelling to care for the pastors and people. A tall, big-boned man, with strong features below his full head of dark hair, he had an air of authority and sanctity; he could also have us collapsing with laughter as he recounted some of his experiences. We loved it when he made his visits to Mundri. With his driver and Yona, his helper of many years, his truck would rumble into the College and very soon a *tukl* or an empty staff house would be set up with his camp equipment, though he joined us or other staff for his meals.

While resident in the College, Bishop Allison made sure he saw all the students individually for discussion and prayer about their future ministry, time well spent for when it came to decisions on their posting the Bishop knew them and their particular gifts. Although he was a bachelor himself - just as well, for what wife could possibly have endured such a nomad for a husband - he was adamant that the clergy he ordained to the priesthood must be men already married and so protected from irregular relationships they might find hard to resist.

The 'Bish' was an interesting and appreciative guest, particularly delighted when he had listened to his radio and could arrive for a meal bursting to tell us the latest BBC World Service news. A report of a coup somewhere or other was what excited him most. It was strange really that living as we all did in a country where the

Government was far from secure, he should have had such a thrill from political collapses elsewhere. Looking back, it was perhaps even more strange that his radio was the only one we ever heard, the only news we so very occasionally had of the world we had once lived in! Mind you, unlike us, he was able to get batteries here and there on his travels.

Bishop Allison at the Chapel door

Despite his bad chest trouble which could make him irritable, he maintained his sense of humour and often an unseasonable though characteristic optimism so that, when he drove off to his next place, he left us encouraged by the strength of his faith in God and the affirmation he had brought to us. For Michael and Katherine there were the splendid stories he told them; I think some students who found him rather *shadeed,* rather strong, would have been surprised to see him crawling around on the floor with the children, all three making the most frightening animal noises they could manage. They would have been even more surprised that one day some years later, when the Bishop was struggling with his breathing and coughing, our young Patrick in Uganda was upset for him. "You must be tired, Uncle Oliver," he said "of always blessing people. Now I'm going to bless you." Quick as anything Bishop Allison was down on his knees with Patrick's small hand on his head and the words were said. "Uncle Oliver, I bless you in the Name of God."

Patrick blesses a bishop

I turn now to the central and special men and women who fill the next chapters. The students at Bishop Gwynne College came from very different backgrounds. Amongst them were trained teachers in secure employment with prestige and income; some would be ordained for pastoral ministry and others would return to their schools with qualifications as specialist religious education teachers, equipped with a manual of 160 pages which John helped to produce. But the majority of the student body had had limited education. A few had completed Intermediate School, but most had been untrained evangelists working with the pastor of the parish where they lived: perhaps with only a few years in a village primary school they had struggled to teach themselves English before they managed to pass the entrance examination and selection for Bishop Gwynne College. At any one time there would be students from at least fifteen different language areas. They had some difficulty communicating with each other though many of them could cope with several languages especially with those akin to their own mother tongue. The main College courses were taught through English, the medium of instruction in the schools and the language of Government in the South; apart from 'southern market Arabic', English was the only language that all students had in common. It must have been quite daunting to have to study new subjects and ideas in a foreign language; I would have found this very difficult.

In 1961 we recognised that something had to be done to meet the urgent need for more pastors. In addition to the courses taught in English we must run special courses taught in the four main vernacular languages. In the first year students from the Moru and Bari areas came with a Moru and a Bari pastor seconded to the College staff as their tutors. The following year was the turn for the Zande and Dinka classes. These courses were designed for older men who had proved themselves as leaders in the village churches but because they had had no formal education could not be taught in English. After their course they would be ordained by the Bishop to be pastors in their own villages where they would continue to support themselves from their own gardens as before. It would be a great strength for people in the smaller places to have their own pastor to lead and minister to them. John and other members of staff produced notes on the Bible, Church History, Worship, Doctrine and Pastoralia which the pastor tutors translated into their respective languages. I had a busy time typing stencils, no mean task in languages I didn't understand! These had to be run off on the hand-turned Gestetner so each student could have his own duplicated copy in his own language. With only the New Testament and the Prayer Book in their own language and no other books at all, these teaching notes were treasured possessions, and vitally important. Though we didn't know it then, these same notes were to prove very useful years later in an emergency course for Sudanese ordinands held outside the country at Mbale in Uganda.

But language issues weren't all the students had to cope with. Their experiences in Mundri opened up a wider world, much of it a world new to them, and that could be disturbing.

16   Training for Ordination

BISHOP GWYNNE COLLEGE

PREACH THE WORD

Bishop Gwynne College was a new world for John too. A classics graduate, ordained in 1955, with a couple of years experience as a curate and a year of missionary training, he was now, with me by his side, far away from all his previous experiences. Students were being introduced to a wider world, but for John the constant challenge was to make the teaching from his wider world relevant to the Sudan situation. He was an able teacher, very effective and much appreciated. The usual theological subjects were taught in the College, but, as everyone knows, the work of a pastor cannot all be taught in the classroom. Living and working together, in our homes, in the College chapel, and through ordinary things, we and the students grasped more and more of the meaning of the Gospel and how it affected our lives. Putting the learning into practice was an important part of the training, and to go visiting in the villages was one of the effective ways of doing this. One day John walked with some students on a forest path to a place six miles away where there was the beginning of a Christian community. They had not passed a single other habitation on the way. Shut up on all sides by the forbidding forest, John wondered at the narrow confined world of this place. Two of the men were clearly different, a difference he suspected at once. One had been away at Elementary school for four years. The other man had been to prison in Port Sudan. Prison and travelling the length of the country to get there had widened his horizons; he had seen places and aspects of life he had not conceived of before and mixed with people whose experience of life was different from his own. Going to prison had been an education for him. Speaking in 'market' Arabic, groups of students went out every week to the neighbouring villages to make friends with the local people and learn from them of their joys and sorrows. They would preach and talk about their faith and the difference it had made to their lives, and afterwards there would be discussion with the tutor who had been with them. Later in the year students had their special concentrated time of practical training with a tutor in their home areas and in their own language.

Visits to the villages made for contact with happy times, a wedding, a new baby, wild dancing and singing to drum beats, feasting for the harvest, but also suffering and death. Sometimes from the forest we could hear the sound of wailing, high-pitched quivering notes piercing the still air of the evening and floating for miles over the tops of the trees. We would know that someone had died not far away, most likely in a village where people were not yet Christian. The wailing would go on for hours, perhaps even for days. The College was not without its sad times too. After the child of one of the students died there was a calm and dignified funeral when the little body wrapped in a white cloth was lowered gently into a grave beside the College Chapel. I remember the silence of mourning as the grave was filled in and then, softly at first, the singing began, staff and students and families joining in a range of languages, "There'll be no sorrow there, in my Father's house," and then "Blessed assurance, Jesus is mine." There was grief then singing, instead of desolation and fear in the face of death, the Christians' peace and hope. The Easter story again proving its power.

Seme Solomona

Most of the students had very little experience of the world beyond their own villages, very little to set as a background to any new information the staff presented. How could the beauty of the Temple in Jerusalem be conceived if no building bigger or more beautiful than Lui Hospital could be imagined? Could Church History be taught in such a way that the young Church in Sudan recognised it had a part within the worldwide Church? Would Christians in Sudan today feel supported and encouraged in knowing how other young Churches had fared through the ages in times of growth and in times of persecution? Can God be appreciated as Creator through mountains and the sea, as in the Psalms, if neither of these are known to you? On the other hand there were gains. Rivers and cool air or shade under a tree described the attractions of heaven to Sudanese believers more vividly than to us, and little known accounts in the Old Testament were found to have a meaning we missed. Dreams, as in the Bible, carried great weight. Many an ordinand was convinced of his vocation by hearing the voice of God calling him in a dream. Through dreams God guided, comforted, and warned of impending danger or the need for repentance.

Not knowing much of the wider world or its history and having to study in a language not their own were difficulties enough for students, but learning was made even harder because of misconceptions about what went on between teacher and student. Most students thought they were only learning when they were actually sitting listening to a teacher and they only liked to work on their own when the work had been set by the staff. There wasn't a student who didn't believe he had limitless capacity if only he had the chance of education; if exam results were poor, it was the tutor who was at fault rather than that the student hadn't done the work or didn't have the ability or aptitude. Books were to be read because they were set books on the course and necessary for the purpose of examinations rather than for the sake of the knowledge they contained and, because fiction seemed totally irrelevant, opening up new ideas through reading a novel for interest and relaxation was rejected. The general opinion was that education was complete when the final exams had been passed. One student in his first year in the College was puzzled when he saw John was still reading books. "Did you not finish your training?" he asked. For tutors at Bishop Gwynne College it was best to know what students expected from you and how much of their progress was your direct responsibility!

John was looking after the library, for him always a joy of a job, which gave him the pleasure both of handling the books and of advising students in their choice of what to read. Sometimes I worked with him in the relative coolness of the library in the rounded west end of the lovely Chapel building, sorting and listing the books and arranging them on the mahogany shelves made at Lainya, zinc-lined to protect against termites.

The library

We faced the problem of getting rid of books which were no longer useful, a tricky action on account of the students' reverence for the printed word whatever it was. If we were seen destroying a book, either by burning it or throwing it into a pit, it was interpreted as deliberately depriving a student of a source of wisdom. Some of these 'sources of wisdom' were Victorian Sunday-school lessons sent as gifts to the College and long past their 'sell by date'! John wrote about what was involved in 'Forming a library at Bishop Gwynne College' in the Sudan Diocesan Review in 1961. At the time he was very excited that a grant from the International Missionary Council's Theological Education Fund had arrived and that it was his task to spend it on books geared to the needs of the students and staff. Not only was the choice of book difficult but with slow posts many months elapsed between the sending of an order and the arrival by surface mail of a parcel from England. John was keen for students to have some basic books of their own so he ran a College bookshop where he was able to sell books at half price, thanks to gifts of money from some of our supporting parishes in Ireland. In particular the book fund relied on generous gifts from Papa's parish in Ballinderry. All this would have been straightforward only that, as he wrote,

"the kind of book that the students really need as a text-book hardly exists. In their own languages there is virtually nothing beyond the New Testament and Book of Common Prayer. Up to the present written Arabic is impossible for all our students except the few from the Northern provinces, so that even the Arabic translations of the World Christian Books are of little value to us. We use English in class, but the students' proficiency in the language has been such that, though the text-books we provide are in the simplest English we can find, there are few who can fully comprehend them. So in fact the text-books from which they learn most in College and which they will treasure and digest during the years of their ministry are the foolscap duplicated notes which the staff produce for each lesson."

In addition to owning some books of their own, students needed to have access to a wide and varied library with reference books, and this was needed too for the staff; some of the money grant would be used for that kind of book. But that wasn't all. For the library to be effective the art of using it had to be learnt.

"Besides, to use a library effectively a student must know how to use books - how to find what he wants, how to select the wheat from the chaff, how to evaluate, criticise, and if necessary reject a writer's opinion, how to make notes and summarise. None of these things can our present students do. The art is only acquired at a higher level of education."

But encouragement was on the way. Soon there was a response to the need for ordinands of a higher educational standard and a course to prepare these men for the Certificate of Religious Knowledge of the University of London was set up by David Brown. Now there would be pastors who could address issues about the Christian faith at a deeper level. Now we hoped and prayed that there would be men prepared and ready to fill the teaching posts at Mundri if the time came when we were no longer needed or no longer permitted to stay.

Issues to do with their studies were one thing but John wrote of others as well.

"Getting into the minds of other people and trying to see what is really there and understand it is the job of the missionary, and not made any easier by the circumstance of his different culture and different language. But occasionally a glimpse is given. One of the students came to see me in our house. He was not in the best of humours. He had taken exception to something I said in class earlier in the morning and had told me so at the time in no uncertain terms. Now he came to re-open the matter. I let him talk as he wished. Before long it came to light that the real trouble was not what had happened in the class that morning. His real burden was something he heard the staff had been saying about him, despising his abilities and questioning the genuineness of his call to the ministry of the Church. The morning's incident in class was only the spark that fired off all the hidden feelings that had been building up over some time. Then he told me something of his thoughts. These things usually only come out in moments of strain. He revealed the strong urge that was in him to be a pastor and the conviction that God had given him this work whether the staff of Bishop Gwynne College thought so or not. He said rash things. He had made up his mind to leave the College. He would go and minister the Gospel to his people without the College training. He said we could reject him from the College, but we could not stop him preaching to the people of his tribe where Christians are few and mostly poor. He referred to one of the pastors there and said he had just had a letter from him in which he said he had only received 35 *piastres* of his salary last month. (It was a barter rather than a cash economy, but even so receiving just over 2% of his expected salary was very difficult) "That's the life of a pastor in my tribe," he said, "Do you staff think I have chosen that life because I can't get a better job?"

"I was glad to say that he had been misinformed. The Staff had said nothing of the kind. After a good long chat it was all cleared up, and he no longer wanted to leave the College. He apologised for using angry words in the morning and told me that all his tribe were known for their hot temper, but he was struggling with the help of God to overcome it. I told him that the Irish tribe had the same reputation!

"This particular storm had blown over. But the College was never calm for long. Little incidents and encounters, disagreements and misunderstandings, sullen expressions, anger, a burst of laughter made up a large part of the life of this isolated community of many tribes. But it was out of these that deep fellowship and understanding grew. Mind meets mind, sometimes violently, and usually something goes across from one to the other, in a two-way traffic. The Staff were constantly trying to put something of their knowledge and experience across to the students, but achieved nothing unless they were ready on their part to receive something of what was in the minds and hearts of the men they were teaching. We were not likely to doubt that student's vocation. But more than that, from our glimpse into his feelings we saw afresh the power of the Gospel to call men to self-sacrifice and poverty and devotion to the cause of Christ. He knew what the life of a pastor in his tribe would be, and nothing would stop him from giving himself to that life to do the Church's work in a dangerous and difficult outpost."

In 1953 the American Presbyterian Mission, which had been at work in the Upper Nile area of Sudan since 1901, combined with CMS to provide some funding and one American missionary tutor for Bishop Gwynne College; from then on a number of Presbyterian ordinands were trained together with the E.C.S. ordinands. This was a good move and enriched the College by introducing students to two different forms of church order but with the same goals. CMS was true to the 'three-self' missionary principle of Henry Venn, formulated as early as 1854, that Churches should be established as self-governing, self-supporting and self-propagating. It was CMS worldwide policy to supply and pay for missionary personnel and give grants for special capital needs but not for running expenses. We couldn't help noticing that some of our American colleagues felt less constrained and were more than ready to respond to the wants as well as the needs of their Presbyterian students. Themselves on higher allowances than the rest of us, and particularly the Sudanese staff, they were very generous in their gifts but it could be irritating to see Presbyterian students riding about on new bicycles wearing flashy shirts and smart long trousers, with shiny watches to tell the time! These unequal conditions in such a small community raised uncomfortable comparisons, sometimes anger against us and CMS for not providing more.

It was obvious that compared with local people and even the local chiefs we from overseas were well off. One student thinking about this came to his own conclusion. He told us he didn't believe we really wanted to train Sudanese leaders because these leaders would do us out of a good job. He was being perfectly logical but it was the way it questioned our motivation that was upsetting.

The safia race

At the end of each term there was a lovely time of closeness, of fun and games. We set aside the hard work of studying and teaching and instead staff and students gave themselves to entertaining each other! Two-legged races requiring the co-operation of men of markedly different heights, sack races ending in pile-ups on the course, relay races with runners drenched by their head-loads of *safias* of water, drama with actions mimicking members of staff, singing and learning each others' songs, playing locally made musical instruments which produced sounds quite different from an organ or piano. John could not contribute his favourite classical music on these occasions since we had neither instruments nor a gramophone; unlike Archdeacon Shaw who had included an organ in his baggage when he sailed up the Nile in 1906 on his 'Noah's Ark', we brought no such instrument on the Salween!

17 Lusi Died

All through my childhood and the years of medical study I dreamed of lancing abscesses, sewing up wounds, delivering babies safely, performing operations, giving medicines and injections, preventing illness. That, I thought, was how I would live my life as a missionary doctor in some far off place. But that was not how it was turning out at all.

It was obvious that when John and I fell in love and married, I was no longer the single woman doctor CMS had accepted as a recruit and expected to locate overseas. Wherever we went now, the main job would have to be either for John or for me. Our offer for service with CMS was an open one, we would go wherever we were sent and stay for our whole life or for as many years as we were needed. While we were in missionary training our future posting was often discussed with us. Was it to be medical work for me in India with a less specific post for John, or a theological teaching post for John in Sudan where there might not be medical work for me? We were drawn to Africa, where both of us had had missionary relatives, teaching in a theological college would fit in with John's vocation and seemed the right place for him to use his scholarship and sensitivity in relationships. I could content myself, I thought, in caring for our children, knowing the students and engaging in College tasks. I expected that it wouldn't be long before I would have a licence to practise where there was a need for my skills. Sudan, both John and I were sure, was God's place for us and we were very keen to go there.

But, from our very first day in the country, we wondered how long the Sudan Government would allow us to stay, how long we would retain the entry visas and work permits we had been granted. Only a week or two before our arrival Bill and Lois Anderson, American

Presbyterian missionaries at Mundri, had been expelled. Church leaders, anxious not to lose any other expatriate teaching staff at Bishop Gwynne College, urged us not to do anything which would risk our expulsion. We were needed to help in the training of Sudanese pastors for as long as we were permitted to stay. I was particularly warned that until I had a medical licence I must not give even as much as an aspirin to a Sudanese person. Informers, I was told, were everywhere and anything I did could be reported. Another missionary doctor without a licence had recently treated a Sudanese patient and, when he pleaded with Ali Baldo the Governor of Equatoria Province that he only wanted to help the sufferer, was told that he had better then do so in some other country. He had been given a week to pack up and leave Sudan.

It was one thing for me to accept in England, where there were full medical services, that I might not be allowed to be a doctor in Sudan, but it wasn't so easy when I found there were no doctors at all for the people living around us in Mundri. How I hankered after that licence! I wanted one thing more to add to my happy marriage and my place within the life of the College. I could not abandon the picture I had of myself as a doctor responding to the needs of people who were sick and in pain and, no matter how unlikely it was, I kept hoping Dr. Zaki at the Ministry of Health in Khartoum would act. In the meantime I knew that as a good missionary I was supposed to be accepting and tolerant and calm, but I knew too that those were not my characteristics. I liked to reform things, to organise and to be in control. It's not surprising that in Mundri I was sometimes restless and very frustrated.

Worst of all was when we were still in our first year in Mundri and two-year-old Lusi fell ill. Her name in her birth-language Moru means 'God-with' and indicated that she was a precious child, the child of her parents' later years. Her father, Canon Ezra Baya Lawiri, the Vice-Principal, was in England on a year-long study course at the time. Her mother Hana, without his support, was quite distraught. She took Lusi to Lui Hospital about 15 miles away. This hospital, as I have already said, was founded by Dr. Fraser as the first CMS hospital in Equatoria, but had been taken over by the Government and was without a doctor, besides being very short of medicines. Some days later Lusi died. That was the beginning of a dreadful time for Hana and her other children and it was a terribly distressing time for us too. While the little girl was ill in her house near ours I had not visited for it could have been reported that I had gone to treat a sick child which would have been to risk our expulsion. Perhaps there would have been nothing I could have done, but from Hana's point of view I hadn't even tried. What, she asked, did I mean by saying I was a follower of Jesus Christ who went about healing the sick and I, a doctor, hadn't healed Lusi? In her loss and distress Hana was very bitter, shouting abuse in my direction whenever she saw me, far away or nearby. "That is the one who says she follows Jesus, but she let my child die." I had wanted more than anything else to be a proper missionary doctor, to do anything I could to save Lusi's life, but saying so and explaining I had no medical licence would have been no help to Hana in her terrible anger and sorrow. I was torn apart by grief and sadness and frustration. The path to Hana's garden passed by our house and so the dreaded shouting occurred each day as she made her way there and as she returned. For month after month I had to endure the shouting and abuse. For month after month it stung like salt in an open wound that the fact I had done nothing for Lusi was so misunderstood.

Had I really made the right decision in accepting our posting to Sudan? Had I been mistaken in my confidence about God's call to be a missionary doctor? How was it that I was so isolated and helpless in Mundri instead of being somewhere else where I could follow my particular vocation? My comfort came from John's constant support and from remembering that even the suffering of being misunderstood was known to Jesus, my dear Lord.

Then Ezra returned from the London College of Divinity. The whole atmosphere changed. He and Hana grieved together over the death of little Lusi and I was no longer the one Hana blamed. Ezra would not hear the chatter of his small daughter ever again, but in a remarkable way he accepted that it was right I hadn't attempted to treat her without a Government medical licence, it was good that John and I hadn't risked expulsion and were still in Mundri helping the Sudanese Church. It wasn't long before we found comfort in the depth of Canon Ezra's faith and love. Time and again he was able to restore my commitment to our life in Mundri and the value of our just being there.

While I still persisted in hoping for a medical licence, John urged me to put my energies into finding the things I could do and then get on with doing them. "Nobody uses all their gifts at any one time," he reassured me, "things change and don't go on the same for ever." And of course John was right; that was how it would turn out. In the meantime his understanding and the prayers of our supporters propped me up.

18   The Snake in the *Tukl*

The Doll's house was so small that John was given a *tukl* to use as his study. It was a small round mud hut with a thatched roof and had been built as the College guest house. It was cool and peaceful, away from household noises. Not where he would have expected to have a new experience, an experience which has grown in the telling.

The sun was high overhead, the sky pale and hazy with heat. The leaves were drying on the trees, the grass was turning brown, the air was still. Sitting at his work in the *tukl* John was preparing lectures and reading his books. Soon it would be time for him to return to the Doll's house for lunch. The wood plank door and a small window were behind him and in front he looked out on the garden through a bigger window above his desk. It was cooler in the *tukl* than outside. It was also much darker.

John gathered up his papers and turned towards the door. Silently and not noticed by him he had been joined by a snake. Relaxing in the lower temperature of the *tukl*, the 4 foot snake was lying on the cross bar of the only door, its colour brownish against the wood and not easy to see in the dim light. John was a prisoner, what was he to do?

"Tell us again about Daddy and the snake," pleads Katherine. "Do snakes eat Daddies? Was Daddy afraid the snake was going to eat him?" Michael asks. It is time for the routine of the bedtime story and I have a book in my hand, but a real live story is always preferred. This story has been told before, but each detail is checked, nothing must be changed or left out. John up on the desk, tearing out the mosquito wire of the window, jumping down onto the ground outside shouting 'snake' and running for Ro'ba who comes with his long-handled hoe. Calling out the news of a snake, Ro'ba is joined by a group of men who seem to gather from all directions.

After some quick action the snake is killed and held up dead and draped on the end of the hoe, its skin no longer lustrous but bedraggled and dull.

"Wa'allah," "Mush kwayyis," "A very dangerous snake." We were not keen on snakes and we didn't know if this was a bad one or particularly poisonous. The men, however, as they never failed to do, talked and shouted all at once, exclaiming on what a dangerous snake this one was and how they have seen such snakes cause bodies to swell, double up with green vomiting and quickly die. We agreed they had done an important job in killing it, though we felt a bit afraid and wary that its mate might come looking for it.

"I'm sorry the poor snake got deaded," said Michael. "I'm glad Daddy didn't," said Katherine. "And," she added, "that's a true story, isn't it?" Katherine is always keen to check on whether a story is about something that really happened, the kind of story she likes best. "Yes, it is," I agree. We say thank you to God for keeping Daddy safe. "He loves us all and looks after us." "Why is God a boy?" Katherine asks.

But that is another subject altogether and for tonight I avoid it.

19   Health and Hygiene

It had rained in the night. Not soft rain but a storm and rain that lashed down and pounded on the tin roof of the Doll's house, that slanted in through the shutterless windows. In the brilliant flashes of lightning the sky was lit up and we could see the water rushing by and eroding the land. John and I snuggled down in bed in the damp cooler air and hoped we wouldn't have to get up; perhaps it would be enough to move things away from the windows and mop up the water in the morning; perhaps Michael and Katherine, who were stirring, disturbed by the rain spraying on their faces, would stay asleep. But just when we had persuaded ourselves the rain was passing, there were further claps of thunder and a torrential downpour, like the heavens opening it was so noisy and so wet. And, yes, the children were calling for us. There was nothing for it. We would have to get out of bed, comfort our little ones, brave going outside to untie the rolled-up canvas blinds at the windows, and we would certainly get drenched ourselves.

From very early on, after that kind of night, I wasn't too pleased to hear the cocks, for all the size of them, crowing like mad in some distant place, and then the clang of the iron bar announced it was time to start a new day. John, in dry clothes, had already gone to his study *tukl* to read his Bible and pray, the students were hurrying to fit in all that must be done before Chapel, before lectures and classes, and the students' wives too had a lot to 'cope up with' as they said. Like their husbands, they too wanted to get the most out of their time in the College. Their helpers, most of whom were quite small girls or boys and scarcely more than children themselves, looked after the babies and toddlers and did some household tasks while the mothers were off at the Wives School for several hours each day. I often saw a little group of these helpers walking about, each one carrying a heavy baby wrapped in a cloth and tied to her back, or with a toddler sitting straddled on a protruded hip, and I was pleased when I saw them in the shade of a tree taking a little break for their own play with others of their language group. They didn't have much time off. With no cots or play-pens, I wondered how they managed to care for the small children and keep them safe from danger, especially the common danger of falling into open cooking fires. Even with all the watching accidents sometimes happened. There were no nappies and it made us smile to see a child being quickly held out for toilet purposes when somehow his carer sensed an imminent need. That saved a lot of washing.

Tito and I had sorted out the food for the day, Elizala was busy banging around with his duster and knocking the legs of the chairs as he swept the concrete floor in our small rooms, while Diya got on with washing the children's clothes in last night's bath water. With a hug and a kiss for me and a cheery 'Bye' from Michael and Katherine, John went off to the teaching he loved, while I, not allowed to do the medical work I would have loved, prepared to teach the students and their wives about common illnesses, prevention and simple remedies.

So back to today. The breakfast things are cleared away and I get out a precious piece of card to make a diagram for the men. Several of them have suffered from bilharzia; they have had unpleasant courses of injections at Government dispensaries but what they want to know is how they got infected. I draw a diagram to show the life cycle of the parasite, part of it in a fresh-water snail and part in its human host, both phases essential to it. In water which has been contaminated with the urine or faeces of a human sufferer, the ova of the parasite enter fresh-water snails in rivers and lakes and develop to their juvenile form; then, as free swimming cercariae, they are ready to enter through the skin of any human host who comes in contact with that water, and so the cycle is repeated. The chronic ill health, pain and blood loss due to bilharzia is wide-spread. The diagram is beginning to look interesting and Michael has his ruler ready to help me by drawing lines and Katherine offers some of her crayons and asks if I am drawing blood and can she colour it for me. I could get on better without their help and it is a relief when Diya comes to take them off for a little walk. I ask them to collect leaves for me and see how many different shapes and colours they can find. I have to hurry to finish and then set off on my bicycle for the classrooms.

Rushing off to teach

Each week I made charts for the sessions on Health and Hygiene with the men. I loved to teach about how the human body works, to give new and strange information which amazed many of the students just as it still amazes me, though that didn't stop them questioning some of the things I told them. I gave details of the life cycle of the various parasites which were endemic and then invited the men to identify the points where the cycle could be interrupted and broken. This was not a hopeless task. As I showed on my chart, in the case of schistosomiasis commonly known as bilharzia (named after Theodor Bilharz who identified the fluke involved) the cycle could be interrupted by elimination of the snail population, a hopeless objective; or by the use of latrines to prevent the snail population being infected in the first place; or best of all by avoiding contact with infected water. There is evidence from Egyptian mummies that this disease has been around the waters of the Nile since the time of the Pharaohs so its eradication will be a tremendous achievement, and is not expected just yet. Until then bilharzia will remain a problem, an increasing problem because irrigation programmes and the building of dams provide additional breeding grounds for fresh-water snails essential in the life cycle of bilharzia.

Classroom block, later extended

Leprosy has been known throughout the ages. In Bible times sufferers were isolated to stop it spreading, and indeed in English medieval churches there is the evidence of slit windows through which, when the disease was endemic here, the priest gave the Holy Communion to men and women excluded because they suffered from leprosy. Through immunisation smallpox has been eradicated worldwide, the incidence of polio has decreased dramatically with improved sanitation, hygiene and the advent of polio vaccines, and the World Health Organisation looks to a future when malaria and several other diseases could become past history. If Mundri students could work out for themselves some ways to reduce ill health, suffering, and untimely death then my teaching about prevention, basic remedies, and first aid for injuries would be worth while. Perhaps more useful than curative treatments.

The simplest and most important measures were already well known even if not always followed - boiling drinking water, washing hands and the use of deep pit latrines; these would help prevent gastro-enteritis, diarrhoea, and amoebic dysentery and reduce the number of ova from intestinal worms blowing around in the dust. Most Sudanese children, and indeed adults too, were anaemic because of hookworm (ancylostoma), a blood-sucking parasite living in their intestines whose ova, excreted in the faeces, matured on damp ground to enter as larvae through the skin of the next barefoot human to pass by. Students readily appreciated that the use of latrines would put an end to this pest. Wearing shoes or perhaps flip-flops made of old tyres would help, though not immediately for shoes and sandals were kept for special occasions like going to church, not for digging and cultivation.

Tropical diseases, the deformities of leprosy and polio, blindness from trachoma or from an organism carried by a small black riverside fly, sleeping sickness carried by the tsetse fly, chest infections and pneumonia, fractures and accidents, spear and arrow wounds, torn flesh from mauling by animals, snake bites, not to mention the perils of childbirth and the infant mortality rate: it was a formidable list. The men loved to have the opportunity to learn what I could teach, and I was flattered when they protested that these sessions were over too soon and long before all their questions had been answered or discussed. But it could be depressing for them too, and I hated to think how little could be done when they faced illness and death and indeed the fear of illness and death. Although I was upset that I was not allowed to be a doctor, the students seemed more ready to accept the situation and believed that anyway there were many mysteries about illness which remained unsolved and might not respond to Western medicine. When I explained that the malaria parasite was carried by the mosquito from one infected person to the next person whose blood it sucked, I was presented with a deeper question to answer. "Why then," Matayo wanted to know, "is it that when there were many mosquitoes around the one carrying the malaria parasite was the one to feast on me?" I had no answer to that question. Perhaps it was an illustration of a fatalistic attitude - there is nothing you can do except take what comes your way, or was it to do with the spirit world, or the curse of an enemy? These mysteries remained unresolved. Scientific explanations were not the whole story but would be part of a continuing study of traditional and Christian approaches.

I could not forget that the area in Nigeria where my relatives had worked for decades was known as the 'White Man's Grave', and that with little immunity Westerners too died of tropical diseases. Graves of expatriates, including the graves of small children, could be seen throughout the tropics. We took as much care as we could: we always wore shoes or sandals, we always had boiled water to drink, we never ate fruit without first peeling it, and we ruled out salads altogether. It was awkward to be so strict over these things but it seemed the best way to remain healthy.

As in most groups, teaching about sexuality and reproduction was high on the request list. Most of what I offered was received with nods of agreement; most that is except when I taught that the sex of a child is determined by the father and not the mother. That was uncomfortable for some of the men who preferred to believe the mother was the one to be blamed for childlessness, too many sons, or worse still too many daughters. For marriage arrangements it was very important that a family had the right balance of boys and girls. In a complicated system of compensation for his loss of her and a safeguard for her wellbeing, a father received a settlement called 'bride-price' for his daughter when she married; she then belonged to her husband's family. When his son took a wife, the father used the 'bride-price' he had received for his daughter to help his son with the settlement required by the father of his son's bride. If he only had daughters the father's family ended when all of them married and belonged to their husband's family not his. If he only had sons he had problems in finding the bride-price for them to marry. I wondered if my information about a baby's sex was shared around the fires in the evenings, and if it eased the tension in some households, so I was a bit annoyed when I gave the same fact to the women in the Wives School and found they were slow to accept it. They gave examples of men who failed to have sons with one wife and then with another wife produced a line of baby boys. Just like the mosquito's choice of victim, there was mystery in the race of the sperm. These things were not explained by science alone.

20 The Long, Long Surplice

I stand in front of the class in the Wives School speaking in short and simple sentences; teaching through translation is tedious and slow and it is difficult to know just what gets through. What I do know is that these women, twelve or fifteen of them, will surprise me by some of the ways they view things and annoy me by being so ready to accept they must be subservient to the men. John would have an easier time if I had the same temperament! Just imagine how wonderfully exciting it is for these wives to have time off from caring for their children, cultivating the land, carrying water and preparing food, and instead find themselves with others in a class where they are being taught all sorts of interesting things. Most of them have had very little schooling but are able to read as that was required of them before they were baptized. Now they are attentive, enthusiastic, ready to learn. They come from many different birth-languages but that doesn't dampen their exuberance; market Arabic and the sign language we all manage to invent ensure the Wives School is filled with endless talk and laughter and loud exclamations. Teacher Alisi, a Moru woman teacher seconded by the Ministry of Education on Government pay, teaches in the Wives School and also translates for the expatriate staff. It encourages us that the work of teaching these adult women is valued by the Government and that the influence clergy wives will have in the parishes is recognised.

Student wives took it in turn to lead prayers at the beginning and end of their school day and with practice and preparation learned to do this effectively and with confidence instead of shyness and giggles. I was present years later when Mary Hassan, whom I remember as one of these student wives, led prayers for the huge congregation gathered in Salisbury Cathedral at the time of the 1998 Lambeth Conference; it was great to hear her strong voice ringing out in Arabic so all could hear, and to see her total confidence. The wives learned of the life and teaching of Jesus Christ in the Wives School, reading from such parts of the Bible as were available in their own languages, and they prepared for what they would be doing later on in the parishes. My job was to teach them hygiene, child care, and sewing.

Student wife and child

Breast-feeding was essential to the baby's survival in areas where cows could not survive and substitute dried milk was not easily available, so I was glad to see all the babies were breast-fed, even for as long as two or three years. It looked very strange to us to see a fair-sized child running to its mother, perhaps even in the Wives School, for a quick top-up suck! To ensure the mother's milk supply until the child was weaned, abstinence from sexual relationships was accepted as necessary. This was easier for polygamists than faithful monogamist Christian couples. Because the next pregnancy didn't follow too quickly after the previous one, all the time we were in Sudan I never saw a child with the reddish hair and bloated abdomen of protein-calorie malnutrition, also known as kwashiorkor. The strange name of this condition comes from Ghana and describes 'the sickness that the older child gets when the next baby is born'. That observant local diagnosis in West Africa predated the researches between the 1930's and 1950's of people like Dr. Cicely Williams in Ghana and Dr. Hugh Trowell in Kenya and Uganda. Another important factor is that a sad child, abruptly separated from the comfort and milk of his mother at the onset of her next pregnancy, usually refuses the substitute food offered to him, food of low protein and calorie content. In countries where breast-feeding lasts only a few months before the conception of the next child puts an end to it, kwashiorkor is all too common and responsible for the death of up to half of all children under five years of age. There were no family planning services in Sudan but perhaps this was just as well, for, however it was managed, a pregnancy did not seem to occur out of 'proper' time as might have been the case if contraceptives were relied on and failed.

I taught about simple remedies for common illnesses such as how to deal with dehydration from vomiting and diarrhoea in gastro-enteritis. This condition was common and in tropical heat death came quickly to small children, but lives could be saved if water which had been boiled with a small amount of sugar and salt and then allowed to cool was given to the sick child teaspoon by teaspoon. This rehydration was soon seen to work, and was life-saving information easily shared.

I think I enjoyed the sewing more than anything else. We taught the wives how to cut out and make comfortable and attractive clothes for

The Long, Long Surplice

themselves and their children. The cotton materials available in the local Greek merchant's shop were brightly coloured and looked striking against the rich dark skin of the women though sometimes the quality was poor and we were disappointed when the dresses wore out quickly. We didn't make men's shirts and shorts for these were expertly and cheaply made by the shop tailors.

Making surplices was another matter. The usual garment worn by the clergy when conducting services was an ankle length white cotton surplice, which was cool and convenient over shorts and shirt and easily washed. Each wife was helped to mark out and cut a pattern for a surplice for her husband and then sew it and be capable of making replacements.

"It is good for you, Marata," said Rachel. "Your husband is not so long. And for you also, Fibi," she added. Voices rise in the class of fifteen as one wife compares her lot with another and clearly women whose husbands are short for once have the advantage! We are in the Wives School and I am busy with the making of surplices. Rachel has a point. It is certainly a long way from shoulder to hem of a surplice long enough for her husband Reuben and she protests. "Anyway what is this Run and Fell seam?" I laugh and explain the quick running stitch and how one edge is folded under and hemmed flat. Mary, Cham Adhom's wife, is of the Shilluk tribe, a handsome woman decorated with keloid scars stretching like a string of beads from temple to temple just above her eyebrows. She comes from the area where American Presbyterian missionaries have worked for decades. Clergy in her area have no tradition of wearing surplices so Mary spends her time going round and teasing the other wives and boasting she has no long seams to sew. I give her some cloth to embroider and make into a little bag for her husband's Bible instead, and she gets to work. All the sewing had to be with needles and thread but I hoped a time would come when we would have sewing machines and no more long, long seams.

I was mighty glad myself to have the sewing machine John had given me as my present the first Christmas we were married. A Singer with an electric motor, it also had a hand-turned mechanism, another handle Michael liked to help me to turn. In the heat and humidity of Mundri, our clothes faded and wore out quickly and had to be replaced with garments I made from the collection of materials I kept in a tin trunk. It was an odd selection of plain coloured cloth and patterned cottons but also of materials that made me wonder why I had ever bought them. All sorts of garments flowed from that Singer: small shirts and trousers for Michael, frocks and bonnets for Katherine and her dolls, a pale yellow dress I was wearing when John took a photo of me holding an angry young leopard cub, a pink one with white spots which had such a deep decorated hem that a visiting senior missionary laughed as she asked me if I was still hoping to grow, a 'Mundri Model' dress for Beatrice Coggan. Beatrice was a missionary nurse at the CMS Hospital in Omdurman and the sister of Donald Coggan, later Archbishop of Canterbury. At our invitation she had travelled all the way to the South of the country where she had never been before. One day we walked together to Mundri to the shop of the Greek merchant, George Frangos. In its dark and dusty interior we found a sophisticated cotton material in ambers and russets, colours which looked lovely with Beatrice's pale auburn hair and were just right for the dress I made for her. Neither of us could work out how this beautiful cloth, made in Czechoslovakia, had ended up in that small store in Mundri.

The leopard cub

The wives not only sewed clothes but followed their own ideas when they produced elaborately embroidered table cloths with drawn thread work and crochet edgings. Bibles were always protected by being carried in small embroidered cotton bags, and these were favourite projects. They wove mats following their traditional crafts and they tried to teach me to make the fine baskets in common use for sifting grain and storing seed. Their sewing was miles better than my baskets.

One of the College jobs the wives took responsibility for was cleaning the chapel every week and arranging leaves or flowers for decoration. I called in each Friday to admire their work. Though very clean, sometimes not a single bench was placed straight. I found this very irritating but when I had straightened them all nobody could see the difference! I think it was Tabita who, with a sparkle in her eye and a broad grin, had the solution. "You paint lines on the floor for the place of each thing and we'll do it the way you want. In Africa we do not have these lines; they are not in our African round houses." I feel relieved that even if furniture is placed topsy turvy in the chapel, Elizala has no difficulty in putting ours straight in the Doll's house, but then I remember that of course that's different - the Doll's house isn't round!

It really must have been a great experience for these wives to have time to learn and follow new skills, wear new dresses and laugh together instead of the endless repetition and hard work of their home lives. In his Principal's Report on the College for the year 1960, referring to the students' wives, David Brown wrote:

> "There were fifteen women on the Wives' Course at the beginning of the year, increased to nineteen at the end. They were taught Scripture, how to lead Women's Meetings and had classes in simple Arabic, vernacular reading, sewing and hygiene. They were commissioned by the Bishop at a special service in Chapel and awarded College Certificates."

To have had all the interest of learning new things and the fun of their years living in the College and joining with women from other areas of the country would have been enough, but to have Certificates too made them go to their parishes and their new ministry very happy indeed. But other women and girls who were not the wives of ordinands, how were they to have opportunities of learning, of being literate, and developing their potential for leadership? A chapter about that will come later.

21   Supper Parties

There is nothing like sharing a meal for the way it encourages friendship and fun; that's why it was our favourite way to spend time with the students. Each week John and I, like other missionary members of staff, invited students and their wives for an evening meal with us in our house.

Picture us then on one of those evenings. It is term time and there has been rain; the air blowing in through the mosquito-wire of our windows, which have no curtains or shutters, smells fresh and is a bit cooler. This is the wet season and food is more plentiful than it will be later on when for five months there will be hardly any rain at all. Tonight we look forward to good talking and good eating together, even if we are a bit tight for space in what we are right in calling the Doll's house. The small room where the children sleep is to the left and our bedroom to the right, both doors closed. Opposite the front door the meshed window to the back gives us a view of the outside thatched kitchen where Tito is cooking. The table takes up most of the space in the room and is set for six, for we have two student couples coming to join us.

Two-year-old Michael and Katherine have had the first use of the limited bath water and, their supper and prayers over, they are already asleep in their cots behind the door just a few feet away. John had the next use of the tin bath and now looks refreshed and handsome, his skin tan against the white of his shirt and shorts, his feet bare in his sandals. The students, who like to swank in long trousers if they have them, find it strange that their teacher prefers to be a little cooler in shorts and has no inflated view of himself. My simple cotton dress is made to a pattern which I have adapted for the women in the Wives School and use to teach them to make their own. They are always interested in examining mine and especially to see if I, the teacher, have finished my seams and facings properly.

The Tilley pressure lamp resting on a tall stand makes a gentle hiss as it gives out heat which we don't need and light which we do. There is an oil lamp hanging on a nail against the wall in the outside kitchen and, its glass clean and its wick trimmed level, it gives Tito a fair light. Elizala has a hurricane lantern with a long handle to light his way as he carries the food from the kitchen to the house. Later he will wash up in a basin of water for there is no running water supply.

So near the Equator, dusk and dawn come about 6.00 p.m. and 6.00 a.m. all the year round. Now it is dark and we see the dim light of hurricane lamps carried by our guests as they make their way from their houses to ours. The lamps are a safety measure for there are snakes and the possibility of a leopard. Tonight we welcome Benjamina Yoane and his wife Mary, and Henry Mabior and Elizabeta his wife. We have only observed one student couple eating together; for the rest the custom seems to be that the husband is served his meal by his wife at the front of their College house and later she eats with the children at the back. So for Mary and Elizabeta this meal is a bit embarrassing though for all of us it is a special occasion, a sort of feast with far more food than we usually have.

Benjamina and Mary come from Yambio near the western border of Sudan and Congo, 300 miles west from the Nile at Juba. They belong to the Zande tribe and are short and stocky with warm brown glossy skin, their faces often rounded and crinkled up because they delight in laughing and joking. Mary's hair is close to her head in eight or ten small plaits each side of a central parting, the ends turned up in tight curls. It must have taken ages to arrange. Last week in the Wives School Mary tried to plait my hair like hers but gave me up as a bad job. We had to laugh for no sooner did she move on to do the next plait than the one she had just finished escaped. She wasn't the first or last African friend who attempted to improve my hair and appearance.

Benjamina and Mary and family

Henry is very tall, as is Elizabeta who is young with a beautiful face and figure and a different pattern of finely plaited and oiled hair. Both of them have the blue-black velvet-like skin typical of their tribe, and Henry bears the traditional markings of scars across his forehead from ear to ear, part of the Dinka rite of initiation from child to man. Because of their long legs Henry and Elizabeta seem to be a long way from the table, and in any case our customs of cutlery and a dining-table are strange. We all laugh as we recognise and value our differences, wanting to respect and learn from one another. The Christian gospel has made some changes in how people of different tribes and languages in Sudan get on together.

Though perhaps at heart they still consider their own tribe the best, even those who have been traditional enemies are finding Christ makes it possible for them to live and work together in peace. Such sharing and exploration is not common in many other settings. So here we are, six people of about the same age though as it happens the majority of the students are older than John and I are. All of us have different life experiences but we are united in our faith as we say the Grace together to thank God for our food.

First we have ground-nut soup - just as we have ground-nut soup for supper every night and John wishes we could have it for ever! Earlier in the day Tito's wife shelled the nuts, then Tito roasted them turning them on a hot pan so the skins could be rubbed off. Next came the grinding between two stones to make a paste which was added to softly cooked onions and stock. We have bread today so Tito has gone to the trouble of deep-frying croutons in oil to serve with the soup. After the soup there is meat, tender after long slow cooking as a pot roast, and with it we have cooked leaves of perpetual New Zealand spinach from our garden. We pick off the fleshy green leaves of this most useful plant which just goes on producing perpetually. It can't be an Irish meal for there are no potatoes - the climate is too hot to grow them here - but we have cassava cakes instead. Mary thinks these must be some kind of imported European food so I tell her how Tito makes them. Cassava is a locally grown root, the basis of the tapioca we had as a milk pudding when I was a child. Peeled and cut in pieces and boiled it softens and can be pounded to become like mashed potato or mashed parsnips. Tito pats it out to make flat round shapes and then fries these in oil. It is a lot of work but the result is crisp and good, though without much nutritional value. It is much more to our taste like this than the local way cassava is prepared, particularly how the Zande people like to cook it. First they soak it in water for some days to rot off the poisonous outer skin and let it develop its own distinctive pong and flavour, then it is cooked and pounded, and mixed with millet to form their staple diet like a thick porridge. The Moru people do not like cassava mixed with their millet and there are ructions in the College dining room when they are served millet prepared in that Zande way; there are ructions from the Zande students when cassava is left out!

The College dining room

For dessert tonight, a special treat, there are guavas fresh off the trees. This fruit is about the size of a kiwi fruit with a tough brownish skin, and inside a layer of pink flesh surrounding a central mass of inedible seeds. The flesh of the guavas gently cooked with sugar and cooled reminds us of the taste of strawberries, especially delicious tonight when we eat them with cream taken from the top of today's milk. I tell our guests that my mother when she ate food she particularly liked used to say she wished her neck was as long as a giraffe's so she could enjoy the taste of it all the way down. That was easy for us all to picture, for giraffes are among the local wild animals and stretch out their long necks to reach and eat the leaves of acacia trees and, who knows, perhaps taste them all the way down too! Tomorrow Tito and I will remove the skins and seeds of our guava crop and thread the half fruit on strings and hang these up to dry. Later when food is in short supply we'll be able to soak them and have something nice to cook and eat.

We have coffee to end our meal. The coffee beans had a narrow escape in their bright cotton bag when a tin of paraffin leaked on the lorry from Juba. Washed, roasted and ground we say nothing and don't detect any taint of paraffin. Benjamin is very pleased we have sugar and wastes no time in putting three heaped spoonfuls in his coffee before Mary stops him, but Henry has four spoons and Elizabeta just laughs. She raises her hands about a foot apart. "Henry is like this more high than Benjamina," she says, "and that takes more sugar." None of them can think why John and I don't have sugar in our coffee. "Do you not want to be sweeter?" Henry asks!

Elizabeta, Polycarp, Henry

Henry and Elizabeta belong to the Dinka tribe, the largest tribe in Southern Sudan and the tribe where response to the Christian message has been very slow though as early as 1905 Archdeacon Shaw arrived as a missionary among them. The people rely on cattle for their way of life and at this time see no virtue in moving into a world culture where reading and education are important. We are reminded of our travelling on the Nile steamer through the land and villages occupied by the Dinka people and their spectacular and much loved cattle. Henry tells us that his friends are advising him to join the Police or the Army and so have the security of a Government job. So far he is sure that God wants him to be a pastor even though he knows he will never get even the small set salary. Of the six Dinka students who started in Mundri with him he is the only one still here.

Next week our guests are to be Eluzai Munda and his wife Fibi, and Benaiah Poggo with Lois his wife. Eluzai with his finely chiselled features and alert expression and Fibi direct and calm belong to the Mundri area, of the Moru tribe, whose language Sapana is helping me to learn. Eluzai and Fibi are very close and eat their meals together always. They seem to accept their childlessness though Eluzai's relatives, in a country where infertility is always considered to be the deficiency of the wife, must be urging him to take a second wife, and give up training to be a pastor.

Benaiah and Lois of the Bari tribe come from Kajo-Kaji to the south of Yei and west of Juba, the second largest tribe in the South. Benaiah has been a Government forestry officer. He is certain he must be a pastor but choosing to train for ordination at Mundri means a considerable loss of income and security for him and his family. A big well-built young man, Benaiah is very fond of his wife who looks so small beside him and is soon to give birth.

There is no end to what we need to learn and understand and these evenings when the students are so patient with us are a great help. Friendships formed in those years have lasted. Although we have never ourselves returned to Sudan we have been able to keep in touch with a number of the men and women we knew in Mundri.

Benjamina, now a bishop, and Mary have suffered and survived the continuing war between North and South in Sudan. Benjamina now uses a hand-carved Zande walking stick because of a painful hip but he and Mary with her neatly plaited hair are just as friendly and smiling as they have always been.

Some years after his ordination we heard that Henry stopped being a pastor and became a policeman and then was killed in the continuing war. It was a sad loss of a good man torn in his life choices and by the times he lived in; we know nothing more of Elizabeta or their son Polycarp. What we do know is that now, after the long years of resistance, the Dinka Church is bursting with life and song, and by 1993 there were more than 100 Dinka clergy caring for huge numbers in new congregations. Dinka Christians have been the missionaries to their own people just as Archdeacon Shaw long ago believed they would be.

Eluzai and Fibi were well known to us over several years, first in the College and then when they were working in the local Moru parish; later John helped with the arrangements and grants for their further studies in Nigeria. Eluzai, now Bishop of Mundri, is still bright and alert and full of plans for the development of his Diocese and Fibi has her own plans as she leads the Mothers' Union which is very active and effective in Sudan.

Benaiah became a remarkable pastor. At the height of the war in Sudan, along with many thousands, he fled to Uganda where we were present when he was ordained priest in exile. He cared for a parish of Sudanese refugees in Bugerere, not far from where we then lived, and turned up regularly on his bicycle at our house intent on getting supplies of books for his parishioners; influenced by John, he knew how essential these were. When the Addis Ababa Agreement of 1972 brought a short term of uneasy peace, he returned to Sudan with his family, as did many other refugees. After serving first as school chaplain in Rumbek and then Loka, Benaiah had two years of theological study at Ridley Hall, Cambridge, before his appointment as Principal of Bishop Gwynne College in Mundri in 1980; when it was later destroyed utterly in the war he set up its replacement in Juba. He is remembered as the man of peace for the way he required differences between tribes and individuals to be talked over and resolved in the College, with staff and students sitting on together in 'reconciliation committees' for as many hours as it took to reach agreement. He was sure that this was the only way forward for real followers of Jesus Christ, a proper witness and example.

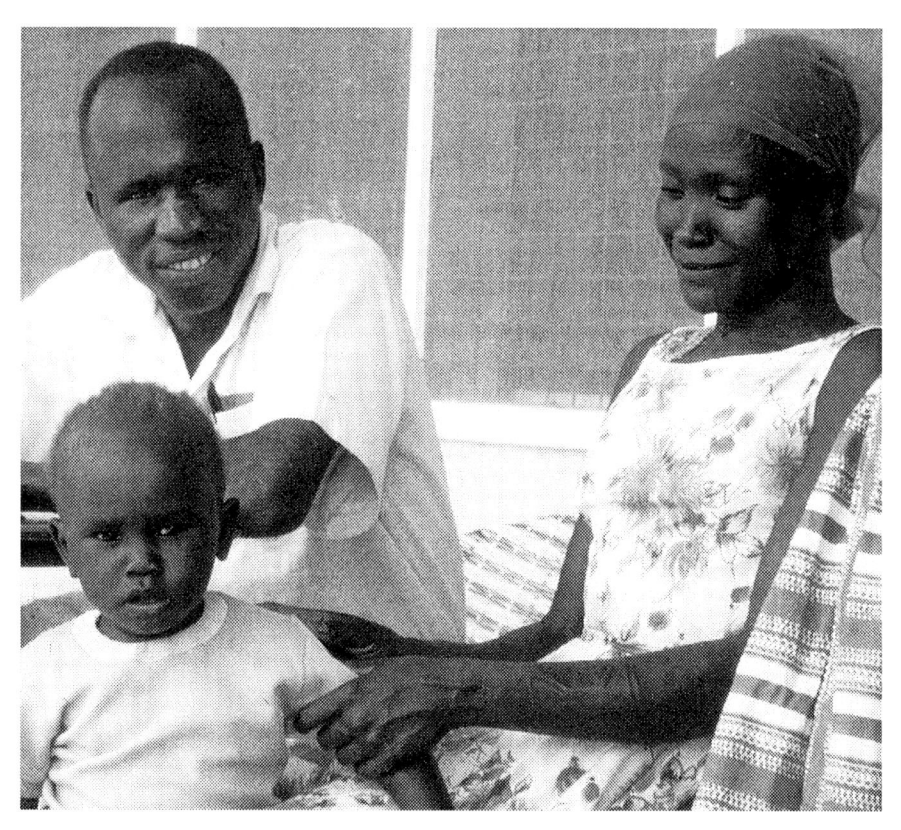

Benaiah and Lois and Anthony (in Uganda)

He well knew that in a time of war personal vendettas could hide as political action. Benaiah died in 1992 of the malaria which had given him serious episodes of illness all his life; Lois remains in Juba where she is loved and supported by their children and grandchildren.

Their son Anthony Poggo, pictured right, is Director of the Sudan Literature Centre in Nairobi which, since it was set up in 1989, has produced more than a million items of literature in a variety of languages for use in Sudan in education and Christian teaching and worship. So Benaiah and all he stood for lives on.

When several of our former students, now bishops, and their wives came to England for the Lambeth Conference in 1998 John and I went to meet them again in Salisbury, an English Diocese with a special link with the Episcopal Church of Sudan. They spoke of their love for us and how they could never forget us. We knew that as well as the good times there had been disagreements and misunderstandings but these seemed to have been forgotten and, taking their place, were warm and loving memories of small kindnesses we had done. Above all there was an overwhelming and embarrassing appreciation of the fact that we had left our comforts and our own people to share our lives with them. "Without you our lives would have been nothing," one by one they declared. We had not thought we would ever receive such affirmation. In our retirement, we were being told that bothering to unpack even for a short time while trying to do something in response to God's call had mattered. Was this a foretaste of heaven we wondered, the excitement, the deeper recognition of each other in love, the forgiveness.

22   How I Fume

News of our arrival in Mundri brought applicants who hoped we would employ them. They stood around in the shade of the ficus tree, the top pockets of their khaki shirts bulging with glowing references of how well they had done their work for expatriate officers during the years of the Anglo-Egyptian Condominium. Domestic work was popular. It offered a cash wage and the opportunity to learn English and other skills from Western employers. A vacant post had many wanting to fill it. Whatever we thought about having our domestic work done for us, we knew that if we were to do any of the work we had come to Sudan to do we would have to employ helpers. We did well in choosing Tito to cook for us and Elizala to do the housework. Ro'ba produced vegetables in the gardens and Bunya set out each morning to forage for firewood and to fetch our supply of water. To their delight, Diya came to look after Michael and Katherine in the hours while I was teaching.

It makes me tired now when I think of living in that heat, but when I admitted to our supporters in churches in Ireland that we employed so many people, they thought we must be living a life of luxury. I took some trouble to explain that they had many unseen 'servants' too who made sure they had their water supply and other services, not to mention proper kitchen facilities and readily available food supplies. In fact it was easier for us later in Uganda when instead of helpers we had taps and electric switches and were one step removed from the services done for us.

Managing the house and garden smoothly took some doing. Our helpers, trained in a former era, had learned to keep very clear lines of demarcation where their job began and where it ended, and they were rigid in not crossing those boundaries. Elizala really wanted to have the prestige of being the senior of our helpers and was quite cross when we pointed out that there wasn't room in the Doll's house for him to have an assistant working under him. While setting the table for the evening meal one day he grasped at a chance to show me that he was qualified for a more elevated household than ours. "Where, Madam," he asked, "are the grapefruit spoons?" Even though we knew we might lose our wedding presents, John and I had decided to take most of them abroad with us. I remembered how we laughed when we packed a small black box containing six initialled silver grapefruit spoons resting on a blue satin padded lining, exactly what Elizala had asked for. I handed them over with a flourish. "There they are, Elizala," I said. He was not too pleased and I soon felt ashamed of myself. In the dry season when the grapefruit ripened, the water was low in the wide Yei river and Elizala liked to take a short cut home over stepping-stones. He had delayed to confront me over the spoons until it was almost dark and now I worried he would be in danger from the crocodiles. "Ah, Madam," he said, seeing my concern, "Yes, crocodiles in river, big, big ones. *Mush kwayyis.* Not good. I see crocodile take man in river. Too much blood, Madam, too much blood. Thank you, now I go." Next morning I could have hugged Elizala, I was so relieved to see him turn up, safe and well, cheerful as usual. Our American colleagues had their own solution to the rigid job boundaries which could leave them stranded when one of their helpers was sick or perhaps had gone to the funeral of a relative or to deal with a family problem. They employed an extra person whose job it was to do the work of any absent one. Before long the advantage of that solution was spotted; as far as I remember there wasn't a day when the 'spare' man wasn't doing the work of one of the others, absent for some reason or other of his own!

John and I wanted to be fair to the people who worked for us. We were uncomfortable when we thought of Elizala or Tito having to light the fire to make that early morning cup of tea which we could do without and which was not, in any case, an Irish custom. But in omitting this usual practice we were having an effect on others in the community. We made this worse when we went further and gave Tito and Elizala a day off on Sundays, good for them but good too for us to be on our own and for the children to help a little with preparing simple meals. I'm not sure that John and I, still in our twenties, fully recognised the ramifications of our thinking and actions on this and other matters, for inevitably our decisions affected other missionary households whose staff envied ours. No bed-tea and no Sunday work disturbed established patterns. This was not how young and inexperienced missionaries should behave. It remained a problem for others that we were not conforming, and a problem for us because we thought we should be free to make our own domestic decisions.

Though we tried to be sensitive to the lives of the people who worked for us we didn't always get it right; that was certainly the case at the end of a visit from John and Helena Parry. They had been our guests for four or five days, had packed up and gone after breakfast handing me the hospitality money as they left. This, as was usual, included some money intended as a gift to our helpers in recognition that they had had extra work, a gift our helpers knew I would hand on to them. Though it was perfectly understandable, I hated to see Tito and the others looking out for this extra money and loitering around at the point when guests were departing. I wanted to deal with it differently and avoid what I thought of as humiliating, so I placed the 'tip' money in envelopes on the dining room table, an envelope for each of our helpers. Though the envelopes were collected, I couldn't help but notice that all was not well. An air of gloom hung around. Tito was hovering in the background, neat and smart in his well-ironed khaki shirt and shorts and making the most of standing tall, but definitely not in a good mood. His face was full of darkness not from pigment but from anger over something, and it looked as if it was something to do with me. He was not ready to tell me yet, to have it out. The grim atmosphere persisted all day. I wondered if it was because his wife had gone to their village to cultivate and he was missing her. Or was he considering again that the only solution to their childlessness was for him to take a second wife, even if that affected his church membership? I knew neither of these were new issues: it felt more like something I had done, or not done, something which had him seething with rage inside. I racked my brains. The guests had been appreciative of Tito's cooking, had thanked him and shaken his hand as they left. Up to then we had all been happy. Could it be the tip? His grievance and anger surged within him all through that long hot day until the evening when in the end he exploded: yes, it was to do with the tip, that was it. The gift money had been in envelopes, not handed to him by me direct in the proper way for people. I had been quite wrong in what I had done, even though I had specially thought it up to avoid the servile response a tip invited. Yes, I had got it wrong. What I had intended as thoughtful and sensitive was for Tito inhuman and insulting.

To eat salads or not to eat salads, that was another controversial issue. In the Sudan climate, salads would have been just what we felt like eating but, with no form of local sanitation and the ova of intestinal worms and amoeba blowing about in the dry dusty winds, I knew raw foods were best avoided. I did not have any confidence in the supposed effectiveness of soaking salads in potassium permanganate solution, so we relied on cooked food, peeled all fruit, peeled tomatoes, and sometimes resorted to Vitamin C tablets. John and I composed a little ditty, the last verse of it still in my notebook, which would not have made some of our colleagues any happier for they thought us unnecessarily fussy and perhaps we were:

O hearken ye living to those who rot!
Salad is cool but Hades is hot.
Though for years you've escaped that's no guarantee,
Be wiser, take tablets of Vitamin C.

"One of the first principles of keeping fit in the tropics is that you avoid salads," was the strong advice of the London School of Tropical Medicine and that was the advice we followed even when it made us awkward guests.

There was a lot of humbug around. I couldn't stand it at the time though later I could see it belonged to the extraordinary isolation of our small expatriate community in Mundri. "Never," I was warned, "walk about carrying a storm lantern at night if you are in a long skirt unless you are wearing a slip as well." "That," said John, "is to stop anyone from seeing that your legs join at the top!" Some of our colleagues were concerned lest the western dress of women missionaries would be an affront to Muslims. Our clothes were in marked contrast with the clothing of Muslim women, mostly living a thousand miles away in the North, who were covered from head to foot whenever they left the confines of their compounds. One day I was taken aside by another missionary to be told that my dress was unacceptable, it was not fair on the men, not right for this country. The dress was one I had made myself with a modest neckline, but its defect was that it was sleeveless. I was so hopping mad that I couldn't restrain myself. "Can't you see those women," I almost shouted at him, pointing at a line of local women who fortunately happened to be passing just then, bobbing along in single file on their way to cultivate their gardens, "What's wrong with my dress?" I raged, "Just look at them! All they are wearing is a bunch of leaves fore and aft."

I knew it was important that there should never be any impression among us of improper relationships, but I didn't think it needed to be taken to excessive lengths. "Sapana who is teaching you Moru," I was informed, "cannot be in your house unless John is there with you." I found it hard to see what the risk was, for these language sessions were in the afternoon when the children and Elizala were around and our windows had no curtains. The matter of a chaperon could be applied to the men too. On one occasion a male missionary was making an official visit to a single woman missionary a hundred miles away, and he required John to accompany him so that he wouldn't be alone with her at her place. In her husband's absence, one wife invited John and me for an evening meal because, without us, a male visitor to the College couldn't be alone with her as her guest, that is alone except for her cook and house helper!

For a brief period a supply of water from the river or well was brought each day to the staff houses on a kind of two-bin cart by a College porter. There was great competition to be the first house on Monday morning to have a water delivery. I thought this was daft. Monday, as the traditional washday in England, made very little sense when clothes dried very quickly in Mundri and in fact every day of the week was a wash-day. I was not often off the front line when it came to exploding over behaviour which I thought ridiculous, but this was one skirmish I didn't need to be involved in. But I could feel that my indifference to it was somehow annoying too.

From time to time I tried my hand at baking. Odd ingredients and equipment could produce good cakes but I soon learned it was more acceptable for me to have my share of failures. For the sake of good relationships I decided sometimes to burn a cake rather than have too many freaky successes. "Did you deliberately burn that cake?" is a question still asked in our family when I'm suspected of plotting an outcome going my way but achieved by devious behaviour.

When this kind of humbug annoyed me beyond my control, I was too quick in my responses and remarks and made ordinary situations more difficult than they need have been. Then I felt cross, cross that living in Mundri could be so annoying, so unlike the life I had imagined for myself working as a missionary doctor, cross that even with my certainty of God's presence with me I couldn't be an easier person. John was very skilled at cooling me down, but that was just what I didn't want when I was feeling frustrated. I wanted to storm or wallow for a while, to feel I was right to rage and be furious. Unknown to John, in the heat of those times I started a notebook, 'How I fume,' where I wrote about the things and the people who made me mad. Forty years on, when I read those pages the feelings are no longer as hot as they were then, but I'm still in touch with them all the same. At the time that small notebook was a defusing device, a device I've used ever since and which I like to recommend.

But I wasn't cross all the time! Cooped up as we were, respect and close friendships with our colleagues grew and conflicts were faced and, by the Grace of God, resolved. John and I had many a laugh at ourselves and laughed too with the others while all of us found our individual ways of adapting or not adapting to this strange life. John, although he couldn't do much about it, was always aware that in marrying him and in accepting our posting to Sudan I wasn't able to follow my own doctor vocation, that my life was more limited than was easy for me. This was certainly true, and when I was in despair about the medical licence I used to cling to John's confidence that something would change. Meanwhile his constant love and understanding, and the delight we had in each other and in our children, was enough to keep us happy in this place where we were serving God as best we could. I appreciated what John wrote in an early 'Annual Letter' to CMS in August 1959.

"Dorothy's time is taken up largely by looking after the children and managing the house and keeping her husband full and happy! We try to make the students feel 'at home' in our house, and we are coming to see that this part of our ministry to the College is worth even more effort than we have been giving it. Nevertheless Dorothy does find time for other activities which include language study - she is learning Moru - and teaching Hygiene to the Ordinands and several subjects in the Wives School. She is also making use of her easel and oil paints.

"I am sure that one of the things that would strike any European most forcibly on coming to Mundri is the extreme isolation.

Transport is extremely difficult, communications with the outside world are slow, there are very few people of a comparable background to our own in whose company we may relax the tension of being foreigners. I do not mean to write about the difficulties of being a missionary here, because they are not so great as to depress us, but if we do face them openly I am sure the greatest is isolation. This is especially true for the wives; their husbands quite often have a change of scene when they go out to the villages, they can enter into a deeper relationship with the students, and their work is all absorbing and probably more satisfying. But usually the wife's horizon is much more limited perforce, and it must sometimes be difficult for her to see just in what sense she is a missionary."

And in much the same way I wrote my own version later, in 1962, by which time we and the Gills were the only expatriates left on the Mundri staff:

"The most difficult aspect of life here is the extreme isolation. For months at a time we go no further than a mile away and we see no other English speaking people at all. This gives us very little outlet of any kind. It is difficult to make real friends amongst the students as their culture is so different from ours. We are not able to speak in their twelve or more different languages, and they do not speak English well enough to make ordinary conversation easy."

Despite our isolation, we had a good balance between work and play in our first year or two in Mundri. Mary and David insisted on time off for all the staff on Friday evenings each week. We gathered in one or other of our houses by turn, and ate a meal as special as we could make it. The women wore long skirts, some of the men sported cummerbunds while others wore traditional Sudanese robes. Talk about work, the College, the students or politics was banned as we relaxed in the soft hot lamplight. If we felt energetic we played silly games, we sang folk songs or engaged in fierce debates.

Two or three times a year we hired the College lorry and went for a staff picnic at Jebel Mundri, an outcrop of rock rising out of the flat surrounding scrubland three miles away. It made a wonderful treat. With baskets of food and hats at skittish angles, we climbed aboard, three in the cab and the rest of us holding on at the back. Every truck passing along the main road between Juba and Yambio, to the far west of us, was required to report at the police post in Mundri village. That was the first thing we had to do. The police, the senior ones Northerners, didn't know anything about picnics and were reluctant to believe us when we told them we were going to Jebel Mundri to have tea there. It was more likely, they thought, that we had plans to hand over guns and ammunition to members of the anti-government Southern resistance movement suspected of hiding in the rocks nearby. So, instead of granting us a pass, a policeman was appointed to accompany and observe us, a duty he seemed to find rather pleasant for while he stood at attention with his gun we shared some of our food with him. When we returned after hours in the sun, John and I rushed the children off to bed and, feeling exhausted and sleepy, were wonderfully happy that these small outings could refresh us so much.

I go back in my mind to that time. We have no telephones, no newspapers and with batteries almost impossible to get, none of us has a radio. Our airmail letters from U.K. often take a month to reach us. I hear Michael and Katherine talking in an unusual way in our bedroom and go to investigate. There the two of them are in front of a photo of Papa Lowe. "Well, you see," Katherine explains, "we wanted to look at Papa's picture and tell him not to be sad because we're going to see him very, very soon." They have not heard his voice for a couple of years and neither have we. Brian de Saram who, without telephone contact and with irregular and unreliable postal services, cared for and managed about 30 missionaries scattered over a huge area, used to joke that he would revert to earlier times and hire a runner to send notes to us inserted in cleft sticks!

23 Our First Christmas

"An *arabiya*, an *arabiya*, Mammy, a 'normous *arabiya*." Michael aged two and a half rushed in, hopping with excitement. An *arabiya*, a lorry, was one of his favourite things. This one was huge, made of heavy metal to survive the rough roads, and parked now just outside the College office.

End of term

It was November 1959, the end of term, the end of our first year in the College. Students had been busy gathering their possessions for the journey to their home areas where they were going for pastoral work experience, holiday, and to cultivate their gardens. This particular group were off to Yei, the centre of the Bari area. Michael wasn't the only one excited. The student families were rushing around with excitement too for soon they would be reunited with the children they had had to leave behind at school when they came to Mundri seven or eight months ago. They would have a lot to describe about their life in the College and their new experiences and there would be news and gossip to gather of what everyone had been doing in their absence.

The packing was not done in an expert way, not categorised or sorted, but somehow when the loading was completed most of the bedding was on the top for sitting on. Round the truck stood men and women with small children and babies as well as the driver and his mate, almost all of them talking and shouting at once. Staff and other students, not leaving for their holidays just yet, were standing around too, ready to be helpful and making sure nobody was left behind, no farewells left unsaid. As was the custom, a hymn was sung at full volume and then one of us prayed for the driver, the conditions of the road, the weather, and a safe arrival for everyone. No journey began in Sudan without this call to prayer, a reminder of God's part in our lives whatever the outcome might be. Then the lorry was away with its load of baggage and passengers; we could see the heads of forty or fifty people bobbing about high up at the back, chatting and singing as they went. We waved until they were out of sight but we could still hear the singing long after. By the end of the week the College houses were all empty. In the vacation they would be used for short courses run by the local parish.

The dry season while the students were away was the obvious time for expatriate staff to have an annual break; as required by CMS we had a month of local leave in Kenya or Uganda one year, and the next year four months of U.K. leave of which one month was holiday and the rest was for visits to our supporting parishes in England and Ireland.

As it happened 1959/1960 was the U.K. year for David and Mary Brown and for Richard Gill. At the same time Noel and Violet White were leaving finally to work in Ireland, Canon Ezra was on a year's study leave at the London College of Divinity and the rest of the Sudanese staff were away supervising students in their pastoral work. By the end of November, John and I were the only staff left at Bishop Gwynne College. And John was about to go away too. With a small case of books and a knapsack for his clothes local people were amazed to see him, a white man his skin tanned brown, climb up to sit with 49 others on the back of the *busta*, the post lorry, for the 130 mile journey to Yei where he was to help for a month with the Bari students. That left me with Michael and Katherine, then two and half years old, on our own. I wonder now if I failed to register properly how isolated I was. All these years later I can hardly credit it. No transport, no phone, no radio, no other expatriates nearer than a day's lorry travel away even supposing a lorry was available, no emergency medical help, and not yet a year in Africa! I can't think now how I don't remember a moment of feeling concerned or fearful. We were where we believed God meant us to be and surrounded by the people we had come to help, and the year of missionary training - or was it mind-shaping? - had prepared us well. Michael was a little less patient. He didn't like John being away. One day I found him stuffing his pockets with nuts as if to sustain himself for a journey. "And where are you off to?" I asked. "I'm going to Yei to find Daddy," he said, confident that for such a goal 130 miles would not be beyond him.

Alone in the Doll's house in that quiet place without the sound of a truck or an aeroplane, it was strange how the deep rumbling of an engine cut into my consciousness or was I imagining it? Could it be that our special visitor was about to arrive? Elsie Ludlow, a younger sister of my mother, had been a Methodist missionary nurse in Nigeria for 30 years, since 1929. When her local leave was due, with her usual adventurous spirit she decided that there was nothing she wanted more than to make a visit to the other side of Africa to spend Christmas in Sudan with us, and experience the Nile steamer for part of her return journey. We didn't know when to expect her. She would fly from Lagos to Khartoum and then take another flight south to Juba but how she would get from there to Mundri neither she nor we knew. It seemed to make no difference to her that she was already over sixty years old. John had been away in Yei for two weeks when the groan of a Landrover broke the silence one night and I was out like a shot with a great big hug for Auntie Elsie and huge thanks for the Government officials who had spared a seat for her on their journey.

Auntie Elsie had really come. There she was, small and energetic and wonderful company. It was obvious from the attractive dresses she had made for herself that she minded what she looked like. Not for her, and not for me either, the aertex shirts, gathered skirts and Clarke's sandals recommended as a kind of missionary uniform by the staff at Foxbury, the CMS Training College! It pleased us both to have our individual style!

Elsie was thoroughly immersed in her work and life in Nigeria and I loved to hear her talking of her experiences there. In her early years she, like Auntie Joyce, had been shocked and distressed by the horrendous mortality rate of small children living around Ilesha Hospital, more than half of them dying before their fifth birthday. She had seen the great improvements which treatment, monitoring and immunisation had brought through the Under-Fives-Clinics. The clinics were acceptable to the formally trained Auntie Elsie; what was not so acceptable was the change in ward management which arrived with Dr. David Morley. He brought new understanding of sick children, and insisted they must have their mothers or known relatives around them when they were in Hospital. "Everywhere there are groups of people," Elsie, the Matron, told me with some heat, "sitting on the beds, lying under them and all over the ward and getting in the way of the nurses, and not always clean." How I would have loved to be working as a doctor myself! Even untidy wards would be no problem for me.

Elsie could be very witty and amusing and wise, but perhaps most of all I appreciated just having her there; it was an almost incredible relief to have in her a safe person to talk to and one who could listen to me and understand when I told of things I found difficult. As well as being ready with wise advice for a young missionary niece and her husband, Auntie Elsie, as my mother's sister, had a special proxy-grandmother relationship with Michael and Katherine. They loved the stories she told them when she went walking with them. Katherine was later to adopt her as substitute grandmother and remain very close to her for all the years until she died aged 98. Our local friends, as was their custom of respect for older expatriates, repeatedly thanked Elsie for sending us to help them and, although she didn't think the thanks were due to her, she always smiled graciously and nodded in agreement!

Christmas Eve, our first in Africa, and still no news of John. Elsie and I sat in the lamplight, trying to work up an atmosphere by playing carols on a wind-up gramophone I had borrowed from a colleague then on leave. Where was John? Was he having trouble with the truck he was driving back from Yei? Was he sick? Was he dead? There was no answer to these questions until 11.30 p.m. when we heard the sound of an engine. John at the wheel of the College truck had been frantic to get to us, delayed by puncture after puncture and the tough work of mending them which had almost defeated him. You can be sure that he got his usual rapturous welcome from me! After four weeks in Yei, he was just in time for all of us to be together again for this our first Christmas in Mundri. Michael would not need to make his trek to Yei after all, for Daddy was back. Stockings somehow were filled with small gifts and in the morning we joined with a huge crowd to sit on the pole seating at the parish church for the Christmas service. It was full of joy but also sticky and hot and very lengthy - and in Moru. A feast followed for all the congregation; Christmas was the great celebration and social occasion of the year. We stayed around long enough for many greetings and then went home in the truck for the meal we had prepared for ourselves with the mixture of ingredients we had. The 'plum pudding' was invented out of groundnut paste, dates, and maize flour with an egg or two and oil, and a man had come to the door to sell us not a turkey but a delicious guinea fowl. We had special Christmas gifts ready for the children. No last minute Christmas shopping here in Mundri, but a red tricycle we had bought a year ago in Liverpool emerged from the Ark packing case for Michael who was handy at holding spanners for John to assemble it for him, and he soon learned how to ride it and even to fix it. Katherine had a doll's pram put together and equipped with blankets and sheets and every comfort for her family of dolls and teddies. She could manage all of them but not our cat which annoyed her by jumping out and escaping when she tried to give him the ride she thought he ought to like.

On wheels - John, Katherine and Michael

During his weeks in Yei, John was asked to fill in for a Sudanese pastor who was ill by going to Loka Intermediate Boys School to baptize a group of schoolboys in a service in English. This, in fact, was the only baptism John ever conducted in our years in Sudan. Before the service he interviewed each of the candidates briefly. At the point of Baptism it was common practice to choose a new name, often from the Bible. One of the boys wanted to be given the name John. "John is a good name, and there are several Johns in the New Testament, which one are you thinking of?" he was asked. There was no hesitation. "John, the Apostle ," was the answer. It was an encounter which was to have future significance for us and for that schoolboy. He was John Lasu Kanyikwa, to give him his full name, a Bari of outstanding ability whose life would overlap with ours at other points.

Some years later, with his wife Lilian, John fled to Uganda as a refugee with many other Sudanese, and was accepted as an ordination student at Bishop Tucker College, Mukono, where we found him when we joined the staff there in 1964.

John Kanyikwa's eyes lit up when he realised that the priest who had baptized him in Loka was to be one of his tutors. John and Lilian had been married by traditional ceremony. Who better than John Lowe, they thought, to conduct a Christian service for them! This took place in Bishop Tucker College Chapel in the presence of all the students and staff, followed by a tea party in the College Assembly Hall. It was a great occasion. In the style adopted for Uganda Church weddings, Lilian looked lovely in a long white dress and was attended by four bridesmaids, two of them daughters of the Principal, the Rev. Amos Betungura, and two the daughters of the Rev. Yustasi Ruhindi, the College Chaplain. Misaeri Kauma (later to be Principal of the College) was best man and his wife Geraldine matron of honour. My part was to bake scones for 150 and make a huge two-tier iced cake which I set up on the platform where everyone could see it. During the speeches it wobbled on its pillars and was given a round of applause when it collapsed!

John and Lilian Kanyikwa

Ever since that great start the Kanyikwas and the Lowes have kept in touch with each other: John a clever and diligent ordinand at Bishop Tucker College, Lilian equally impressive in the Wives School. They shared Christmas dinners with us and other Sudanese refugees in our house in Mukono, followed by presents and prolonged games of croquet in the sunshine; later on, there were reports from Richard Gill that John and Lilian were the best curate couple he had ever had in his parish in St. Alban's. Next, on the Bishop Tucker College staff, the Kanyikwas lived in the house next to ours. Difficult times too: one Sunday Lilian saw me sorting out some photographs and suspected that we were deciding to leave Mukono. When I told her this was not so, she looked at me and gave me wise advice, "it is better to leave when you are still loved," she said. She had a harder choice. When the Addis Ababa Agreement brought a period of relative peace to Sudan in 1972, John and Lilian and their family faced up to what a return to Sudan would mean for them. For John there was the post of Provincial Secretary in Juba, but for the four children the schools were not at the level of those they were attending in Uganda. Still, Juba was where they believed God wanted them and to Juba they returned. During the years ahead there were visits to us in Kent and in Cambridge between periods of further study in America and in Ireland. John served as Principal of Theological Colleges in Tanzania and Zambia, and now is General Secretary of the Council of the Anglican Provinces of Africa, based in Nairobi. John and Lilian are a remarkable Sudanese Christian couple and have been a blessing to a great many people and a blessing to us too.

But back to the Doll's house and Auntie Elsie's visit. At the beginning of January we set off to attend the Annual Conference for CMS missionaries which was to be held in the Girls School in Yei during the holiday time for the girls. We travelled there by lorry taking our camp beds and oil lamps and all the other equipment we would need. Bible studies, hymn singing, discussions, meals together in a cooler place and especially meeting about twenty other CMS missionaries, some of whom we hadn't yet met, provided us with a good programme. There was plenty of room, so Auntie Elsie came too and was a guest in one of the missionary houses.

In order to be close enough to the children while we were at the evening events, we were given a dormitory near the classroom where these sessions were to be held. That dormitory had been emptied of furniture and left spotlessly clean by the schoolgirls when they went off at the end of their term, and we soon had it set up as our place, Michael and Katherine in their cots and our low canvas camp-beds on the floor beside each other. What we didn't know was that the thatch of the roof above was harbouring an enemy. A population of bed bugs in it lost no time before dropping down for a feast of blood. Mine seemed to be just to their taste, quite irresistible for bedbugs. I was tormented by them, catching them by lamplight and counting them as I banged them dead on the concrete floor with my sandal, until in desperation I left John and the children, whom the bugs didn't seem to like at all, and went out to sleep in the lorry. Next day, leaving the bloody massacre site of 157 adult bugs beside where my bed had been, we moved to a different building where we had peaceful nights. That was, of course, just one episode in my continuing relationship with bedbugs. I was always simply delicious.

An annual Missionary Conference had been a regular feature of the Mission but was becoming a sore point in Sudanese Church circles. Was it appropriate now for us, expatriate missionaries, to meet together on our own, we who were sharing and working in partnership with our Sudanese colleagues? This was sensitive thinking, but without such times there would be no opportunity for us to discuss the particular concerns and difficulties we faced as expatriates living in our isolated places. We were being buffeted about by the 'winds of change' and so were our Sudanese colleagues. For us it could mean expulsion; for them their future as Christian Southerners was under threat in a Sudan dominated from the Muslim North. Their gatherings did not always include us; perhaps we too needed separate time to encourage each other, even at the cost of possible misunderstanding. I read how Archdeacon Shaw, earlier in the century, was described as having the mark of 'the country gentleman' with his china cups for tea, his riverside golf course and the swimming pool free of crocodiles which he constructed by blocking off a section of the Nile at hot humid Malek; compared with him maybe we, in the years of transition between the earlier times and what was to come, were more reticent than we need have been. Perhaps it was a hidden form of patronising that we put sensitivity to Sudanese colleagues before our own needs. As it was the changes were greater than we had expected, for many of those with us at that Missionary Conference in 1960 had their work permits withdrawn soon after, and were gone from Sudan before the year was out. In our fifteen years as missionaries in Sudan and Uganda this was our one and only Missionary Conference.

24   On Leave

"Will we be there soon?" That is the question Katherine keeps on asking. We have hired the College Peugeot truck. John is at the wheel with Michael and Katherine and me squashed into the cab beside him. "Will we be there soon?" Katherine repeats her question, clutching her favourite Teddy who has to come too. "Well, not just yet," I answer, knowing that we are off on local leave and that there is a long way to go. Tonight we are to stay in Juba, then drive south on untarred roads to cross the Sudan border at Nimule on the Nile, before we reach Gulu in Northern Uganda. There we will stay for the night with Keith and Dora Russell, CMS missionaries who, as is the custom, provide hospitality for others who travel in their direction, especially for those of us from Sudan. The day after that our road will take us through a swampy area, then across the Nile on a ferry, and after a final stretch we join the tarred road and arrive in Kampala, the capital of Uganda. "Not just yet" is a fair estimate!

It is March 1960 and we are on our first local leave, our first time away since we arrived in Sudan a year ago. To preserve our mental and physical health CMS requires us to spend a month in a cooler climate for local leave one year, and to take U.K. leave the other. I feel as excited as can be for we will stay with various missionary friends and best of all with Raymond and Audrey Smith. Audrey is my sister and she and Raymond, also CMS missionaries, arrived in the Kenya highlands just a month ago with Peter who is two and baby Rosalind, first cousins of our children. Katherine repeats her question at each of the stops we make, Gulu, Kampala, Mukono, and after four hundred miles further on I can say, "Yes, here we are, here are your cousins, your aunt and your uncle!" The climate where they live is very pleasant, the grass is green and not too far away the shops in Nairobi are full of goods. We relax and make the most of this respite, especially all the company and entertainment and delicious food Audrey and Raymond provide. The evenings are delightfully cool. I sit one evening beside the wood fire in the gentle light of a table lamp, and I can't help comparing the living conditions of CMS missionaries here in Kenya with ours in Sudan! Not just the comfort but even more the relief of being able to write our letters home without censorship, able at last to tell the truth about the Sudan situation. That, of course, is not to forget that every location has its challenges. Within the last decade in Kenya there has been the terror of Mau Mau.

A new house is being built for us in Mundri. It will be bigger than the Doll's house and we wonder how we can make it more comfortable and attractive. Some new cushions would be a start and what about buying gutters to collect wet-season rain water from our corrugated roof? So along with the good supply of food and household stores bought in Nairobi, we found room for our very own tin gutters and the brown powder cement colouring for the floors which I have already mentioned.

The truck stands ready loaded to return to Sudan. "Will we soon be home?" Michael keeps asking, eager to be back riding his tricycle again. We will miss Audrey and Raymond, miss being free and secure and living so comfortably in Kenya and Uganda, but Mundri is home and we are glad to be back, back in our own place.

By the end of the year our turn for U.K. leave came up. We would go by air, flying over the Sudd, the sands and the sea in a flash compared with the long journey by surface in 1959. We decided we would make the most of the airways concession by which travellers on a long haul flight could deviate up to 600 miles for a stop-over, without incurring extra cost. We fancied a few days in Athens to provide us with a gap between our isolated existence in Mundri and our arrival to be with our parents and friends in England and Ireland. We would soon be very busy meeting with CMS staff at Salisbury Square and then carrying out numerous speaking and preaching engagements in the parishes which supported us; a few days holiday before all that seemed a good idea. We went by lorry to Juba, this time an uneventful journey apart from one breakdown greeted by Michael with "Oh! Goodee, a puncture!", and then on by air to Khartoum next day. This was our first time to be on an aeroplane. Our flight on a D.C.3 was not smooth. The very hot air rising from the ground caused turbulence, lifting the small Dakota upwards and as suddenly giving way and leaving us in free fall or lurching from side to side. We found it hard to face the meal served to each of us in white cardboard boxes; a boiled egg, a piece of cold cooked fish, a round cake of local bread - the only 'convenience' food available at that time in Juba.

After a night in Khartoum we flew on to Athens where a helpful receptionist fixed us up at the Hotel Plaka, central and not very expensive. To make our money stretch as far as possible and save us the price of a meal in a restaurant, I set off for the nearby shops. So lovely, so exciting, so clean. Not a bit like the dusty shops which were all we had known in Mundri and Juba. How do I choose between so many luscious-looking honey cakes and salad rolls? And then anxiety takes over: I haven't reported to the police, they don't know where I've gone. This was the first time I fully realised the restrictive effect of living under surveillance at Mundri, and fully appreciated the marvel of freedom and liberty.

Our three or four days were packed with seeing some of the wonderful architecture and statues of classical Greece. For the children paddling with us in the sea at Sounion was very popular, and so was travelling on an ordinary bus to Corinth in the company of local people with their assorted bundles and baggage, including a basket of squawking live chickens. Perhaps the highlight for John and me was the day we spent wandering around in the Parthenon enjoying views of the sea and the city of Athens below us, and then as we descended overhearing the children's comments on their day: "This must be the hill where Jack and Jill fell down," Katherine told Michael. Both children were more interested in nursery rhymes than ancient buildings, and hills for them were a novelty.

After two years absence it was wonderful to be with my parents in Liverpool and with Papa in Ballinderry, and to see their delight in the grandchildren. Stories, games, endless talking and questions and comments. We had become so used to being in Sudan that we were often bewildered when we went to well-stocked shops. George Frangos's shop in Mundri had a total of 3 dusty tins of baked beans on a shelf when I was there a month before, but here the shops had many tins of baked beans and many different brands of the same thing. Surely that was excessive. It upsets me that the rich parts of the world are so rich and the poor parts of the world so poor.

Three weeks ago we arrived in Ireland and we are staying with Papa and John's sister Daphne in the Rectory in Ballinderry. Papa is a widower with a housekeeper, and works from home. He is out visiting a sick parishioner. His house has been filled up by John and me and our children, and he is amazingly good-natured about it though, as a tidy and precise man used to being on his own, it can't be easy for him. John and I sit at the fire reading, glad that the children seem to be quiet and amusing themselves, as we wait for Papa's return. A key in the door, Papa's voice not pleased. We rush into the hall to see what he has seen. After only knowing bungalows without stairs, the hall and stairway of Papa's house are Michael and Katherine's favourite place. This afternoon Michael has made a discovery. Those triangular oak stair rods can be moved to the right or to the left and then come out of their retaining loops. By the time Papa arrives most of the stair rods are out and Katherine, always Michael's assistant on these occasions, is collecting them up on the landing. The stair carpet has escaped. It takes some time for Papa to restore order and we stand around feeling awkward for he prefers to sort it out himself without the help we offer, but soon it's done. Michael realises that his discovery is not approved, not what Papa wants, but that doesn't deter him from further discoveries and observations, useful qualities for a future researcher.

We were surrounded by love and consideration and a lot of help with the children, and this allowed us to fulfil a strenuous programme of visits to the churches which supported us. In those three months John preached 43 times and I gave 13 talks. On other less formal occasions we projected colour transparencies for small groups of people. We felt very encouraged to find so much interest in all we were doing.

But we could see that making our home with grandparents for four months every two years would intrude too much on their lives. That prompted us to copy Uncle Nelson and Auntie Joyce Ludlow who, when they were missionaries, bought a house in England where they lived when they were on leave and which they rented out when they returned each time to their work in Nigeria. We borrowed money and bought a new red-brick semi-detached house for ourselves in the suburbs of Belfast which, over the years, 'bought itself' with the rent money it earned while we were abroad. It was a very convenient home for us when we were on leave and produced enough capital years later to start us off on buying the better house in Cambridge where we now live.

25   Sapana

In the year of our missionary training with its wide range of subjects, John was included with other CMS candidates in a motor maintenance course at the Ford factory in Dagenham. That was useful when he had to sort out the College trucks at Mundri. Later on after the American Mission had installed their gift of an electricity plant at Bishop Gwynne College, John was the only one able to see to the Lister engine and the generator and stop the fluorescent strip lights from flickering or giving up altogether. But a course on accountancy didn't seem quite so relevant until, almost immediately after we arrived in Mundri, John found it essential to know something about the principles of keeping accounts.

John's main work was teaching but he also had responsibility for the administration of the College finances with the

Sapana and John

help of Sapana Bennsion who was already doing some book-keeping when we arrived in 1959. In the way missionaries did, John, who was not an accountant at all, responded to the need, and soon he and Sapana were managing the office together. Sapana was one of the tall members of the Moru tribe, with inky black skin and an engaging smile, both intelligent and hard working. Although he had it in his strong personality to be warm and kindly, he also had it in him to rise and erupt in response to conflict. If he was treated with proper respect and fair discussion all was well, if not his face could darken and the sparks would fly. He was above all a man with a living faith in Jesus Christ and this had transformed his life. John knew him well through their working together and I had my own contact with Sapana who was teaching me his language, Moru, the language of the people of the area where we were living. We sometimes look back and think that if Sapana with his alive Christian faith and total integrity was the only result of the efforts of missionary endeavour through 60 years, it would still be more than worth it all.

The College sent Sapana to Khartoum for a short course in accountancy and with John's help and support he became the College Bursar. Later, as a refugee in Uganda, he kept the account books for various Church institutions until he was able to return to Juba where he served for many years as Provincial Treasurer of the Episcopal Church of Sudan.

Sapana and John managed the money well in Bishop Gwynne College, aware of how terribly important it was that all transactions should be open and that those who had to do with finances should maintain utmost honesty. In this respect Sapana was exemplary. This is the kind of honesty my grandfather passed on to his family by a custom of his; when he received a letter in the post and saw its stamp was not franked, he would take that 'new' stamp and tear it in two with the comment, "This little stamp has done its work." His small great-grandson, Michael, was quick to be on honesty duty. The Sunday morning service is over and John is left in the chancel of the College Chapel, tidying up. He lifts the collection basket off the

Table and empties the money into his hand. A small voice breaks the silence. "Daddy," asks three-year-old Michael, "did you take God's money, did you?" John is careful to explain that he and Sapana look after the College money and now he is going to put it away. He and Michael walk out together into the bright sunshine and across the grass to unlock the office door. Next John opens the safe with his key, God's money is put securely inside, and Michael is satisfied.

Later because of political unrest this is no longer a safe place to keep money. "Don't use the safe except for very small amounts of money, Sapana," John advises, "just keep the cash hidden somewhere else so if you are held up for the key you can hand it over and not risk your life. You are worth more than any cash." Only a year later a missionary in Rwanda, with a safe in his bedroom, resisted handing over the key and was shot dead by an intruder. Money hidden under books or somewhere else did not give rise to the risk posed by money in a safe.

Early in his years as a student at Trinity College, Dublin, John saved up and bought himself a dark green Raleigh bicycle with a 3-speed gear. It carried him on holidays to Scotland, to London for the Festival of Britain in 1951, and also all over Ireland. At the beginning and end of each term he used to cycle the 100 miles between Dublin and his home in Ballinderry, Co. Antrim, when holiday time came, in order to save the train fare but also because he enjoyed it. Best of all, as far as I was concerned, he on that bicycle and I on mine explored the Wicklow mountains and other places near Dublin. Those expeditions while we were students were a wonderful way to be together and to enjoy the glorious countryside where we walked in the mountains, swam in freezing lakes, sheltered from the rain, ate bread and tins of thick Heinz vegetable soup warmed up on John's folding Primus stove, and shared our thoughts and hopes during the five years of our engagement, at every moment longing for the time when we would be married and together at last. In January 1959, that was the bicycle John took to pieces and carefully packed with other heavy things in the 'Ark' bound for Sudan. My bicycle was too much of a crock to be worth taking!

In Mundri Sapana too had a bicycle, a heavy model with 28-inch wheels, more suited to the rough local roads of Sudan than John's Raleigh with its smaller wheels, but where John had his chain and pedals, Sapana had neither; his had worn out and replacements were not available. With one hand to steer and a long pole in the other, Sapana punted himself quite effectively around the College. Then a great day came. Like John, Sapana had saved up and he came to show us his splendid new bicycle. We were delighted for him. John and he lost no time in arranging a celebration trip. They would cycle to Sapana's home village, about forty miles away. They set out early one Saturday while it was still fairly cool, and enjoyed the freshness of the air and the dew glistening on the scrubby bush beside the narrow track. More than half way there some men warned them that there was a lion nearby and indeed they could recognise the spoor on their path. Lions were no joke. Lions in this area were still a serious danger, a danger Sapana knew all about. (People mauled by lions accounted for the majority of surgical cases treated for their terrible wounds by Dr and Mrs Fraser at Lui Hospital in the 1920's.) Though he felt anxious and responsible, Sapana decided they were now too far away to return to Mundri; they had no choice but to continue their journey. What a relief it must have been when they could see groups of *tukls* under the trees in the distance and knew they would reach the village safely. After a round of greetings and introductions with Sapana's family, a meal was served by the women who, as was the custom, ate on their own afterwards with the children.

Three or four men spent the evening sitting with Sapana and John in the open talking round the fire, aware of the roaring of a lion not too far away. Sapana translated into English for John and the talk went on until it was time for them to sleep in the *tukl* they shared for the night, the lion still roaring in the darkness. The village was an active Christian community and arrangements for the next day, Sunday, had been discussed. It was to be a special occasion. John was to preach and celebrate the Holy Communion, Sapana translating, an event which was only available when an ordained pastor could come. It was always difficult to find an acceptable substitute for bread in this country where the diet was millet porridge, but somehow Marie biscuits appeared on a painted enamel plate and one biscuit could be broken into many pieces. We often wondered how that had come about! The Bishop had given permission in the Diocese for cold tea or a red drink called *kerkade* made from dried hibiscus flowers to be substituted for wine and administered from a shared glass. I wasn't there but I could picture John in his long white surplice standing in the place set aside for prayers, a wooden cross behind him and log pole seats for the congregation. The people, many of them Christians, would be joined by others standing around, all of them keen to see the white man who had cycled to their village with Sapana. John and Sapana returned safely after their trip but we weren't allowed to forget the lion.

We take out the well-read books for the bedtime story. "No, Mammy, not those books," says Katherine, "we want a true story." Michael is already making roaring noises. "Tell us about Daddy riding his bicycle so fast the lion couldn't catch him." And so the story grows, and is joined onto the story of the leopard. That one recalled the time we had a real and very fierce leopard cub brought to us by a man who had found it in the bush. He was afraid of the mother leopard attacking him if she heard her cub mewling, so he decided to solve his problem by getting rid of the cub, at the same time getting some money for it. He knew that foreigners were his best chance, so he hopped on his bicycle to carry the leopard cub about thirty miles to sell it to us in Mundri. While it was in our care we too were afraid the mother leopard would trace her cub and find us. We stayed indoors at night and it wasn't surprising that we sometimes imagined a prowling leopard! Katherine soon learned that this little furry cuddly wild animal could not be wheeled around in her doll's pram, could not be a pet at all for it was always ready to use its four sets of sharp claws and pointed teeth. It was perpetually hungry and especially restless at night; it wore me out trying to satisfy it. In the end I had to resort to bottle-feeding it, tied up in a thick cloth, while it consumed one after another of our precious tins of concentrated evaporated milk. By the time Government officials, in Equatoria to collect animals for Khartoum Zoo, drove through Mundri six weeks later, our leopard cub had grown bigger and, with no milk left, we were more than ready to hand it over to their care.

As for Sapana, all went well for a week or two. We often saw him whizzing around on his new bicycle. Then one day I saw him punting along on his old bike again as he came to the Doll's house for my Moru lesson. "Where ever is your new bike, Sapana?" I asked. Sapana smiled in an accepting way. "My brother has it now, he needs it more than I do."

A young man like Sapana was ready for marriage and we began to hear about the beauty and suitability of Kristina, an attractive local Christian girl. Plans went ahead for the members of both families to do the things that had to be done to come to an agreement over the marriage. But other things were expected too as we soon discovered. When a member of the bride's family, for instance, visited the house of the bridegroom-to-be and admired any of his possessions, he could find it impossible to avoid handing the items over. Visits to Sapana's house became all too frequent and it was clear that he and Kristina would be starting their marriage in an empty house. "Just move anything you want into our house so it won't be seen and admired," I offered, and Sapana did just that. We did the same with any spare money he had, acting as his bankers. He told his relatives we were very strict about withdrawals!

John and I meet Sapana punting his bicycle along the road from the office. He looks a bit weary. I call a greeting in Moru, for he is my language teacher. "*Mi kado ya?* Is everything good for you, Sapana," I ask. "*Aro'boya Lu ri.* Thanks to God, it is alright for today," he answers, "but for tomorrow that is difficult." He now has eleven people living at his house with himself and Kristina and some of them have been there for several weeks. Providing for them all costs more than Sapana can easily manage. During the year, as a man in paid employment, he has met the usual requests from his relations, school fees for two or three boys, a bicycle tyre or tube for an uncle, clothes for cousins, tea, coffee, blankets. His sister hasn't enough milk to nurse her baby and he pays for tins of powdered milk while she and four of her children move in to stay with him. Among the rest are two young men, eating well at Sapana's expense and doing no work. "But Sapana," I say, "isn't that bad for their characters to let them eat and laze about all day talking and sleeping while they do nothing to help? How long do you think they will stay?" Sapana pretends to count how many days, how many weeks they may still want to live off him. Then he laughs and admits that if he gives them work they will quickly move off to some other relative. "But they will speak bad of me there," he adds. As we part he shouts back to us "I'm going home now to prepare hoes for the young men."

Change and development pose difficult questions. We couldn't help but realise how hard it was for a man like Sapana in the rural areas of Southern Sudan, even a man with education and initiative, to make any real change unless he was himself successful enough to carry his whole community up with him. Everything was diluted amongst the extended family and community and there would be a high price of unpopularity to pay if a man stepped ahead on his own. He could not focus on being an individual as we can: he was inseparable from membership of his community. On the other hand the tradition of sharing, including within the wider extended family of the Christian Church, was a lovely thing from which we in the West have something to learn.

26   Maria

"She's there again, John," I said in a tired and irritated voice. "She's there, Maria is there near the path." Yes, Maria had arrived as she did most days, a silent supplicant for money and gifts from the rich missionaries. Withered and old, her face deeply furrowed but her eyes alert, she sat outside the Doll's house. Her back was propped against the trunk of a small almost leafless tree and her thin legs were sticking out in front of her, the skin stretched and shiny over the bones and scarcely covered by the inadequate rags of her dress. Wherever we went, we felt her eyes following us and there was no escape. John went off to teach and Diya took the children out for a little walk. I tried to prepare lectures, to read, but always those eyes were upon me. With no curtains or shutters, being watched like this was driving me mad. I took my book and crawled on all fours to sit on the floor beneath the window in the bedroom. At least now she would not know which room I was in. But soon I could hear her systematically going round the small house and peering in through each window in turn. From the second window of the bedroom she saw me sitting on the floor under the other one! Somehow I would have to find relief, a way of doing the right thing.

To take on an isolated teaching post in Sudan, accept I couldn't work as a doctor, and deal with students was one thing. To adapt to conditions of heat, bed bugs, mosquitoes, snakes, cockroaches and safari ants was quite another, all made worse by the absence of electricity and mains water and familiar food. But to live as rich in a poor world was the hardest of all. As a student on a bicycle in Dublin I often rode past a 'Maria', usually sitting on the pavement of O'Connell bridge with a baby wrapped around with a shawl. In London an evening out could feel spoiled on passing a 'Maria' with a dog or a child in a doorway holding out a card 'Homeless and Hungry', but I could always tell myself that there were some other resources available. But Maria in Mundri was always there, and we were the ones being appealed to for help.

Maria

We had learned to turn to Canon Ezra for wisdom and advice. What should we do? Maria was the only beggar we had come across in Mundri, something that had surprised us. Though we wanted to help in general we knew that we could not help everyone who was in need and we certainly didn't want to promote the indignity of begging. Canon Ezra told us that Maria was one of the oldest Christians in Mundri but he was sorry to say that her begging had been encouraged by missionaries. "Begging is not a custom among the Moru people (his tribe), though it is common among the Dinka," he said. "We Moru people do not like any of the Morus to beg and we do not want this encouraged. It makes us feel ashamed." We were impressed that the force of public and Church opinion could be so effective in a settled rural community like Mundri, whereas we knew that in the cities and towns in Sudan, as in most other parts of the world, it was different: so different that no individual or statesman or aid agency can find a permanent solution. Shifting and mixed populations were often destitute and, far away from the help of family and community, begging was the only relief, the only way for men and women without paid work to survive.

We decided to give some money regularly to Canon Ezra and to the Pastor of the parish who would know who were most in need and be responsible in how they shared it out. This was a personal solution but was not applicable at a global level. It may not have been an easy task either for Canon Ezra and the Pastor, but it was a great relief for us; the pleading eyes of Maria no longer disturbed us, and though we gave her tea when she came we no longer gave money or clothing directly. She was not altogether satisfied with the arrangement however, and when we had visitors she was an opportunist and quickly reverted to her previous pattern. One visiting missionary found her appeals irresistible. That resulted in an unusually successful day for Maria because he gave her a Sudanese Pound (a bit more than the wage of a workman for a week). She cackled with delight and came straight to me to ask for change! At the same time she wanted to show me that in the light of his gift I was indescribably tight-fisted and, as she declared in a loud voice, had not done what Jesus would have done. Actually we had heard that that missionary's handouts in the town where he lived had encouraged a crowd of hopeful beggars to gather on his verandah much to the annoyance of his neighbours. It wasn't everywhere that an intermediary like Canon Ezra was available.

Even in Mundri, it remained a difficult question. Were the most needy the ones who came to beg, and did haphazard giving mirror the example set by Jesus? And should we missionaries exacerbate the situation because it was temporarily easier to give a little than to refuse, easier to give direct than to work towards longer-term solutions? It was impossible to imagine all of us, a mixed bag of foreigners, agreeing to give our gifts only through Church or other official bodies. Such a suggestion would raise a storm of protest. Whether we lived in Africa or Europe, and even if it would be better and fairer, as individuals we would resist any pressure to conform. I doubt that we fully realised at that time just how much we were asking of the Pastor and Canon Ezra. They too had a following of relatives who looked to them for help with school fees, food and money, the cost of weddings and funerals and sickness. We were asking of these Church leaders an integrity which ensured that the needy people for whom our gifts were intended were the ones who received them, while at the same time they had to meet, from their own limited resources, the needs of their own family and dependants. Such integrity, in line with the teaching of the Gospel, explains why it is Church personnel who are most often asked by aid agencies to handle the funds, food and material goods they provide in response to disaster and famine, and for the support of refugees.

The next dry season a drought caused a disastrous famine in the land of the Dinkas to the north of us. The people there depended almost totally on their cattle, drinking the milk and cooking the blood taken regularly from the jugular veins in the necks of their cows. Their attempts at growing food were scant because of their nomadic way of life. When the rains failed there was no grass, the cattle died, and there was famine in the land. Men, women and weak children then walked south in search of food. The Moru people, who considered the Dinkas improvident because they had not learned to store food for the dry season which came regularly every year, were inundated by tall thin skeletal figures dying of hunger. We did what we could in providing food but the starving Dinkas seemed to be everywhere. Instead of Maria sitting under that little tree, John and I, open to view through the wire-meshed windows of the Doll's house, felt imprisoned with everywhere an emaciated face looking in and making it very difficult for us to face eating any food at all.

In particular I remember a young Dinka mother with tiny twin babies. I suppose I identified with her because of our own twins. I gave her food and my favourite yellow cotton dress; it looked lovely on her and she had a small respite of happiness and hope. Four days later she was back, the yellow dress so soiled it was scarcely recognisable and the one surviving baby close to death. I wept for her: her life looked so near its end too, a young mother of twins with none of the advantages which were mine. It was in times like this that I felt utterly despairing; what a tragedy it was that there were such contrasts in the world, some had so much, others so little. I would have been much more comfortable if I had not seen this so close up, if I had not been in Sudan. We were 'rich' in a poor man's world, we were here because we believed it was where God had worthwhile work for us to do.

We longed to make life easier for the people around us. We couldn't do much about relieving famine, but perhaps we could help to make the lot of the women a little less hard.

Here in Mundri women and even quite small girls were the water-carriers. It was a familiar sight to see them place a ring of twisted grass on their head, struggle to raise a heavy earthenware pot or four-gallon *safia* filled with water and balance it on the ring before stepping out. In the dry season they might have a walk of several miles to collect water from a river bed, but even so were faced on their return with the work of preparing food. That involved grinding the flour, making a vegetable sauce and cooking on fires lit with firewood they had collected in the forest. It certainly wasn't an easy life. I thought particularly of Doruka, the Pastor's wife, who had a steady flow of visitors all expecting to be fed. A parish well would be a great help for her, and would provide a safe source of water. A parish well might even convince the men that it would bring benefits for them as well as the women. Perhaps we could help?

I had been reading Neville Shute's *'A town like Alice'* and the thought of providing a well at Mundri parish, like in that story set in Malaya, haunted and excited me. Mind you, there was something special about wells, something belonging to my childhood memories. My father had been involved in just such a project when he went to a new parish in Co. Monaghan and the Rectory water supply was inadequate. The church dignitaries and the Rural Dean in their black suits and overcoats had walked solemnly in procession behind an acknowledged 'water diviner.' With the ends of a forked sapling in each of his spread out hands, thumbs to the outside, and the main part pointing upwards, we watched him solemnly pace around. Suddenly the Y-shaped sapling seemed to have a life of its own, jumped in his grip and reversed to turn downwards over where water was to be found. We onlookers took turns to try our skills as 'water diviners'. I don't understand it, but I know I was particularly pleased when the sapling in my hands also seemed to respond. There was water alright in the selected spot, but had my father known that Andy, the little well digger shouting and cursing all day while he worked, would have to get to 96 feet before finding it, I'm sure the whole project would have been rejected. It has left me with a special memory. A hoist above the well consisted of supports and a heavy iron bar with a cogged handle and ratchet. A thick rope suspended from the bar had a bucket attached to it and, with his feet in this bucket and his hands holding the rope, Andy was lowered down each morning by a workman turning the handle. The earth Andy dug out was winched up bucket after bucket all day and wheeled away in a barrow, and at the end of the session Andy himself, his feet again in the bucket and holding onto the rope, appeared at the top. Then the shuttering for that day's work was put in place and the concrete poured. Before the water was reached my turn came to have the treat of descending to the bottom. Looking upwards from the depths was like looking through a telescope; although it was a bright sunny day I could see the stars! Surely digging a well in Mundri could not be anything like as difficult!

Ephraim and Sapana came to have supper with us and after some general conversation I brought up the subject of wells. Our suggestion that men could easily dig wells in the dry season brought a quick response. "But that is the time that men think they need to rest for the work of the next year!" said Ephraim, to which Sapana added, "It is true that the men sit round most of the day waiting for food to be ready, but that is the custom." I pointed out that if women had a nearby well they would not be so tired from carrying water and, especially at the busy times when they were doing the cultivation, they would have more time to cook food. Really, I felt exasperated. Why was it that this idea had not entered into the heads of the men of itself? Perhaps it was that as long as women were doing most of the work, the men didn't see that any change was desirable. "Besides," said Ephraim, "there is the danger that women could become lazy." It would be a struggle to get a well at the parish church but still it was done. Sapana took the initiative, we gave some money, the well filled up with water and was protected from erosion by its concrete lining. It was named after me and was in use for many years as a wet-season well; much later a bore-hole, which produced water all the year round, was drilled to a greater depth and saved the women a lot of heavy work. I doubt if it made them lazy.

We recognised the food value of the rather small local eggs brought to our door for sale and we thought the people who brought them should be paid more for them, especially as our own chicken-keeping had been so unsuccessful. John and I discussed this with Sapana. We were willing to pay more for eggs; could he encourage the local people to provide more of them, as fresh as possible? Perhaps he could promote this as a kind of co-operative effort? He saw it as a good idea too so all three of us were taken aback when we were met with fierce opposition. Eggs, other expatriate members of staff declared, were already expensive enough, besides being terribly small and often not fresh. Expatriates even if they had the money must not disturb market forces, we were told, though we couldn't really see how this was a relevant issue since eggs were never bought by the local people themselves. John and I failed to get the agreement of the others; if we persisted in paying the local people what we considered a proper price for eggs, it wouldn't be long before all the vendors with eggs would come first to our door. I could just see them watching their eggs being tested in water, then counting the *piastres* we paid and going off smiling with the coins knotted up in a corner of their cloth wrappers. That would make our colleagues, short of eggs, extremely annoyed with us. Once again we were proposing a disturbing move away from the established pattern. It made me furious that this way for local people to earn extra cash was blocked. Sapana, who had been setting up the little enterprise, was as disappointed as we were: in some heat I took out my 'How I fume' notebook to make another entry.

27 Omdurman and Arabic

We thought it would never happen but at last, two and a half years after our arrival in Sudan, we went off to learn Arabic at the American Mission language school in Omdurman. This was more to be in tune with the political situation in Sudan where Arabic was the official language, than that it was needed for the work we were currently doing in Mundri. English was still the language of education in the South and the language of our College, but 'southern market Arabic' was used throughout the South as the common means of communication. The Government was now pursuing a policy of promoting Islam together with the Arabic language which was to become the medium of instruction in Southern schools and the language of trade and government. In three or four years from now students coming to the College would have been taught through Arabic in school and so have to be taught through Arabic by the staff engaged in their theological training at Mundri.

Our house all packed up, we travelled in a hired truck to Juba, the same long road rough with stones and rocks. As usual we came to places where the road was blocked by a broken down lorry, as usual we stopped. "How long have you been here? Can we help?" "Two days, two weeks. Man gone for spare parts. *Insh'allah*, back here one week." Cautiously we left the road to drive in the bush alongside. It was clear others had done so too. Further on our driver lost control and we crashed into the ditch, though when he managed to get us back on the road again, his inspection and ours did not detect any serious damage! This was all a bit alarming for I was three months pregnant, but it was just the sort of journey Michael loved, and for him unusual and interesting problems were better than the common punctures. We lurched along for hours and then broke down ten miles past Lainya. A lorry going the other way took a message which brought Ken Ogden out to rescue us, look after us for the night and get us to Juba next day just one hour before our flight took off for Khartoum. At least we were glad our delay on the road was much less than John had experienced the year before. He told his father all about that in a letter:

"I was asked to go to Juba as College representative on a Church committee concerned with the teaching of Scripture in the schools and set off in the Chevrolet truck with the driver, a local teacher and two other men. Unfortunately about seventy miles from Mundri a tyre burst. The spare tyre and tube turned out to be very poor, the tube having a lot of old patches which kept coming off. We had to open up the tyre and repair it six times before reaching Juba. We left expecting to reach Juba that night. But we slept on the road in the lorry, three of us sitting in the front seat and two in the back, and eventually reached Juba at 5.00 p.m. next day. We were so late that we missed half the meeting. On the way back it was discovered in Lainya that the radiator was breaking loose, so we had to sleep a night there and got a lift to Mundri next day in a Government lorry. Our driver returned three days later after the truck had been repaired."

There were no seat belts on road transport but on the aeroplane we buckled ourselves into our seats for the flight we could so easily have missed, Michael at the window giving us a running commentary on all he could see. It was a small and aged Dakota and as we flew we could see the shadow of the aeroplane on the ground not too far below us. "Yes, I know we're up in the air," said Michael, "but we're not at the top yet."

Brian Lea, a CMS teacher in Omdurman, met us at the airport and took us to live with him in the small mission house at Abu Kadog. Brian never failed in his friendship and good humour, though being joined by us with two small children must have been a great invasion of his life and peace. We often heard him singing verses of hymns early in the morning and knew that his time of quiet had been more secure before we came.

The CMS house at Abu Kadog was dark with a wide verandah, thick mud walls and heavy shutters to keep out the heat of the day. Sophie Zenkovsky, a CMS missionary nurse, had lived here for many years running maternity and baby welfare clinics in the dispensary attached to the house but no longer in use. She was well remembered by the local people for her friendship and her love and care of them and, though the Anglo-Egyptian Condominium Government did not allow her to talk about her faith, the way she lived surely was a sign of it. It must have been very strange for her neighbours to see a single woman missionary living on her own without fear, and free of the kind of restrictions suffered by secluded Sudanese women. The house was hidden from the road behind heavy bolted iron doors with very high mud walls enclosing it in its own small courtyard, and like all the houses nearby it had its small square trapdoor in the wall for the sewage bucket.

There was sand everywhere. As we walked it went in and out of our sandals making it sheer pleasure to plunge our feet in a basin of water before we entered the house. It gave life to the Gospel story of Jesus washing the dusty feet of His disciples. In front of the house a *neem* tree gave some shade, the tree and a small patch of grass and flowers kept alive by waste bath water poured each day around them. Rain in Omdurman is rare and some years none falls at all. The winters are dry, hot and sunny by day and pleasantly cool at night, but as summer approaches the heat can be terrible with temperatures of 115°F (50°C) and more in the shade, and the discomfort of intermittent sand storms. These storms, known as *haboubs*, rush in from the desert at a ferocious rate, carrying sand which pelts down from the darkened sky, so dense that it is impossible even to see across the Nile. The sand penetrates into everything: towels feel and behave like sand-paper, cups in the cupboard, although the windows are closed, are found to be quarter full of sand. One great comfort and a real luxury for us was a good supply of pay-by-the-metre water from the Nile, purified and ready for drinking instead of all that filtering and boiling we had to do in Mundri. It was also safe for Michael and Katherine who spent hours every day in and out of the water in Brian's large tin bath in the shade of the *neem* tree. Electric light was so much easier than oil lamps, food was plentiful in the shops, and there was a wonderful variety of fresh fruit and vegetables in the local markets. Zebedaya, who was our cook, went to buy food each morning and we observed each other's cooking. One day he came back with a most lovely cabbage and I saw him cut it in four at ten in the morning and put it on to boil for two or three hours in plenty of water. By lunchtime it was khaki-coloured and I gently suggested a different way of cooking it. The other way round, it was he who taught me how to cook red and green peppers and stuff them with delicious savoury minced meat and rice.

We enjoyed those first winter months, especially the cooler air at night. Just as others slept in their beds up on the flat roofs of their houses, sometimes we slept out in the open courtyard at Abu Kadog. It was lovely to need a blanket to snuggle down under while looking up at the great expanse of sparkling stars, clear in air not yet polluted.

Unlike in the Doll's house in Mundri, in Abu Kadog we were aware that we had neighbours very near us. We could smell their food cooking and other less pleasant smells as well, the background mumble of conversation went on all the time, and though it was too dry for mosquitoes to find water for breeding, we were plagued by persistent flies. Barking dogs, early morning cocks, noisy goats and a love-sick donkey braying in a particularly discordant manner broke into sounds of domestic disputes or violence which distressed us, while at other times the sounds were joyful with singing, the beat of a drum, and dancing in celebration of a wedding or feast day. Once there was wailing all through the night after a death. I remember a visit from John Taylor, then Africa Secretary and later General Secretary of CMS before he became Bishop of Winchester. He sat on the sand with us under our *neem* tree and seemed to enter into the atmosphere and culture surrounding us. We felt encouraged by his understanding and spiritual depth as he related to us and absorbed the ambience of Abu Kadog. Perhaps he even envied how we lived there in the heart of a great Muslim city.

Throughout our stay in Omdurman we became accustomed to hearing the *Muezzin* calling the people to prayer from mosques all over the city. High up on the Minaret five times every day the voice rang out: '*Allah Akbar* . . ', 'God is great, God is greatest. There is but one God, and Muhammed is the prophet of God.' John Carden wrote of hearing the same call in Pakistan:

"God is great, God is greatest - this is a cry to which the Christian can respond, easily.

"But when the city below gets under weigh, and the sick and the maimed and the poverty-stricken crawl out of their mud houses, and the streets begin to fill up with thousands of people, then that call, God is great, God is greatest, is just not enough, not loving enough, not saving enough. A Christian longs to be able to cry out in a voice unmistakable and compelling, God is great, God is greatest, and Jesus is his Son, our Saviour, the Saviour of this city." (*Empty Shoes* - Highway Press/CMS 1971)

During the years of the Anglo-Egyptian Condominium there were strict prohibitions on any attempts to bring Christian teaching to Northern Sudan because the administrators feared a resurgence of the *Jihad*, the Mahdi Holy War. This policy has continued since Sudan's independence. Brian de Saram writes of earlier years:

"When Dr. and Mrs. Hall arrived in 1900 to put into effect the medical work advocated by Dr. Harpur (the year before), they received little encouragement from those whose chief concern was to preserve peace and order in the Northern Sudan. They went to live . . . in a house in the desert on the outskirts of Omdurman. This house became known as 'The Poisoner's House' by the local people. Some men, not willing to endanger themselves, brought women slaves on whom to try out the doctor's skill and medicines before they would risk their own bodies. By 31st December 1902, 50 patients a day were being treated. .... The Town Council's confidence was now shown by the grant of a gift of land on which a hospital could be built. The buildings were ready for use in 1914 and a chapel was added in 1924 ... So began the witness to the love of God through the ministry of healing which has continued down the years, and included treatment for leprosy, care for the elderly and blind, and the opening of maternity and baby welfare clinics at Abu Rof and Abu Kadog."   (*Nile Harvest* - Brian de Saram 1992)

Living amongst the local people and loving and caring for them, CMS missionaries like Sophie Zenkovsky, May Bertram, Beatrice Coggan, Ruth Pakenham and many others on the staff of the CMS Hospital in Omdurman, though they were restricted in speaking about their Christian faith, were witnesses in their work to the love of God, the love which was the reason they had come to be in Sudan.

John comes in for lunch and brings Ulrich Portman with him. Ulrich is from Switzerland and was with us in our year of missionary training in Kent. He is a forthright character and finds it hard to slow down to the rate at which things happen in Sudan. He is the Manager at the CMS Hospital in Omdurman and he has come to the end of his tether. "I have told them many times and they do nothing, nothing at all. These Government people don't even believe me. They say there is no leprosy in Sudan, so we do not need money to support these people. I tell you, NO LEPROSY! They do not come to see. So today I take eleven men and women crippled and maimed, with missing fingers and toes and bad skin, and I put them in the hospital van and I drive them myself to the Government Department. I tell them to sit all round in the room there. We will not leave until this matter is settled." The officials were not pleased, but by the end of the day Ulrich's dramatic action worked where talking and writing hadn't. A support grant was given, although officially there were still no leprosy patients anywhere in Sudan.

[The CMS Hospital was taken over by the Government in 1971 and is now used as Omdurman Psychiatric Hospital. The former clinic at Abu Rof is a clinic for treating leprosy.]

Life in this sprawling Muslim city could seem captivating, but it would be superficial to discount the fear, pain, and suffering that can lie beneath the mystery, and fail to notice the restricted lives of the women within their high-walled courtyards. Women living near us took a great interest in seeing a young white mother walking around freely with two small children, and sometimes I was invited into the seclusion of next door to drink *limoon* and to practise speaking the little Arabic I had learnt. They took an even greater interest in the way John and I shared the care of the children and some of the house jobs which had to be done. I wondered if they put it down to our different culture or to our Christian faith. One or two of the local young men had their own view and, despite my pregnant bulk, when I went out on my own in the shared taxis they were ready to flirt with me and be a nuisance.

The Language School was in a more prosperous part of Omdurman, and we used the 'shared taxi' cars to get there. *Sitt* Josephine, an over-weight youngish woman, was my teacher and I was not her best pupil! The main thing I remember about her, as she tried to put some words of Sudanese colloquial Arabic into my head and out through my mouth, was not the Arabic I learned but her unique and effective method of continuously catching flies, using a quick one hand cupped action!

Language learning for John was a more serious matter. His brief was to learn Classical Arabic as well as to speak Sudanese colloquial Arabic which is distinctive to Sudan, just as Egyptian or Palestinian or Tunisian colloquial Arabic is distinctive to those countries. All colloquial forms have developed from Classical Arabic over the centuries and are languages of speech, but never written - a good job for me because in learning a little colloquial Arabic I didn't have to learn the Arabic script! All writing must be in Classical. Could you imagine me jotting down my shopping list in Classical Arabic like as if I had to write the words for sugar and meat and flour in Chaucer's English! Classical Arabic remains as it was written in the *Qur'an*. For help in learning to read and understand it, John went regularly to the house of an Arabic scholar, an old man who sat formally in his house, wearing a long white *jallabiyah* and turban to receive his pupil and study Classical Arabic with him, both the *Qu'ran* and modern Arabic writings.

Although John's previous studies in Classical Arabic at university made reading and writing the script not too difficult, the spoken language was a new challenge. Since his academic experience of Latin and Greek and other ancient languages had been almost entirely paper work, he found it took a mighty long time for the Arabic in his head to reach his lips. The children and I didn't help much when we laughed and imitated the guttural sounds he was trying to produce.

Still, by Christmas Eve he was ready to take his part in the service in the Church in Omdurman, assisting Pastor Philip Abbas by saying the words of administration of the Holy Communion in formal Classical Arabic.

The short six months in Omdurman were a start to what John hoped would be years of learning Arabic; seven years would not be considered an excessive time to master such a difficult language, but it seemed unlikely that we would be in Sudan for as long as that. Another difficulty was that in the South where we were working there would be little opportunity to practise it with others in its correct form. The 'southern market Arabic' widely used as a second language in the South in trade and between people of different language groups was regarded by Arabic speakers of the North as a debased form, scarcely recognised as Arabic at all. As missionaries we knew well that we could be out of the country tomorrow but still we must go on planning and working as if we would be around for years. In faith, even if it involved learning a difficult language, we had to take the long view and make preparations for the future.

We were very interested to meet Roland Stevenson, a CMS missionary, who was living in Omdurman at the time we were there. He had gone to the Nuba Mountains to teach in 1938 and quickly put his exceptional linguistic gifts to good use; he became fluent in more than ten of the languages spoken in that region and it was he who produced the first written forms of them. Sitting in his small house in Omdurman, surrounded by his enormous collection of dusty books, he read the English and Arabic daily papers but also, since he was fluent in Russian, he read Pravda and was able to talk in their own languages with expatriates of many different nationalities who were working in Sudan at that time. He served as consultant with the Bible Societies, and later held University appointments in Khartoum and Nairobi. Alas, not all of us were like Roland Stevenson.

"Mammy, Mammy, come quickly." Katherine rushed into the house, her feet hardly touching the ground, the words coming out in gasps. "Michael's foot is very, very, very sore and he's crying like anything." We run out together. Michael certainly is very upset and I soon see the cause. He has been playing in the sand, as usual building his complicated roadway systems and flyovers, and has disturbed a scorpion and been stung. He sobs with the acute pain and shivers, his skin cold and clammy. I wrap him in a blanket, take him on my knee and comfort him, Katherine hovering anxiously beside us. Some tablets for pain and a short exhausted sleep help. "Did you dead the scorpion, Mammy?" Michael asks on waking, "'cause I don't want him to sting Kathy." These two children were always concerned for each other. Both still remember the day of the scorpion.

Life in Omdurman and life in Mundri were very different. Not just the cooler 'winter' weather, the water supply, the electricity and the food, but that we had the company of others and the freedom to get about. We attended services in English at Khartoum Cathedral, travelling in battered yellow and black taxis which functioned like small buses filled with passengers who shared the cost. At the Sunday evening Supper Club at Clergy House we met other expatriates (there were perhaps as many as a thousand in Khartoum at that time) and educated Southern Sudanese Christians. We went swimming at the Sudan Club and even visited the Zoo one day where we wondered if a leopard we saw was the one we had cared for as a tiny cub in Mundri.

While we waited for a taxi one day Katherine sat down on the sandy path with her favourite Charlie Teddy propped against the high mud wall behind her. When we reached our destination, we found Charlie Teddy had stayed behind on the sand. This was a tragedy for Katherine and for many years, perhaps still, she thinks with sadness of that day, that loss. We never found Charlie Teddy again, but his supposed adventures and new friends and journeys featured in our 'pretend' stories for many years. Katherine always believed that whoever knew Charlie Teddy would love him as she did.

We had exciting experiences too. John and I had never been to a midnight picnic before, so we were delighted when a friend offered to look after Michael and Katherine for the night while we were included in a group of our Cathedral friends going out into the desert to a remote place called 'Gordon's Tree.' We went in two or three cars taking ample specially-prepared food with us, including roast pigeons considered a local delicacy, spicy kebabs, and *halwa* made of almonds and honey. That was a night to remember. The full moon casting ghostly shadows of us on the sand, the clear sky, the bright stars, the cool refreshing desert air. Sitting close by John with his arms around me, I felt we were very small in that wide empty space as if we were the first people on this bit of God's earth. The tree where General Gordon used to pray and reflect eighty years before connected us with others who had come to Sudan, this vast and special country. They, like us, longed for peace and justice in this land, for the end of slavery, for prosperity, health, and stable government and to see women given fuller recognition and freedom. Above all for God's love through Jesus Christ to be known.

We sit around the dining room table for lunch at Abu Kadog where our windows are very small, the walls brown mud. Brian enjoys cooking and he has made a special pudding today. He puts it in a glass bowl and with a flourish sets it on the table. The pudding is yellow and looks just like custard. Michael dips his spoon into the helping he has been given and opens his mouth wide. The look of happy anticipation of his favourite custard changes, the little face is crumpled. "Mammy," he whispers, "the pudding's GHASTLY." It was not custard but lemon soufflé. Forty years later Michael is no longer a child but as far as our friend Brian is concerned he is still 'Michael Ghastly.'

28   Can Open Mouth Very Wide

We had a difficult decision to make. John had had some bouts of severe abdominal pain, which was diagnosed as almost certainly appendicitis. His symptoms settled and left us with a dilemma; should he have an operation in Khartoum in conditions far from ideal or do nothing and hope he would have no further trouble? A recurrence back in Mundri could put him at risk like John Bates, a CMS teacher in Yambio, who died in 1950 from a perforated appendix, but an operation in Khartoum could pose a risk too. I find it strange now that we didn't consider travelling to Kenya or England if an operation was needed, but only thought of the choices we had in Khartoum. Was it to be in the Government hospital where conditions would be fairly basic but the surgeon Mr. Davy Crockett (of the same name as Disney's 'Davy Crockett, King of the Wild Frontier') was known to us, or in a more comfortable private clinic where we didn't know who the surgeon would be?

The decision made, and accompanied by our friend Dr. May Bertram of the CMS Hospital in Omdurman, John and I arrive at the Government hospital at noon and walk down long corridors to the theatre for the operation set for an hour later. It is an anxious time for both of us. John is wheeled away and, as I wait with May, it feels like hours until Mr. Crockett emerges to say all is well and certainly that appendix needed to be removed.

We follow the trolley when John, not yet fully conscious, is taken to a six-bed male ward on the third floor. The ward is crowded. Each patient has a relative to see to his needs, to sit around by day and sleep under his bed at night. Pregnant as I am, this doesn't seem possible for me so, reassured John is alright, May drives me back to Omdurman to be with Michael and Katherine. "Where did you leave Daddy?" Katherine asks. "Is he all bloody?" "We want to see him in the hospital, we want to see him in the hospital," they chorus. Next day they are not too pleased when I leave them with a friend and board a yellow and black taxi to go back to John. His breakfast waits untouched on a tin plate on his locker - a cake of local bread, a slab of cold cooked fish and a hard boiled egg in its shell. I quickly decide I can look after him myself back home in Omdurman. The hospital has done its part, I can do the rest. Katherine is very pleased Daddy is back. "But I didn't see him in the hospital, Mammy," she laments. Michael, who doesn't like blood, doesn't want even to see John's plaster, but Katherine watches closely a week later when I remove the stitches. "I'll hold your hand, Daddy, so it won't hurt much," she promises. We were thankful it happened when it did, before the flight to Kenya the following week.

It's another clear dark night. The air in Khartoum, cool from the desert, blows softly on our faces as John and I with Michael and Katherine wait at Khartoum Airport. The B.O.A.C. flight from London is said to be on time and due in at 2.30 a.m. When that DC8 takes off again the children and I, now seven months pregnant, will be on board on our way south to Nairobi. I don't like the thought of being separated from John for more than two months, though I'm quite glad I can abandon the Arabic study which I have found very difficult. Large aircraft always landed and took off in the hours of darkness to avoid the heat turbulence of day time, so our arrivals and departures from Khartoum were always in the middle of the night. As the huge plane took off that night John marvelled that such a weight could be airborne taking, as he later said, 'all my people' with it. When his Arabic course is over he will join us for his local leave in Kenya. In fact it would be nine weeks before we were together again.

Raymond and Audrey (my sister) meet us at Nairobi Airport and drive us to Limuru where they are CMS missionaries on the staff of

St. Paul's United Theological College. Limuru is about 20 miles from Nairobi and in the highlands. What a place! What a contrast with Omdurman! The grass is soft and very green, the climate a delight of bright sunshine by day, the nights cool, though there are times of the year when the College is lost in mist and there is a lot of rain. The gardens are beautiful and Raymond takes such an interest in planting trees that his nick-name is *Bwana Miti*, the man of the trees. We join the Smith family, eating delicious food provided by Audrey day after day and we often talk and laugh into the small hours of the night.

"It was just wonderful," I wrote to my parents, the grandparents of the four children, "to have Audrey and Raymond's company and help during the three months I was in Kenya. They were so cheerful in accepting an invasion of Lowes for so long in their beautiful house and surroundings. They looked after Michael and Katherine for the four and a half weeks I was in hospital, three of them before John's arrival. Their two children, Peter (4) and Rosalind (2), shared their bath, their bedroom, their parents and everything else with our two and apart from some skirmishes they were all great friends."

If only John was with us to enjoy it all too. He was having a problem over the re-entry visa which he must secure before leaving Khartoum; without this we would not be allowed back to Sudan. Our letters were full of how frustrated we were by the delay. At last, the document in his hands, he rushed to the airport and took off on a flight to Entebbe Airport near Kampala in Uganda. That was on Sunday the 8th of April at much the same time as I was on a trolley being wheeled to the hospital theatre and wishing John was by my side. Instead he was still on the way, delayed on the 400 mile train journey from Kampala to Nairobi because heavy rain had washed away a section of the track. Late next evening Jesse Hillman, the CMS Secretary, met John at the station and drove him straight to the Agha Khan Hospital to see me and our new baby, born by Caesarean Section the day before. There he was, our Patrick, wonderfully and perfectly made. He was a contented and easy baby, whom the nurses described as 'a little Christian gentleman', and we all loved him. Two-year-old Rosalind was a bit confused by John's arrival and called him 'the other Daddy,' but her comment on Patrick was clear. "Can open mouth very wide," she announced.

Patrick keeps an eye on his mother

After my discharge from hospital we had a further two weeks at Limuru and a two-day trip to make. We all squashed, four adults, four children and a baby into the Smith's car for the trek to meet

Mrs. Nicholson who ran the Rift Valley Correspondence Course. She was a teacher married to a highland farmer and, recognising the need for a specially adapted home education course for children whose parents lived and worked in isolated places, she had gathered a small staff of other teacher wives and organised the course we planned to use in teaching Michael and Katherine. It was a bit like the P.N.E.U (Parents National Educational Union) course used in England for children being taught, often by governesses, at home.

Michael and Katherine were to be the most isolated of her pupils. Postal services to Mundri were so erratic that, instead of parcels every two weeks, she sent us all the equipment, books and supplies we needed for a term at a time. She also returned Michael and Katherine's corrected work and forwarded reports from their teachers which guided us and kept up our confidence that we were doing alright.

With the help of the Rift Valley Course during the years of the school in the *tukl* in Mundri, I settled down to being a teacher though I hadn't forgotten I really wanted to be a doctor. Perhaps my settling down had something to do with a little plot I was hatching; perhaps I could do some medical work when we were next in Uganda on local leave?

29 The *Tukl* Primary School

We would all stay or we would all go. That was always our answer to questions like -

"Isn't it time you took the children back to Ireland for school?" or "You know, children over five don't do well in this climate, they don't thrive." By this time we were the only CMS couple in Sudan with small children. "It's a good thing, isn't it, that while John goes on teaching in Mundri, Dorothy and the children can live in the house they bought in Belfast, and Michael and Katherine will be able to go to school there!"

The tukl school

They all had their concern and advice and solutions, none matching ours. John and I and the children were an indivisible bundle. Whatever sad partings former missionaries in Sudan had endured, for the present we would all stay or we would all go. "Time for school." I ring the bell and wait at the door of the thatched mud hut we use, the *tukl*, for my two pupils to arrive. Patrick is in the care of Diya, treated more like an African baby than was ever possible for Michael and Katherine, for Diya's job is to carry him, or push him about in his pram, or sit around watching him play. I also am more like an African mother, making sure of his milk supply by breast-feeding him until we go on leave when he is ten months old. In our new house Patrick's cot is in the same bedroom as Michael and Katherine's beds so he always has their company. "Time for school," I call again and ring the bell for longer. Katherine, a pretty vivacious little girl with a head of dark curly hair, has already danced her way over to the *tukl* and is at her desk but Michael's other activities are of more interest to him than school. Perhaps, observing the world with his big blue eyes open, he has gone exploring somewhere, or could he have decided to hide? The two of them approach school differently but for both the first thing I require is that they fill in their diary. Before they are able to write for themselves I must write what each child tells me; later, without my help with spelling, they write their sentence or two

Diya and Patrick

themselves. It is good if they have noticed something they want to write about; if not we have to walk about to find some little creature, a bird or animal or plant, to satisfy their Rift Valley teacher in Kenya.

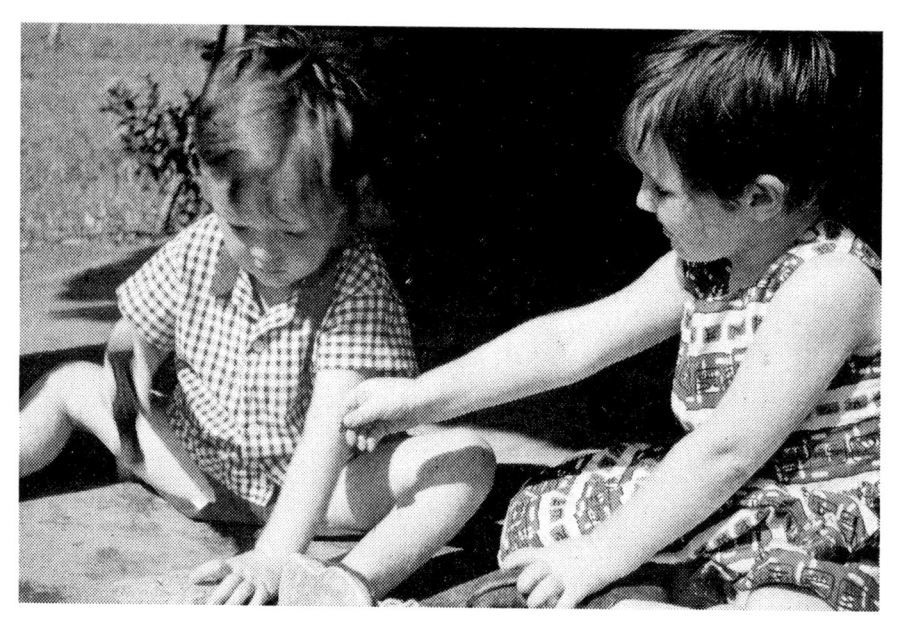

A nail for you Michael

Formal lessons follow, reading, writing and 'rithmetic, art and craft, and later some history and geography and nature study. It only takes an hour or two, or should only take an hour or two. Katherine applies herself fully. Michael on the other hand does not. He has to be encouraged to concentrate on his school work instead of thinking about what he is planning to do later when school is over, such as how to make a needle out of a thorn for the College gramophone with its wind-up handle. I don't want to have to stay in school all day so in desperation I resort to a reward system. A kitchen timer is set, giving a reasonable period for a piece of work to be completed. Finishing before the timer pings earns a star and ten stars earn a reward. A little competition and a 'carrot' work though I have to watch out for Katherine deliberately slowing down so she doesn't get more stars than her brother. By September 1963 they were six and at the beginning of their fourth term at 'my' school and I wrote to the grandparents:

> "Michael and Katherine had two weeks between their school terms and then pleaded with me to start school again! They can now read very well and it is hard to keep up the supply of books. Home education is working out so far with the help of the Rift Valley Correspondence Course we use."

We still have two bulky parcels of Michael and Katherine's work, sent to their Rift Valley teacher and returned with corrections, and their reports and paintings have survived, fascinating evidence of their years of being taught by their mother. Here are some diary entries:

> "There was a hornet on the window of our school. It was caught in a spider's web."

> "A man killed a water buck with his bow and arrow and I went with Daddy to see it."

> "I have a gumboil and it is hard to eat meat and toast."

> "A black ant crept under my dress and bit me."

> "Daddy went up my ladder. Two steps broke and he fell down. Daddy did not hurt himself and I hope he will fix my ladder soon."

> "I saw a lot, hundreds, of ants in the bathroom and they ate a hole in the curtain."

> "I saw a lovely yellow butterfly on the grass."

> "The dead lizard is gone today. The ants must have taken it away."

And then there were the sad comments. "I am very terribely (sic) sad becose (sic) one rabbit is dead and the other ran away"

(Katherine, age 6). "Auntie Elizabeth had 11 baby ducks and now she has none. 2 died because the mother stood on them. A hawk took 4 of them when the mother duck wasn't looking. 3 were left out in the rain and they must have been drowned. That leaves 2 and they got lost. Perhaps a dog ate them. We are sorry that Auntie Elizabeth has no little ducks now." (Michael age 6, in a form that reflected his father's Farmer John sums).

John's help, usually over lunchtime, with mental arithmetic has not been forgotten and neither has Farmer John, the imaginary character his sums were centred around. Farmer John had a selection of fields and sheds and was forever moving his animals from one to the other. "How many are left in the long field when 2 sheep escape and 5 cows go to the shed to be milked?" John asks. These exercises are easier for Michael than for Katherine who protests, "Please, Daddy, not again! Not more Farmer John today." Katherine (later herself a teacher) is imaginative and prefers language work and I notice she reflected her opinion of sums in her diary entries when she was seven. Monday: "Peter Teddy is going to begin school today. I made him a uniform." Tuesday: "Peter Teddy did not enjoy his first day because of the sums." The system for counting in the Moru language is based on words for the numbers one to five, as if on the fingers of the hand. The rest of the numbers go like 'a hand and one' for six, etc. to twenty which 'consumes a whole person,' all the fingers and all the toes. When I was at school there was trouble for any of us who dared to use our fingers to help with counting, but I wonder now if using her fingers would have eased Katherine's struggles in the beginning. On the other hand Michael's early liking for number work led on to the ability which has been so useful to him as an adult. John's presentation of sums to be done in the head before calculators were invented may have been a valuable first step.

Apart from the individual attention they had as a two-pupil class with one teacher, there were advantages for them in living in a different culture. They had to adapt to different food and conditions, and they learned to amuse themselves by making up their own games and learning that if they wanted something they didn't have, it was worth trying to make it themselves; these were skills that would remain with them. Michael loved exploring the forest paths with John and even on his own, keeping his eyes open for snakes and wild animals and noticing how to find his way home again. Katherine was a great reader, always happy and content when she had a book in hand, and she loved to make up stories. She loved too to sit on her father's knee when he read '*Winnie the Pooh*' by A.A. Milne or better still the '*Cautionary Tales*' by Hilaire Belloc. These were read and quoted repeatedly in the voice John developed specially for them, and the actual copies are still on our bookshelves, now in use with grandchildren. Both children had their favourite books and entered into the lives of the children and animals they read about. Perhaps because they knew of the happy ending, it was often the stories which distressed them that they turned to again and again, such as about a small dog called Ruby in a circus not properly cared for, and more often than any other the Gospel story of the lost sheep being found. The small book containing that story was read so often that it became tattered and worn.

For schoolwork in Mundri it was a help that Michael and Katherine were the same age and doing the same lessons, but they were short of early mixing with other children, team games and music. Michael and later Patrick were fascinated by the marvellous lorries made by small Sudanese boys. These were of millet stalks pinned together with thorns to make the body-work, sides, doors, floors and other details, and then small branches of wood cut across in slices to make the wheels which were threaded onto thinner stick axles. A bark string joined the lorry to a length of bamboo enabling the proud owner to walk along with his creation, his very own *arabiya*. Michael enjoyed playing with these clever boys and they taught him how to make a model for himself. This was good fun and so were ball games and running races and attempts at weaving and plaiting, but it was inescapable that by this time Michael and Katherine were the only children who were not African, that they had very little language in common with the others, and that their life experiences in Mundri were quite restricted when compared with what would have been normal for children of their age in Ireland.

Missionaries should identify with the people in the foreign country where they are working. The missionary should 'sit where they sit' was what we were being told. An issue of the CMS magazine at that time had a picture of an agricultural missionary in India, squatting down as he and a hen in a coop looked at each other, eyeball to eyeball. The Adam's apple of the missionary and the hen in profile made them look as if they were indeed identifying and John and I hooted with laughter. But, of course, it wasn't that we were to take up the posture of the missionary with his hen, but 'sitting where they sit' was about our integration in the country where we served. The 'wind of change' was blowing in Sudan as it was in the rest of Africa and critical questions were being thrown at us. "If you were really identifying with us and the life of the people around here in Mundri you wouldn't be teaching your children at all at this stage," an intelligent student told us with some anger. Gently we pointed out that our children belonged to another country and had to be made ready for where they would live later on. "We want to be here," we told the young man, "but you know the Government may throw us out at any time." We had no security of belonging in Sudan, a fact he well knew.

These misunderstandings could be very disturbing. Life for us in Mundri was not the easiest we could imagine and I, always more hot than John, felt like raging and saying so.

As well as other subjects John taught Church History. Students were very interested to learn of men and women of former centuries who had been Christians, and who had suffered and been put to death when they refused to deny their faith. These accounts matched what they knew of torture and persecution in Sudan in their own lifetime. Knowing how earlier Christians had fared gave strength to Sudanese Christians when they were faced with resisting Government pressure and inducement to deny their faith and turn to Islam.

Five babies are baptized in College Chapel

Names from Church history influenced student parents and influenced us in the naming of our babies. Four babies of students and our Patrick Allen were baptized on the 30th. September 1962 in the chapel of Bishop Gwynne College in Mundri by Canon Ezra Lawiri, three by the pouring of water and two, including Patrick, by the alternative of immersion. For this we used a tin bath decorated with mango leaves. In her school diary about that day, Katherine asked me to write what she wanted to tell her teacher:

> "We are busy getting ready for Patrick's baptism. All the students and their wives and children are coming to have tea with us after it."

> "Yesterday Patrick was baptized in the big kneeling Church (our College Chapel). Four other babies were baptized too."

Benaiah and Lois gave their baby girl the name Blandina after a young Christian woman martyred at Lyons in the second century. Blandina was 'filled with such power that those who by turns kept torturing her in every way from dawn till evening were worn out and exhausted,' but she still regained her strength enough to say before her death by being thrown to wild beasts and devoured "I am a Christian." Henry and Elizabeta's baby was named Polycarp - perhaps Polycarp's declaration at his martyr's death in Smyrna in 156 A.D. was unforgettable.

> "Eighty-six years have I served Him, and He has done me no wrong: how then can I blaspheme my King who saved me?"

"And why have you chosen the name Patrick for your baby?" the students ask. "Well," we tell them, "you know many children in this area are called Fraser after the first missionary to bring the Christian Gospel to the Moru people; the first missionary to our country was Patrick, so we have named our baby after him." Patrick had not been a martyr but he had been taken to Ireland as a slave and later taught the Irish people the Christian faith he had brought with him. He is the Patron Saint of Ireland.

Patrick is walking but not yet steady on his feet. I see him toddling along the verandah, going to see what Michael is doing in the sand pit. Patrick stands watching, suddenly his legs give way and he loses his balance. He is sitting looking a bit surprised but comfortable, Michael's latest construction completely demolished beneath him. I see some reconciliation is needed between our two sons. "I'm so sorry," I say to six-year-old Michael, "but you know Patrick is only one year old and he loves to see what you're doing because he thinks you're great."

The budu

We were not so sure he should see everything his brother and sister do. Only the day before after heavy rain a worm wriggled up onto the warm damp concrete of the verandah. Michael and Katherine, who shared everything, took a great interest in this worm. With a spade from the sand pit the worm was soon in two halves, "one for you and one for me," said Michael. "And," said Katherine, watching in excitement as each half moved, "they still work!" We were sometimes glad of Michael and Katherine's help in understanding Patrick; he had invented his own language and they were able to interpret it for us. From that early language of his, Patrick for a long time held onto his name for himself, 'the budu'.

The shelter for the two College trucks - a blue Chevrolet and a grey Peugeot - was near our new house. Patrick escaped there as often as he could, giving chase to any chickens he found pecking around on his way, and with total absorption he inspected and admired each detail of the trucks; perhaps his later career was beginning already.

John and I were glad that we could be so close to our three children. Life in Mundri was so uncomplicated, the routine of each day so settled, and they were surrounded by the love and goodwill of the people we lived amongst. Michael and Katherine's schoolwork was going well. For the present we could continue as we were.

Tomato harvest

30   It's Hard to Belong

A Sunday morning. John and I feel free, for today we have the house to ourselves and the children, while Tito and Elizala have the day off. We boil water on the oil stove for tea and take out the special tin of sealed Quaker oats to cook a pot of delicious porridge, without a weevil in sight. A day like this is a treat for all of us.

The drums at Mundri parish church call me. That's where I'm going this morning while John reads stories with the children and hopes he will read his own books too. "You mustn't forget your stool, you know, Mammy", says Katherine carrying the small *gba'da* made of wood and bamboo. Michael reminds me to take the stones and helps me to fix everything on my bicycle, the one which used to belong to Violet White. A quick wave and I'm off. Off in the bright sunshine through the College and down the slope, across the bridge over the Mori river and up to the wider road, then turn left to the parish centre.

The drums sound louder now. The road is filled with happy smiling people of all ages, each one walking in the direction of the church and each one, from tallest man to smallest child, carrying a rock or a stone for the new church about to be built. The existing church, built when Canon Ezra came here to start Mundri parish ten years ago, is now too small for the number of worshippers so it must be made bigger. I feel the excitement of the people that their church is so alive and growing, and I know they will enjoy working together to make the building both wider and longer. Teams have been selected for the various tasks; skilled men to make sure the stone pillars are strong enough to support the heavy pole framework of the high-pitched roof, strong men to cut and carry huge head-loads of long-stemmed thatching grass, others of all ages to sit around laughing and joking as they tie the grass into smaller bundles. For the thatching, a line of experienced men will stand inside and outside on flimsy platforms and, starting at the lower edge, pass bamboo 'needles' threaded with bark-string backwards and forwards between them, singing in rhythm as they pull hard to make the thatch secure. There will be teasing when men on the ground fail to aim well enough as they throw bundles of tied grass up to the thatchers, while every day the roof will soar higher and higher. Grass bundles will be placed in the traditional pattern of this area, one layer of cut ends about nine inches higher than the previous one, and an upright ridge at the top. When the roof is finished, walls will be woven of wood branches and plastered with puddled mud, but only waist-high so air can blow through to keep the church cool and make it easy for any overflow congregation outside to see what is going on and join in. Poles are already stacked for seats; each one will rest on several forked branches stuck firmly into the beaten earth floor, rows of seats on the right for the women and children, on the left for the men.

Comfortable pole seats!

Susana Yoane and some of the other women are busy embroidering a special cloth for the Holy Table which is to stand near the east-end wall below a window in the shape of the cross. The new building will be made beautiful to the Glory of God. The whole parish is engaged in the building, the whole parish will worship in it for years to come. I am pleased to put my stone in this Sunday's pile, and one each for John and our children.

Mi kado ya? Is everything good for you?" The greeting and hugging and high-pitched voices make me feel very welcome as I enter the church. My friends all speak Moru and encourage me in my attempts to speak and hear it myself. I will do my best today to understand the service and follow it in the Moru Prayer Book which I have brought with me. I join the others but instead of perching on a pole seat I place my more comfortable *gba'da* beside where Miriamu and the other women sit crowded together as we wait for the service to begin.

The starting time is never precise but after a last vigorous crescendo the drums are now silent and so are we. Worshippers come and go during the next two hours of readings, prayers, hymns and sermon. There are several entrances and exits, handy for mothers tending their children; sometimes handy too for a straying chicken or dog which comes in and is quickly chased out, and perhaps for a bird distracting us by taking a short cut through to the other side of the church. It is cooler inside and seems dark after the bright sunlight. I look around at all these people; some of the women and children in brightly coloured clothes, the men in their places with well-ironed shirts and shorts or trousers, and less well dressed people here and there. Some are bare footed, but many have rubber sandals or shoes, and some of the women wear headscarves over their finely plaited hair. Sunday and Church are for wearing the best clothes we have and I am wearing a dress I made for our honeymoon, a dress with pink roses on a white background to match my white sandals. I look up high into the roof, dark and mellow with its woven branches and poles, and joy and thankfulness well up in me that this community has come together to worship God and that it includes me.

There is plenty of life in this church. There are more than four hundred people here today, half of them outside for the building was already full by the time they had walked many miles to get here. They will be glad of a bigger church with room to be inside instead of out in the burning sun. It's the same every Sunday in this church and, what's more, there are forty worship centres in the outlying villages which belong to this parish and all of them are well attended too. Today Pastor Elinana will not be here for he is ministering in one of those village centres. I think of him and his wife Doruka (Dorcas) and their care of all these people. He travels on his bicycle and celebrates Holy Communion for the Christians in each village centre and manages to visit all forty of them once a year. On the other Sundays the congregations meet together and one of their number, usually a Lay Reader, leads the worship. This morning our service in Mundri is being taken by Yereboma, who is employed as foreman of the College workmen, and who is also a Lay Reader. He has been a believer for several years and has attended some of the teaching and training courses Pastor Elinana holds about three times a year, some for men, some for women. Literacy classes are also an important feature of the parish. Moru men and women who attend courses are particularly active in passing on the teaching to others in the village centres where they live, and so the churches grow and are built up.

How wonderful that this man Elinana, God's man for the job, is the pastor here at Mundri! He was only three years old when the Frasers arrived in his country in 1920, attended one of the first Moru village schools, became a Christian and was baptized in a local stream by Archdeacon Shaw. He was a teacher before his ordination. When, later, he was chosen to succeed one of his relatives as the Chief among his own people, he decided with Doruka's support that he could serve his people better by continuing to be their Pastor. And that is how it has turned out; he is an effective minister of the

Gospel, well able to organise, to inspire and enthuse his congregations. John and I were not surprised that in 1960 Elinana Ngalamu was appointed as one of the first two Sudanese Archdeacons, subsequently consecrated Assistant Bishop in 1963, and when the Dioceses of the Sudan were formed into a Province in 1976 it was he who was elected the first Archbishop.

But back to Mundri parish church. Yereboma uses the Moru Prayer Book and I am glad to follow the form of service so familiar to me, for it is a translation of the 1662 Book of Common Prayer used in all the churches I attended while I was growing up in Ireland. The readings and psalms, the prayers confession and absolution, and the blessings. In a way it is strange and perhaps parts of it are not quite relevant for this congregation, but it has its advantages. Because it has been translated into the main languages where CMS has been active and also in many other places throughout the world, I know that as I worship God here in Mundri many others are worshipping God in other places in much the same words. And even when I know none of the languages being used around me, if it is a Prayer Book service I can follow what is going on and join in the prayers in English. This is true for Sudanese Christians too. Even if away from their home area, the Prayer Book gives them the strength of belonging to each other and of belonging to the worldwide Church whatever language they use.

From the time of their arrival in Moru country in 1920, Dr. and Mrs Fraser stressed the importance of literacy, making it a requirement for baptism that a believer learns to read, and possesses his copy of the parts of the Bible already translated into Moru. It can't have been easy to produce the first written form of the Moru language and begin to translate the Bible, but that was what they did in conjunction with Andarea Apaya and Ezra Lawiri, keeping to the orthography agreed at the Rejaf Language Conference of 1928. The first complete edition of the New Testament in Moru was published in 1952 incorporating revised sections of earlier translations; my Moru Prayer Book, a 1959 edition, was first published in 1934. The

Book of Psalms - *Longo Dawidi ro* - came out in a revised translation in 1963 while Canon Ezra was still engaged in the daunting task of translating the Old Testament. When completed, the whole Bible in Moru would be received with great joy by the people here; Bibles and Prayer Books are precious possessions in constant use and always carried around in small embroidered cloth bags specially made to protect them.

Next the sermon, a real test for the learner of Moru. I could manage while the Prayer Book was being used but now it's beyond me. Eliaba who knows some English takes pity on me and comes over to translate some of what Yereboma is saying. He will have to do the same when I discover there is a second sermon to follow, but before that we will sing.

Yereboma   *Abarayama*

We stand when the number of the hymn is announced. A small drum to keep the time is beaten with a thin stick by one of the men and soon the whole church and everyone outside is in full voice. Many of the hymns and songs are new, the words and tunes composed by Moru Christians and now replacing the earlier translations of English hymns. There is new revival life around and the singing is part of it, a new spirituality. Moru is a tonal language and many of the translations from English hymns make no sense at all when the tune takes a high-pitch word onto a low note! The new indigenous hymns are attractive and are sung with great gusto; various booklets of Moru hymns and choruses were published in 1952, 1957 and 1960 and I am helping to gather up a further collection of the new hymns for the next printing. The service over, the people are slow to leave. So much news to exchange; babies to be admired, growth of the church to be talked about, reports of sickness, death, disaster and of prayers answered. I don't linger long, for later in the week I will come here again to share with the women in their Bible study and prayer. One after another we will tell of God's blessings and perhaps of His special help in a time of difficulty or temptation or suffering.

As I ride back home my head buzzes. This place is a hive of activity. The parish church, outreach to 40 church centres, fellowship meetings, teaching and literacy courses, and the training of Lay Readers, as well as the parish garden where food and cash-crops are grown to support the Church. Pastor Elinana and the Church leaders certainly keep busy. 'A Christian home in every pagan village', was what Dr. Fraser prescribed. We see evidence of homes transformed by the teaching of Christ and how other families are then attracted. We sometimes visit a clearing in the forest about half a mile from the College where a small group of Christian families have prepared a little garden under a tree with flowers and pole-seating. In that clearing they meet for their prayers and hymn singing at dawn and sunset every day and, when the wind is in the right direction, we can hear them from the Doll's house. We are told the same thing is happening in many other places. This is the way the Gospel catches on, and it's very infectious.

All these things are spontaneous, of the Spirit of God. Mundri parish itself has always been the responsibility of the local Christians alone and has not been dependent on either missionary finance or leadership. This is an important factor in its life and growth. Other parishes in Equatoria are growing just like Mundri and in many of them hundreds of converts are baptized every year. As many as 5,000 new Christians are confirmed by the Bishop in the Diocese annually. That's great, but we are concerned that without more clergy and trained leaders these new Christians only have the basic minimum of teaching.

On one of Bishop Allison's recent visits I had a wonderful day when he set off for a Confirmation service at a village about forty miles away and took me with him. A huge crowd had gathered under a grass shelter erected to accommodate them, and in a very long service with vigorous singing and prayers Bishop Allison laid his hands on the heads of a hundred and thirty five men and women, confirming them in their faith; then there was a feast and the rain poured down and everybody clapped and saw it as a sign of God's special blessing on all of us.

Moru Christians have travelled far and wide and, wherever they have settled, Christian churches have sprung up. Their practice of passing on to others what they have been taught has made them key people in the spread of Christianity outside their own tribal area and into the far corners of Sudan.

We are blessed in being here. But can we really be accepted as ordinary members of such a congregation? Eluzai has come to see me. He was ordained recently and is now assistant to Pastor Elinana in Mundri parish. He suffers many interruptions when he wants to study so comes to read in the College library whenever he can. Yesterday I was at the parish church for a special service to give thanks for the harvest, and now Eluzai has come to apologise that I wasn't placed with the honoured guests. He was very upset about it. It was the fault of the women, he told me, because they kept me with them and then took me to be with Doruka in the Pastor's house. He insisted that this was not how it should have been. "But Eluzai," I reassured him, "it was better that way. You know the first time I attended the service at the parish church a special chair was brought for me to sit on, but now I sit anywhere among the rest of the congregation. Anyway all the other guests were men! Coming from another country it is nice to belong as an ordinary member of the church." Eluzai was still not satisfied that due honour had been paid to me as an invited guest and, in spite of what I had said, I wasn't really satisfied either. It is very difficult for me to be seen as an ordinary member of the Moru congregation. John and I are from another country. In the College we use English, the only language students from so many different areas have in common, and even if I learn to speak and understand Moru more than I do, I doubt if it is possible for me to be fully integrated within this parish community. Inside myself I feel peripheral and isolated, unable to enter at depth into the lives of the people around us; I do not pretend it is otherwise.

In the background I could hear Michael. He had moved some of the furniture and was climbing up. "I'm on my way to Heaven", was part of the chorus he sang. That's the place where I'll be an ordinary member of the multitude praising God.

31   Money for the Cooks

I saw them coming, a line of thirty-four teenage girls and eight women Church leaders all carrying their bedding and food for their ten-day course, and about to stay in the houses of the College students while they were away for their holidays. Courses like this were becoming very popular and it looked as if there were more than ever on this one. The girls were chosen by their village churches and then walked to Mundri, some from places even as far away as 75 miles. On their journey they stayed at one church centre after another where they were helped on their way with food and shelter. "We come to learn of God," they said as they arrived. They had been gathering at Mundri parish church from different directions all day, and meeting the others for the first time before they walked together to the College. Amongst these adolescent girls some were fully mature and soon to be married, others were small, shy and quiet, none expensively dressed. The confident ones were talking without cease in high-pitched voices and made a great deal of noise while they sorted themselves out to share houses with their particular friends. The eight women leaders would be teaching and were responsible for the safety and good behaviour of the girls but it was clear that they too were enjoying every minute of this exciting event. And so was I!

Most Sudanese women had a hard life, every day filled with doing what seemed more than their fair share of heavy work. The first missionaries in Southern Sudan were upset about the position of the women and girls and decided that providing schools would be the best way to improve their lot and bring about change. Literacy would mean power and confidence which in turn would enable women to take a more decisive place in their own homes and also in the community. Girls' schools were established and missionary teachers struggled to attract girls to attend. Only a fairly small number did so; for them it was a big step to be released from their accustomed duties of cultivation, water carrying, preparing food and caring for younger children, and it was a success in itself when fathers paid the required fees to enable their daughters to have a few years at school. It took time and patience but slowly the strategy worked and missionary teachers were themselves encouraged when, as a result of their teaching in the schools and the work of the Mothers' Union in organising courses at the parish centres, a number of women became teachers themselves and effective Christian evangelists.

Mothers' Union leaders: photo CMS

Jean Drinkwater, a Mothers' Union worker and CMS missionary, built on the earlier work in schools and also set up courses in churches throughout Equatoria for women who had not had a chance of education. In 1960 Bishop Allison, at a great service of celebration, commissioned the first Sudanese Mothers' Union workers, each one to have an important role in her parish. The distinctive 'uniform' of these M.U. workers was a white dress with a blue sash tied diagonally over one shoulder and we used to tease Jean by calling them her Blue-Band girls after the only brand of margarine we could buy in Juba! Susana Yoane was one of them, well known to me when she became a Church leader of Mundri parish. One day I waved at her as she set off sitting sideways on the carrier of a bicycle, while the man she had hired pedalled hard to carry her and her books to a distant place. She was going to lead a womens' meeting and run a course! This was a sight that would have delighted earlier missionaries though they might have found it difficult to imagine! The gifts of leadership, enthusiasm and devotion of many marvellous women were to play a major part in the survival and growth of the Church in Sudan in the years of suffering ahead.

Pastor Eluzai was very enthusiastic about the courses run in the College during the vacations in previous years and so was his wife Fibi. They wanted to have more of them. Towards the end of 1963, Eluzai came to see me about arrangements for two courses he had in mind. One was to be in December for adolescent village girls who had never been to school and, as well as Christian teaching, would include marriage preparation to replace some of the former traditional rituals. A second course in March would be for girls who were attending schools, but would enjoy meeting other Christian girls, receive more teaching about the Christian faith and have an opportunity to affirm it for themselves.

"I think we need to make some changes this time," Eluzai said before the December course. "The girls spend too much of their time on preparing food; if we get some of the Christian women of the parish to do the cooking, these girls can concentrate more on their course." The suggestion that the parish women would give their time and work, as a service and without pay, impressed me and I quickly agreed, "and you can count on me to see to the notebooks and the materials for the sewing", I added. At a committee meeting of the Moru Rural Deanery it was decided that the course was to be led by the local women Church leaders, I was to be asked to help with the teaching, and some of the women of the parish would do the cooking voluntarily. With this underlying co-operation, Eluzai and I settled down to discuss a full and interesting programme. His part was the Bible study; he planned to set frequent tests to make sure that what he taught was being learned and understood. The women leaders were to teach about Christian family life and behaviour and to instruct and support each girl as she took her turn in leading the chapel services every morning and evening. For me it was health and hygiene teaching and joining with the women leaders in the sewing and craft work in the afternoons. Singing and story telling would follow the evening meal, and there would be acting out of Bible stories too.

The course was very successful; the Bible tests showed Eluzai's teaching was getting through, and the girls were delighted to have the small Health and Family booklets and *'The Life of Jesus'* which I had typed in Moru and duplicated for them. It was a novel experience for the women and girls to be eating food they had not had to prepare and cook and I felt happy for them that after their long walk with heavy loads under the scorching sun they were having such a good time. The course was taught in Moru, the women leaders and Eluzai teaching direct and also translating for me, though for the sewing and general conversation I managed on my own in Moru.

Coming to Mundri for a course was a most exciting venture for these girls and an opportunity to see more of their own country. They chatted and joked and laughed with other young girls and back in their villages they would have many tales to tell of all they had seen and done. I think most of all they were really thrilled to have learned some of the new hymns being composed by local men and women and set to Moru music. The joy and enthusiasm of the girls was infectious, so that when I heard the beat of a drum to keep the time I too joined in as together with swaying bodies and dancing feet we sang the new songs straight from our hearts. The song and music of worship had sprung not from the missionaries but from within the living Sudanese Church of this area.

Pastor Eluzai Munda

Before their baptism these girls had to be able to read; they would make good use of the books we gave them and would soon be teaching the new hymns and songs in their villages. At the end of their course they set off to return home, and we listened to their joyful singing until they were too far away for us to catch the lilt of their voices. They would have a happy homecoming. And there would be many wanting to be included in the next courses the parish planned to run.

It had all gone so well. Now the girls were on their way home, and we had packing to do for we were setting out on our local leave to Uganda the next day. Another visit from Eluzai came as a surprise. "I've come for the money to pay the cooks," he said, looking troubled. "But, Eluzai," I blurted out in amazement, "the Moru Rural Deanery committee discussed it all and agreed that your idea of having cooks was a good one and the work would be done voluntarily, as a service. What has happened?" He told me how a member of the Rural Deanery committee had returned half way through the course and declared that the cooks should be paid seven *piastres* a day for their work. For the ten days for two cooks that added up to a total of one pound and forty *piastres*, not a large sum, and though I had no special funds I could have paid it personally. That would have been much the easiest response. It would have relieved Eluzai's fear that if the money was not paid to the cooks it could cause a set-back for them in their faith, and it could mean the course planned for schoolgirls in March would have to be cancelled.

But there was a serious issue at stake for this young Church at a time of persecution when the presence of missionaries in the years ahead was extremely unlikely. If that member of committee said the cooks were to be paid, then he must take responsibility for where the money was coming from. It could not be right to simply turn to the missionary to rescue the situation. Eluzai didn't lose his temper when I failed to produce the money he had asked for, but he was very upset. I was very upset too.

The rest of the day passed and I kept busy with the packing and producing tea for various callers who came to say good-bye to us. After dark three women leaders from the parish arrived and we sat around drinking tea together. Then they produced a parcel and a letter for me. Inside was a flat grain basket and inside that an embroidered cloth wrapped around small coins: one Sudan pound in *piastres* and *tarifas* - a present for me, as the letter said, from the Christians of Mundri parish to help me on my journey. I was overcome. It was almost impossible to say a word of thanks. This was cash from a community without a cash-crop. They have so little, we so much. Even worse, I had refused that very morning to give one pound and forty *piastres* for the cooks. I still have the basket and the letter, reminders of that day, that gift.

I was still troubled when we reached Juba, on our way to Uganda, so I wrote to Canon Ezra to tell him all about what had happened - he was the Moru Rural Dean but had not been in Mundri at the time. I also asked him to vote some money from the Moru Rural Deanery budget for the course for schoolgirls to be held in March. Canon Ezra, on our return from leave, thanked me for refusing to pay the cooks. "That way," he said, "you would have crippled the Church. These courses are part of the work of our Church and we must be responsible for them."

Now I felt better. Canon Ezra had taken on the CMS principles (laid down by Henry Venn) on which our work and witness in Sudan was based; the Church was to be self-supporting (pay for the cooks), self-governing (be in charge of the course), and self-propagating (plan a course for schoolgirls in March). These principles underlay the continuing growth of the Church despite the pressure, violence and inducements of the Government's Islamization policy. With men like Canon Ezra the Christian Church would survive when it no longer had the presence of expatriate missionaries.

32   Do You Think You'll Like it Here?

"Do you think you'll like it here? Do you think you'll stay?" This was a familiar greeting between missionaries, said partly in joke but also knowing that we had no choice in the matter for the Government could withdraw our permits at any time. In Mundri, for Sudanese Government teachers from the North it was different. They had been posted to work in the South whether they liked it or not. Although some believed they had an important contribution to make to the development of a unified Sudan, others just longed for the moment when they would have completed their time and could return to teach in Khartoum or indeed anywhere else in the North where they came from. To some teachers it seemed pointless to make the effort to teach black Southerners whom they despised, and also politically dangerous; but there were those who believed their work was worthwhile and they did not spare themselves in what they did for their pupils.

We lived and worked almost entirely in the South, but our months in the North helped us to understand the difficulties two very different groups of people had in belonging to one country. John and I had walked about in Khartoum and Omdurman and seen a little of the life of a great Muslim city, the capital of Sudan. Its population, speaking Arabic and cherishing the ancient culture of the Arab world, for the most part followed the Muslim faith. The University, modern shops, wide streets with splashing fountains and bright lights, large Government buildings, mosques, hotels, the Anglican Cathedral and other churches, made of Khartoum an impressive city. Across the Nile was Omdurman, the ancient capital, with its miles of mud walls and houses and its wonderful *souk*. The Tomb of the Mahdi in the centre of Omdurman kept the memory of a former era in mind, and in both Khartoum and Omdurman there was always a mosque in sight, its tall slim minaret reaching upwards to the sky. And there were always men in their long white *jallabiyas* and turbans responding to the call to prayer when it rang out over the city. It wasn't hard to understand that the Northern teachers posted to the South missed all this enormously, this world so different from the steamy huddle of Juba and the undeveloped vast expanses of the rural Southern Provinces.

During the fifty-eight years of the Anglo-Egyptian Condominium, unlike colonies such as Kenya, British officials recognized that Europeans would never settle permanently in a country with the climate and conditions of Sudan. They concentrated on developing the infrastructure and training for Sudanese in the professions and in administration. Self-government and independence in the future was their goal though, as it happened, it came sooner than they expected. Historically North and South started from different points of development. At the time of Independence, education, training and achievement in the North were a long way ahead of the South which was left with no time to catch up. This disadvantage of the South is at the heart of the conflict between them.

The British contribution to prepare for future independence was in marked contrast with the performance of some other European powers in Africa. John and I were in Mundri in 1960 when the Belgians abruptly abandoned the Congo, leaving that huge territory bereft of services and with no nationals trained to take their place, not a single Congolese doctor for instance. (Unlike Sudan, where the Kitchener School of Medicine for training Sudanese doctors opened in Khartoum in 1924.) A flood of Greek and Belgian merchants and other expatriates and their families fled across the borders into Sudan, and groups of them, frightened, despairing, exhausted and hungry stayed with us on their long dusty journey to Juba. They told us they had been taken completely by surprise, that there had been no alternative plans ready for the end of Belgian rule, that their lives were at risk with the breakdown of law and order.

Their trucks were laden with all they could salvage of their possessions; any which broke down while covering huge distances on such rocky roads had to be abandoned. A year later when we were in Juba on our way on leave, we saw those trucks, lorries and luxury cars, rows and rows of them, parked in the *merkhaz* and covered with dust, some of them vandalised. They had been rounded up and confiscated by the Sudan Government when their owners had no option but to travel on by air to Europe.

We had been courteously treated everywhere by the Northern Sudanese officials we had met, both in Port Sudan and in Khartoum. Dr. Zaki at the Ministry of Health had been very affable and respectful in how he related to me and Dr. Trub. On the train and the Nile steamer we had had good conversations with the Northern passengers, some of them merchants but most of them teachers who spoke English. They liked to talk with us of issues beyond the confines of their place of birth and we could enjoy discussing the affairs of the wider world and of our culture and theirs. We shared our games, pitting our wits in competition with each other to find the best use of the Scrabble letters, and sharing our books.

The only blur on all this good experience was our embarrassment on the steamer when we saw the disrespectful way some of the Northern passengers amused themselves, throwing empty bottles and pieces of bread for Southern villagers on the banks of the Nile to catch. It was not the way for brothers, already not on good terms, to promote their belonging to each other in a united Sudan. As we all travelled on the Nile, the Northern passengers kept to themselves, and if they spent time with other passengers it was with us and not with the others, the Southerners. In Juba the Arab merchant had been helpful and polite and had served us the traditional small glasses of coffee while we shopped in his store.

This had been our limited contact with Northern Sudanese people until we lived in Mundri and met teachers at the Intermediate School where the Headmaster and all the senior teachers were Northerners and Muslim, usually referred to in a rather hostile way by the local people as 'Arabs'. This was a boarding school making use of the premises of the former Mundri Teacher Training College, now evacuated to the North because of the unrest in the South. Set on the other side of the main road through Mundri village, it had spacious buildings and playing fields, with a fair number of shady fig and mango trees. John went there regularly with the Mundri Pastor to conduct services for about 120 Protestant schoolboys and to join in their discussions.

It was through those visits to the school that we met several of the Northern members of staff who were always very friendly to us. Special among them was Ahmed Awad, a handsome and well-built young man with dark skin which hinted at some Southern forebear. He invited us to games of tennis on the school court; I have a note of one of these games, when I think my tennis partner must have been a champion, for I wrote "I played with Hezekiah against Ahmed and John. We won! The ball boy spent his time pushing Patrick in the pram." When we went to study Arabic in Omdurman, Ahmed wrote to his mother and we were invited to have tea with her. We found her two-storeyed house easily, in the older established part of Omdurman, and soon we were in her shady courtyard sitting below an elaborately carved balustrade and having tea and cakes served by one of her family. Michael and Katherine got past the shy stage and she laughed when they imitated her son Ahmed playing tennis. I hoped they wouldn't go on to include me in the imitation; she would not have liked to know I played too, she would not have considered that acceptable behaviour for a woman.

John was learning Sudanese Colloquial Arabic and he liked to join the Northern teachers on Saturday mornings in the *souk* in Mundri where they spoke Arabic together while drinking coffee served by the enterprising shopkeeper. Tea parties were a favourite way of entertaining in Sudan, and for us and the children trips for tea at the Intermediate School made enjoyable outings.

Some of the teachers had their wives with them and I often tried to imagine what it was like for them in Mundri. Although they and the local people were all Sudanese, Northerners here were much more isolated than we were; they could feel the hostility towards them and were often afraid for their lives in this place not of their own choosing, while on the other hand we were made very welcome in Mundri and were where we wanted to be.

One of the few acts of defiance schoolboys, and indeed University students, could engage in was to go on strike. These strikes could be about the food, or some unwise statement made by a teacher, or against some new Government order, and easily got out of hand ending in the school being closed, sometimes for many months, so nobody really gained anything. But there could be violence as well. John and I were having tea with some of the schoolmasters one day when they talked about their fear and showed us how they kept a gun behind the sitting room curtains in readiness to protect themselves, and also slept with a gun beside their beds. They could not forget the mutiny of Southern troops in Torit in August 1955 which resulted in the killing of 261 Northerners throughout the South. One of them was a teacher shot dead while teaching a class in this very school in Mundri. (75 Southerners also were killed, 200 were executed for their part in the mutiny and over 1,000 imprisoned). Men and women, used to being able to have a clear view of everything in the sandy open deserts of the North, hated and feared being surrounded by the alien scrub bush and uneven ground of the South. They dreaded being attacked by someone hidden and waiting for them, and they feared violation of their wives by intruders. Perhaps most of all they missed being near their families and friends, mosques and cultural activities.

Apart from returning to their homes in the North for their annual vacation, I doubt if the wives of these teachers ever left the school except when they and their husbands came by truck for a social visit to the College or to have tea and cakes with us. I remember those occasions well, and the very young wives only recently married to their young teacher husbands and so far without children. They wore long white clothing alright but the cloth over their heads did not quite cover either their hair or their attractive faces, as if while they were in the South they could enjoy some degree of freedom from the tighter restrictions imposed on them in the North. They were very interested and curious about the details of our house and possessions and, like our children, they loved looking at my cookery books. Without most of the necessary ingredients the main use we had for these books with brightly coloured food pictures was when Michael and Katherine ate 'pretend goodies' with me while we wove them into our stories of parties and journeys. A few of these Northern women, who knew a little English, copied recipes for baking cakes when on leave in the North where they would be able to buy a wider variety of foodstuffs.

The teachers liked to examine Michael and Katherine's school-books with a critical eye and get them to read for them. They were very particular that when a page had been read, the little reader could tell them what it was about, to show it had also been understood. Some accepted our invitation at the end of term when we held a Visitors service in the Chapel and afterwards the College students entertained the Northern teachers and their wives to tea. We hoped that the social occasion of drinking tea together would do a little to help Northerners and Southerners in how they related; we hoped too that these events would give our Muslim friends a glimpse of our Christian faith and way of life.

One of the Northern teachers in the school, whom we knew well, asked me how I was enjoying life in Sudan. "Among other things," I told him, "I'm learning the local language, Moru." His reply was instant. "That," he said, " is not a language. That is the speech of animals." There was a long way to go for Sudanese 'brothers' to be united in one nation North and South.

There was also a long way to go for 'brothers' in the South who had no wish to be united with those in the North. "When we get separation, every year we will wage war on the North and bring back Arabs to torture and put to death," one Southern Sudanese schoolboy told me.

I found a small spark of encouragement in a note I made at that time.

"In the evening," I wrote, "we joined the ordination students for a debate in the College on the motion: 'That this house considers it right for nations and individuals to take part in warfare.' Many very good speeches. The Dinka students voted for fighting - hardly surprising - but the vote was against the motion."

Although it was hard to be optimistic on this small spark, please God a way will be found to a peaceful future in Sudan, North and South at peace not war.

33 Arabization and Islamization

At the time of Independence in 1956, the South had expected a measure of autonomy and political freedom, together with economic justice and respect for black African culture and goals, while the North expected that Independence and the end of the Anglo-Egyptian Condominium would result in North and South being clearly one country, all of it ruled by Northern Muslims. It was impossible that both these objectives would be achieved.

The Government, predominantly Northern and Muslim, pursued its policy of promoting Islam and the Arabic language and culture throughout North and South. This was how the Sudan would be united as a single Muslim state. The decision was reached without consultation and without the agreement of the people of the South.

Under the Anglo-Egyptian Government, Christian Missions, as the pioneers of education in the South, were given funding to support the schools. Boys and girls, educated by missionary teachers, became teachers themselves, staffed the hospitals, served in the administration, the army, the economy, and agricultural research. The most able of them were admitted as students to Khartoum University. A year after Independence, under the Education Act of 1957, Church schools for boys were taken over and controlled by the Government, and in them Arabic and Islam were promoted. Northern Muslim headmasters and senior staff were posted to Southern schools. For a time the Church girls' schools were allowed to continue unchanged.

At primary level, *Khalwa* schools, based on the *Qur'an* and using the Arabic language, were introduced by the Government; no fees were charged, making these schools available to any boy who wished to attend (there was no education for girls in *Khalwa* schools). However, that could involve a change of name. A Christian boy might say "My name is James," only to be told, "That is too difficult, we'll call you *Mahmoud* instead!" Small boys in long slightly dirty *jallabiyas* and embroidered round caps could be heard reciting the *Qur'an* in chorus and reading the Arabic script out loud. This seemed to be all they were taught, and no doubt it contributed to the failure of these schools, the ruins of which soon littered Southern towns and villages.

It was all a long way removed from the former general Mission school education in the South where the vernacular languages and the Roman alphabet were used in teaching a range of subjects in the lower classes, and English was the language further up the school. Southerners were far from happy with the changes in education and resisted them. Coping with different languages was made more difficult still when there were two scripts, the Arabic script for Arabic and the Roman script for the vernacular languages and English.

Schools, Lui Hospital, and the Church Agricultural Training Farm at Undukori all became Government institutions. The Church bookshop in Juba, supplying Bibles and Christian literature, was closed on the grounds that Missions were forbidden to trade, though Bishop Allison's intervention gained permission to sell Christian books at cost price.

In 1960, the Government decided that the official day of rest for the whole of Sudan was to be Friday. The Christian Sunday would no longer be the day of rest in the South. Clearly it would be easier to administer the whole country that way but Southerners were outraged and saw it as a direct attack on them and their wish to stay in tune with the rest of the Christian world. Three students at the Secondary School in Rumbek wrote a letter of protest and were sentenced to 10 years imprisonment, others were expelled. In time however Christians in the South had to settle for the Friday holiday but continued to observe Sunday, the day of the Resurrection, by attending their churches in the very early hours of the morning before starting an ordinary day at work. In Khartoum no change was needed. The custom there had always been to have the main worship services on Sunday evenings at the end of the normal working day. I see from the pack of their school work that Michael and Katherine made entries in their daily Diaries on Monday, Tuesday, Wednesday, Thursday and Saturday showing they too had a holiday on Friday.

Further harassment followed with the Missionary Societies Act of 1962. Its purpose to end the presence of missionaries within Sudan was obvious, but it soon became clear that the Act was mainly intended to control the Churches which the Government considered were really only appendages of the Missions and would have no hope of surviving without outside support. The Act was designed to establish Islam and Arabic in the South and hasten the end of the Christian presence and resistance. Permits, not readily granted, were now required for the construction of churches and also for any repairs such as the renewal of thatch when roofs leaked or the replacement of wooden supports in church buildings when these were eaten away by termites. Licences for Church leaders and their locations had to be renewed every year and could be refused, and there were new regulations affecting the publication of pamphlets and books, both Christian and educational. One by one missionaries would be out of Sudan; not all at once, which would have caused protests and trouble in the South, but quietly and unobtrusively by refusal of visas or expulsion for supposed misdemeanours.

All these Government actions provoked a response in the South. If there were no peaceful negotiations nor a fair resolution of what was called 'The Southern Problem,' then there would be armed conflict and war. Bishop Allison spent a night with us in Mundri on his way from Rumbek to Juba. His customary optimism had at last collapsed. "They have done it now. They have gone too far," he said as he told us of the terror, details of horrific tortures and deaths he knew about. He told us also of the Anyanya, a guerilla force made up of Southern ex-soldiers and other resistance fighters. They did not believe that Southern aspirations would ever be achieved by political means. "Our patience has now come to an end and we are convinced that only the use of force will bring a decision . . . From today onwards we shall take action . . . We do not want mercy and we are not prepared to give it," was their statement in 1963. Force was to be met with force.

But no force could overcome the problem at a deeper level. Northerners wanted the whole country to be Muslim and Arabic-speaking alright, but that would not solve everything; they felt different and knew they were different, they belonged to another world, another culture, and far from feeling close to their Southern fellow countrymen, they despised and feared them. We had seen for ourselves in a small way the lack of respect and the unfortunate arrogant attitudes of some of the 'Arabs' and guessed the Southerners would have no immediate forgiveness to offer them. If the two parts were ever to be really one, great changes would be needed. The North, Arab and Muslim and looking towards the Middle East, and the South with a significant and alive Christian Church alongside traditional religions and looking towards Africa, would each need to look more kindly towards the other.

In the North, the Government was convinced that without the missionaries and money from outside the country the Christians of the South and the Nuba Mountains, who were a progressive and growing element of the population, would abandon their beliefs and adopt Islam. It was not appreciated just what a hold Christ had taken on the hearts of many Southern Sudanese people and how they would stand firm whatever inducements or suffering came their way, for it was in their Christian faith that they found comfort, strength and hope. In 1963, John reported in Outlook, the Irish CMS magazine:

"Lives have been revolutionised, customs challenged, fears and superstitions broken. Thousands have found in Jesus Christ a new status as sons of God, a new way of life, and a new vision of this world and the world to come. The Church is growing in

Equatoria at the rate of 6,000 a year and the pace of growth shows no signs of slackening. If it continues ... a very substantial proportion of the population of the Southern Provinces will be Christian."

The phenomenal increase in the number of Christians was good news even if it had to be admitted that in some cases becoming a Christian was less a spiritual move than one motivated by politics, a way of rebelling against Northern Muslim domination.

John's photo, end of term, 1963

34 The New Cathedral

We had been hearing about more and more violent incidents. All around us the Anyanya carried on a guerilla war against the Northern army and Government personnel. Bridges were destroyed, army convoys ambushed, and Northerners shot. The ordinary people, though sharing the goals of the Anyanya, also feared them and, when intimidated into providing them with food, lived in terror of army reprisals. They were caught between the two sides, the army and the Anyanya, both equally brutal and ruthless. Many Southern-born Government officials and employees deserted their posts and disappeared into the forests or across the borders into neighbouring countries, while others who stayed were accused of collaborating and killed by the Anyanya for continuing in their Government employment.

It was a terrible and terrifying situation. The Northern soldiers, far away from their homes and their land of open sandy plains, were right to hate the forests and scrubland of the South where they could be ambushed and shot at so easily. The Anyanya faced forces much better armed and equipped than themselves. When their villages were set on fire, the women and children tortured and killed indiscriminately and the men taken away for worse, it mattered little whether the local people suffered at the hands of the Government army or at the hands of the Anyanya. A few years later we heard from John Kanyikwa (see chapter 23) that in the continuing conflict seventeen of his close relatives, including his father, were massacred in a single raid.

What place, we wondered, does a missionary have in a war like this? We could pack up and go only that always in our ears were the voices of the Sudanese Church leaders pleading with us to stay as long as we could, to help to train as many clergy as possible.

Although it was possible we could be caught accidentally in crossfire, we did not feel at risk of deliberate attacks on us by Government forces because the killing of an expatriate would result in adverse world publicity which Sudan wished to avoid. As expatriates we were potentially 'the eyes of the world', able to observe and comment on what we saw happening, and our presence was some slight deterrent to the worst of the violence. It would have been an advantage to the Government to get us out of the country so that torture violence and massacre could go unreported, but unexpectedly we were granted re-entry visas allowing us to go out and come back in. We went to Uganda in December 1963 for a month of local leave.

Uganda was such a different world and it was a relief to be there. At last, for some weeks at Mengo Hospital in Kampala, I had the thrill of being a missionary doctor. Then we spent Christmas fourteen miles away at Bishop Tucker College in Mukono where we stayed with Charlie and Mary Preston, our Canadian friends. Audrey and Raymond with their children drove four hundred miles in their car from Limuru in Kenya to be with the rest of us. The days in Mukono passed in a riot of activity, huge feasting, laughing and teasing and telling stories, playing games and listening to Charlie playing the piano while he sang a ballad about *'Blood on the saddle'*. We were delighted with our holiday and the fun and games the children had with the others.

All six of us, the Smiths, the Prestons and the Lowes, had been together in missionary training and this was a chance to continue discussions we had started then, talking of the three very different Theological Colleges we were serving. In each of them the challenge was the same; we must make the teaching and practical training appropriate to the needs of the students and relevant for their parish ministry later. Bishop Tucker College, with its beautiful mellow brick buildings set on the side of a hill, was where clergy for the Church of Uganda were trained in rather different circumstances from those in Mundri. We saw the Library, the Chapel, the ordinands' village and Josephine Tucker House recently built for women students. We met Ugandan staff, staff from England and Ireland, from Canada and America, and from India. The contrast with Bishop Gwynne College was enormous. Mary, a doctor, can do as much medical work as she chooses, children have other children to play with, and good international schools in Kampala offer more than I can provide for Michael and Katherine in the *tukl*. Delicious and plentiful food, a glorious climate, and post and telephone services which work well. Even a good bookshop in Kampala.

But somehow we get strength to turn our backs on these congenial conditions and opportunities in Uganda. Our hearts are in Sudan and we are keen to be back there; that is our place and our leave is over. A flight from Entebbe to Juba, a lorry for the long uncomfortable haul which ends as we rattle again across the iron bridge spanning the Yei river, pass through Mundri village, turn left and left again into the College. We are back in Mundri, back home to our house in the College. Only Canon Ezra, Hana and their children are present, the students and the other Sudanese staff are away and the Gills on U.K. leave. After so much company in Uganda it is very quiet, very isolated, and terribly hot and sticky. I picture our friends in Mukono and Mengo and I admit to some feelings of envy.

The house built specially for us in Mundri is a great improvement on the Doll's house. It is good that John is so slick at packing, for, by Mission rules, every time we go on local or U.K. leave everything we have in Mundri must be packed in crates and tin trunks in case we are not allowed to return. We hurry to unpack. First for Michael the trucks and tools his hands are itching for, then for Katherine an assembly of her dolls and teddies, and a pile of her books to read again; for Patrick a ball and then into his cot for a rest for him but mainly a rest for us. Special treats of tinned food and the twelve two-lb. tins of 'Blue-Band' margarine bought in Kampala are put in the store; we have enough margarine now for a tin a month for the next year. When we have finished with the tins, which are coated inside against rust and which we open with great care, they will be much sought after for use as large mugs - in Africa the art of recycling is well established. I put the herbs and spices safely away; they will add variety of taste to our food and will disguise horrible weevil flavours. We give presents of shirts to Tito and the others.

The house specially built for us

For the next couple of months we will have the added heat of our Tilley pressure lamp too, for we must save the generator Diesel for light for the College students when they return. This does not please Michael. He is not keen on the dark so we keep a small oil lamp burning on a high shelf overnight for him. Indeed, considering it gets dark at 6.00 p.m., I am not much pleased either. Being stuck with one oil lamp feels worse now that electricity has made such a difference to our evenings and just switching on a light allows John to prepare lectures and me to do some of the typing it was too hot to do earlier in the day. "Is there electric light in God's house in heaven," Michael asks, "and what I want to know is, does it stay on all night?" That would be his ideal and probably mine too. I remind myself of the day the electricity was first switched on in 1961. Philip Can, one of the students, wrote about it in the College Newsletter which was edited by John and posted twice a year with sermon notes, Bible studies and news to former students who were now pastors.

"We thank God for the gift of electricity," Philip wrote, "which makes everything go easily now. For the service of Dedication the staff and students with their families went first to the Chapel for a short prayer and then out marching and singing hymns to the Electricity Engine House. They stood in front while the Principal read the Bible and gave a short talk about how we can use the machines to God's glory. Mr. Pollock (the American missionary engineer) went in to turn on the machine and then came back out to give the key to the Principal.

"The evening studies from 6 to 8 p.m. are easy now because of the electricity. In the past we used to begin late due to the difficulty of waiting for lamps. The big lecture room has four long tubes high up giving light. It looks as if you are studying in the day- time. When the evening study ends we take home our books and we can continue our study by night until 10 p.m. when the machine is turned off. Many people are visiting the College now to see the machine. We take them round to see the different places having light, the Library, the Chapel, the Dining room, and the Common Room also. We are thankful to the American Mission for this electricity and to Mr. Ted Pollock who worked to install the machine and wires all through the College."

After Mr. Ted Pollock had finished the installation and departed, 'Mr. John Lowe' was the one to function as the engineer, a troublesome and exacting task not made easier by complaints when it failed. The system had its complications. When the larger of the two engines was running, Oloni was employed to watch it to make sure that the three phases were in balance; if too many lights were on in one part of the campus or not enough in another it was Oloni's job to notice this and run around switching off or switching on lights. The smaller engine was used on Sunday nights when Oloni was off duty, as it did not need to be watched, but it was not powerful enough for more than one light in each of the student's houses. It was extraordinary how many complaints and protests this limitation raised from students for whom having any electric light at all was a very recent experience. It was even more maddening for us at first; our new house had not been built when the plans for electricity were drawn up, with the result that John was the 'engineer' for the electricity supply but our own house for a time was the only one without a connection and lights. This was soon rectified.

It was still vacation time. The College was at peace, but the countryside was not. It looked more and more likely that soon the young Church in Sudan would be continuing without the presence of its Mission personnel and support. In a way it was exciting for us to see the Church in Sudan, in this time of unrest and civil war, growing at such a great rate and with such conviction and confidence. It was not dependent on expatriate missionaries and money and would survive without them. It was full of life. Its leadership was strengthened when Bishop Allison appointed two Sudanese Assistant Bishops in 1963. We knew both of them well. Bishop Yeremaya Kufuta Dotiro had been a tutor at the College, while Bishop Elinana Jabi Ngalamu had been the pastor of the large and growing parish at Mundri. Both of them had our full confidence as real men of God. They were called to bear burdens that would crush most, and to do a new job in a country where the Christian Church was under threat, and where it was likely they would soon carry the burden without Bishop Allison to share it.

At such a time, the completion of All Saints' Cathedral in Juba was another great achievement. All Saints' Cathedral in Khartoum had been consecrated in 1912 but most people thought the Cathedral in

Juba would not now be built. *'Mush mumkin'* meaning 'just accept that it is quite impossible' was the usual opinion, amidst the pessimistic forecasts. So it was all the more remarkable that Ken Ogden and Tony Idle, with the skills of men from the Technical Department at Lainya and firms in Juba, erected the impressive new stone-built Cathedral on the site marked with the Celtic cross, where we had walked with Michael and Katherine in their pram five years before.

Assistant Bishops Elinana and Yeremaya

The people of Yambio sent a gift of a Zande 'talking' drum. This drum, on its way to take up its position in the new Cathedral, rested long enough at Mundri for Michael and Katherine to draw pictures of it and write about it in their school diaries. It was 7 feet long and 3 feet high, carved out of a huge tree trunk in the shape of a hippo, and weighed over 2 cwt. Its two side cavities produced different notes, and it would make sure the people of Juba and all around were summoned properly to worship God in the splendid new Cathedral.

Juba Cathedral under construction, 1963: photo CMS

Consecrated on All Saints Day, 1st.November 1963, the Cathedral was an important witness to the presence of the Christian Church in Juba, the capital of the South. It was a tremendous encouragement at a time when Sudanese Christians faced a difficult and uncertain future. Representatives of other Churches, the Government, the College (including Canon Ezra and John) and of parishes all over the country crowded into Juba for the great occasion. Pastor Khedekia Mabior wrote of his impressions:

"This year everyone wanted to go up to Juba. I know I did. I wanted to see for myself about the things we had been hearing. I am glad that I went. Juba is far from my home in Tonj (500 miles). I am lucky to have been there this year. I arrived in Juba on the mail lorry. After getting down from the place where the lorry stops, I made my way to the mission. My first object was to see the new Cathedral. When I saw it, I exclaimed, 'Praise the Lord!' I wanted to jump for joy. Then my heart told me that outward signs are not the sign of an inward blessing. So I praised the Lord quietly for the beauty of the new building which stands in Juba as a witness to Christ and as a house in which to worship God. It also reminded me of the early Church. In the New Testament we read how the Church was founded in the Gentile countries. When St. Paul visited a city and made converts, he also appointed leaders to meet the needs of the people. In that way the gospel became part of the life of the Gentile community. The same thing applies to our Church of Sudan. The gospel of Christ was brought to us by others. Now it is laid on our shoulders to carry on. Whatever the reasons, we know that the Church belongs to us. The work of carrying on the witness is ours. And now, praise God, we have our own Sudanese leaders and this wonderful All Saints Cathedral."

Two new Assistant Bishops, the new Cathedral and, greatest of all, the increasing numbers of men and women who were turning to Christ and flocking into the churches to worship and pray, to seek baptism and confirmation, were cause for celebration and rejoicing but provoked a monstrous response from the Government. A terrible massacre of worshippers was carried out by the army at the new Cathedral in Juba only a year and some months after it had been consecrated.

35 This is the Day that the Lord Has Made

It's an ordinary day in Mundri, and I'm not in my best mood. It's another day when, although I know it's stupid, I'm feeling frustrated again that after five years I'm still waiting for that licence to be a doctor here. It's no help at all to me that my mind thinks back over our local leave when I was able to work as a proper missionary doctor at Mengo Hospital in Uganda. I was out of practice of course, but with the encouragement of the others I had a great time doing what I could. I even donned a green gown and cap one day and took up a scalpel to operate in the theatre, and even here in hot Mundri I smell again the antiseptics and the whiff of ether. And I am sure that lovely Bishop Tucker College at Mukono would suit John with all its students, its library and its staff, and he would be delighted for me to have the chance of doing the work I have always wanted to do. I know it bothers him that in Sudan he follows his vocation but I can't follow mine. One of our Irish supporters wrote last month to ask why we stay in Mundri when other countries are crying out for doctors. That's what I'm asking too, but John always answers that if we were transferred somewhere else no replacement for us would be allowed into Sudan, and we both realize how vital it is for us to hold on here.

Most of the time I count it a privilege to be here, but not today. Even if Mundri is still our place, today I'm feeling trapped and terribly frustrated. In my thinking I go over all this so often, round and round, what I want for myself and what is best for the Christian Church in Sudan.

Then I think of four of my cousins and that makes me feel even more sorry for myself. I can't imagine they are as isolated and restricted as we are. I have to admit that it is really rather extraordinary that, with their husbands, they too are serving the developing Churches on the staffs of other colleges in Africa: Bertha and Don English are at Umuahia in Nigeria, Joyce and Terry McMullan are in Malawi, while Margaret and Brian Beck and Audrey and Raymond Smith are all at Limuru in Kenya. With John and me here in Sudan that makes five of us, quite something our Ludlow grandparents would have been pleased about. But this hot afternoon I'm not pleased about anything, and I'm further aggravated by reading the latest CMS magazine which has a list of places where there is an urgent need for doctors.

I get up. I leave John enjoying his *raha* and the children quiet in their room, and go out to walk on my own, to pray, to think over how my life is working out. Have I been able to do anything at all worthwhile here?

From our front windows I see the *tukl*, the small thatched house which was built first as a guest room for College visitors and where Auntie Elsie stayed when she was with us for Christmas four years ago; later it was John's study where he was joined by the snake which wanted to share it with him. It's where I escape to another world with my easel and paints, and produce vivid green landscapes in the dry season when all around is dusty and brown. Now it's Michael and Katherine's school and every day I am a teacher and, though I'm not always patient enough, I suppose I'm not too bad; I'm glad to be so close to them as they learn, and I'm excited they're making such good progress. To the right the large poinsettia bush is blazing scarlet again; I smell the frangipani flowers, the same smell as at Brian and Eileen de Saram's breakfast table in Juba when we first arrived. I walk out in the burning sun to look around the College, to remind myself of our life here. It is clear that if we had waited a bit, the new house for us would not have been built, not needed. When I come to think of it, it's amazing really that we are here at all; there were fifty three CMS missionaries in Southern

Sudan ten years ago, and now with Government restrictions we are two of only ten who are left.

I pass the house next door where Noel and Violet from Ireland with their small son Ian lived for part of our first year here. I miss them but I smile to myself when I remember how we all, having kissed the Blarney stone, told our tall stories and cracked our jokes. I admire a 'mile a minute' Russian vine covering the front of the house and climbing up into the high thatch, with its froth of small pink flowers so dainty and delicate, not like the tropics at all. I'm thankful I can still whizz along on Violet's bike when I ride to the parish church on Sundays and sometimes to George Frangos' shop in the village even when he has hardly anything to sell.

Another thatched house with a large food garden nearby is where Canon Ezra and Hana and their family live. They call out a greeting to me in Moru, this mad young white woman not on a verandah but out under the scorching sun. Memories come crowding back, vivid memories of our first year in Mundri when Ezra and Hana's two-year-old daughter Lusi fell ill and died while her father was away in England, and the terrible time it had been for Hana, and for us. She had been so angry with me for not treating Lusi. I remember the healing that eventually came, the day when John and I with Michael and Katherine and our new baby Patrick, born in Nairobi, returned dusty and tired after the long lorry journey from Juba. Hana rushed out to greet us with washing water and tea. "Let me help you," she had said, "now you too have suffered." She would never forget the pain of Lusi's death, but she was able to be loving and gracious in her care for me and our new baby.

Round the circle of staff and student houses and dormitories I go, all of them empty and looking a bit derelict, waiting for the students to return. Soon there would be the happy sounds of conversation, laughter, the play and shouts of children. The Wives School and lecture rooms remind me of my attempts at teaching, and it warms my heart when I remember how pleased my mother was with the brightly embroidered table-cloth, edged with crochet, which the women made as a present for her.

Canon Ezra and Hana

I look in through the open door of the College dining room equipped for fifty, where single and married students all eat their lunch together, joined once a week by members of staff. I remember the day when there was nearly a riot. Contrary to their tradition, the men students were asked to help with the washing-up. They were not pleased or co-operative; indeed they were extremely angry and vocal in their resistance. Canon Ezra the Vice-Principal, sitting among the students and exercising his hand as he constantly did to relieve the pain he suffered from a damaged nerve, was the first to rise to his feet and start to wash the plates. That made it hard for the students to continue to refuse. Ezra was only doing what he would have done in his own house where he helped Hana, but it was behaviour in a man which was unusual then. Knowing Canon Ezra was one of the special blessings of being in Sudan.

I glance in passing at the small engine house. The electricity generator is coaxed by John to keep working and has made such a difference to life here. Beside it is the Doll's house, that small house which was our first home in Africa. That was where we unpacked our baggage, and after all our travels were so happy to be on our own at last, wedding presents and all. That was where we first shared meals with students, where we were almost cooked alive between the corrugated iron roof and the hot gusts of air blowing through the wire-mesh windows. So far since we moved out of it nobody has lived there.

Last of all the Principal's house, the house we stayed in with Mary and David Brown when we first arrived; they had helped us a lot but now I feel a bit sorry that I gave them, especially David, a hard time when I thwarted his efforts to tame and control a rebellious Irish recruit. It's Richard and Elizabeth Gill's house now, empty while they are on leave in England.

I've taken my time over this 'memory' walk but I must end it by going into the Chapel, at the centre of the College, just as we did on our first morning here. I sit down in the stillness, out of the glare of the sun and under the high thatched roof. The alabaster cross with the map of the world below it reminds me that this College, the Church in Sudan, the worldwide Church belong to the great multitude of saints from every country, from every age, and I belong too. This is our place. Yes, this is God's place for us. Even if it is not an easy or comfortable life at this point, perhaps only for this one day I know it is where God has put us. I accept now that although I won't be a missionary doctor in Sudan, my life will be taken up with the people around us and the many other things I can do. Loving and caring for John and for our three children comes first. Typing all those pages for the students may have more long-term value than the limited medical work I might manage, especially with inadequate access to drugs; and I must safeguard Michael and Katherine's education by being as good a teacher for them as I can be. My time need never be wasted time. Each day is to be lived for itself and will add to how I am in the future. For however long we stay here, I will no longer telescope my life by undervaluing the present. "This is the day the Lord has made; I will rejoice and be glad in it," becomes the song inside me, an attitude I train myself to return to again and again. I walk back to our house, to John and the children, peaceful and healed, my spirits revived.

Evening after evening in the darkness the children sleep in their beds, while the Tilley lamp hisses on its stand. It casts light on the book John is reading and on the table where, with a pile of papers, I set to work typing notes for the students or a letter home to the grandparents. A hot wind blows through the house. It carries off three light-weight pages which finish up clinging to the window-mesh at the other end of the room. I collect them and weight them down with a stone.

Almost alone in the spread-out College, day after day John and I live quietly and look forward to the return of the students and staff, to the start of the new term.

36   Canon Ezra's Blessing

And so the days go by. We are very cut off; the only news from outside the College is of violent incidents and killings, and the post lorry does not come. It is well into the dry season, there has been no rain for four months. We woke to an unfamiliar rumble. Not thunder. Not the rains coming early. But the groaning of heavy vehicles less than a mile away. They were on the unpaved main road, then we could hear them coming down the narrow track to the College. We dressed quickly, and through the billowing dust made out the line approaching our house. A number of large trucks, two Bren gun carriers, lots of soldiers fully armed and wearing tin hats who quickly jumped to the ground. There they were, the army had come. Our house was surrounded. What was to happen to us? Would the children be alright? Would we be imprisoned, deported, separated from each other? What would become of the College, of the people around us, of the Church?

The young Northern Sudanese officer in charge approached. "I have Government orders to remove you. Send for your second in charge," he ordered. "I can't do that," John replied, "Canon Ezra is the Vice-Principal, and my superior, I can't send for him." The officer couldn't believe that was true. "Who signs the cheques then?" was his next question. "I don't, Canon Ezra does," John declared. "Hand over the truck," the officer demanded. "I can't. It is not mine." The altercations went on. The officer found it impossible that John Lowe, a white man, was not in charge of the College. "Send for your second in charge," he ordered again, beginning to get angry. John calmly repeated his reply, and so it went on and on. This exchange was on such an important issue that though it could end badly, I knew John would not concede. The officer was irritated and frustrated that this defiance of his order was going on with the soldiers and some of the local people watching, but in the end he recognised that he had to accept John's quiet insistence. The tension eased when that proud young officer, smart in his uniform, walked off with John in the direction of Canon Ezra's house and came back with him. It was Leap Day, the 29th February 1964 at 6.00 in the morning. We were to pack up and leave without delay.

The news of the intended deportation of all missionaries from Southern Sudan had been broadcast on the BBC World Service on the evening of Thursday 27th February but we hadn't heard of this. It seems strange now that we had no radio. It would have been quite difficult to get batteries, and radios were few and far between. But it was actually our choice to be without a radio, to be content in our isolation; we were less likely to fall under Government suspicion if we were not in touch with the outside world. We knew, of course, the conflict in Sudan was getting worse but, as expatriates, we did not feel that we were in personal danger; nobody was wanting to harm or kill us. We would stay as long as we could and carry on with the training of the clergy, the task we had come to do. The previous month, January 1964, while on local leave in Uganda, John had written to his father:

"One danger of the present political situation is that the Government might perhaps take the opportunity of the conditions of unrest to order all foreigners out, supposedly for their own safety, but in fact to remove all outside observers."

Just six weeks later that was what was happening.

So the army had come for us. Keep calm like John does, I told myself; treat it as an ordinary day, do the ordinary things one after the other, one after the other. Michael and Katherine, nearly seven, dressed quietly and stood back watching everything as we identified essentials to pack. They chose their essentials too, a favourite truck, a teddy, some crayons and paper, books. Patrick, not yet two, was very excited and I saw him going off with another little boy to explore the Bren gun carriers. Two or three soldiers followed us around everywhere in the house, even in the bathroom; others were watching through our mosquito-wire windows, always with their eyes on us in case we had arms to hide or give to the Anyanya. These soldiers knew what it was like to be ambushed and attacked, but once they could see we had neither guns nor ammunition they didn't seem hostile to us or the children; perhaps there was no need for us to feel frightened?

For Canon Ezra there was every reason for fear and apprehension. Yet he stood his ground. He knew that the coming of the army signalled danger and suffering, doubts about the future of the College and certainty that the Christian Church would be persecuted, yet all that day he remained with us, calm and at peace. From time to time I could hear him repeating his favourite phrase, "but God is not defeated." It was vacation time, the College empty of students, but a group of local people soon gathered. Like at a death they stood around in silence all that day observing what was going on but knowing how powerless they were. I couldn't help thinking that if it had been these Southerners the army had come for, by now they would have been subjected to harsh and terrifying treatment, not the polite approach given to us.

It was a long day. At 9.00 the officer looked through the things we had packed but, for some reason we did not understand, he refused to allow us to take a box of emergency food and toys, and even a container of safe boiled water. We had put these together for we had no idea where we were to be taken, what the conditions would be like, and how long we would be there. It was clear the officer didn't know where we were to be taken either, though he seemed to be getting instructions from time to time by radio telephone. So much not known. Keep calm, do the ordinary things one after the other, one after the other, I reminded myself. But what was ordinary about today? What was to happen to us? What would become of Canon Ezra and the rest?

We were only to take essentials. The officer instructed us to make lists of the possessions we would leave behind; these lists when typed were to be handed over to the Church. We did not hurry with the typing and making carbon copies, for by delaying and slowing down we had a little time to think, a little time to grasp that this was probably our final departure from Bishop Gwynne College. When the lists were complete, the army officer and Canon Ezra gave us receipts in accordance with the Government rules. It was all done in an orderly way, an orderliness which was unexpectedly completed four days later when, by the intervention of the British Ambassador, John returned to Mundri in a civilian lorry with a police escort, for two nights and a day, to pack up the Gills' possessions and ours and to collect his beloved books.

The policy of the Church Missionary Society had been to train Sudanese Christian leaders, to establish a Church which did not depend for its growth and nurture on the presence of missionaries from overseas. Richard Gill, the Principal, was on leave in England on that Leap Day, leaving John the only foreign tutor, John and me the only missionaries and the only expatriates in Mundri. Our colleague, Canon Ezra Lawiri, was Acting-Principal. John constantly made it clear that Canon Ezra was his superior. "But how can this be?" demanded the officer yet again. "How can you be under an African and," he sneered, "a black Southerner at that?" He could not credit that John was not in charge, didn't sign the cheques, and didn't have the keys for everything.

By afternoon we knew that we were to go to Juba. John was seated in one Bren gun carrier with Katherine between him and the soldier driver, and I was in the second Bren gun carrier driven by another soldier with Michael in the middle and Patrick on my knee. There were more soldiers behind in both carriers and all of the soldiers wore tin hats. Our local friends, silent and sad, stood around as Canon Ezra following the customary pattern for all journeys blessed us, praying for those who stayed and those who went, and for the soldiers and vehicles to be kept safe on the road. In travelling with the army we would be in a very dangerous position. There Canon Ezra stood surrounded by the army trucks. Although he looked so vulnerable, he gave strength and confidence to us all by the love of God within him. He would stay to face the consequences of the

Government Islamization policy; for decades to come, he and the Southern population would suffer in a brutal hidden war. Oh! Ezra, Ezra, man of God, our friend: our hearts are heavy for you, you represent so many we have to leave behind as we are taken away. We felt strangely numb to our own situation. Because we were white we were safe from deliberate violence, but when expatriates had been removed the war would go unobserved, the small protection our presence provided would end.

By 5.30 we were off with such baggage as we had been allowed and with the container of water included after all. None of us would ever live in Mundri again.

The road between Mundri and Juba is uneven and rough and there are 180 miles of it. Michael beside me in the Bren gun carrier was fascinated by the driver soldier's uniform and equipment. "What's that for, Mammy?" he asked, pointing towards the soldier's belt. "A bayonet," I said, hoping he would be satisfied, but of course he wasn't. "But what does he do with it?" The soldier didn't speak English but grasped what Michael was asking and I only just managed to stop him acting out the way he would wield his bayonet. The carrier had no doors, just shoulder-height leather straps at each side, and I still remember my fear that I would grow sleepy and in a lurch on the road Patrick and I would fall out, for the strap was too high up to hold me and there was nothing else. I kept my eyes on the road which was empty of other traffic all that dark night, to check through the dust that the other Bren gun carrier with John and Katherine was still ahead and that the road was the familiar one to Juba, for my other dread was that our vehicles could be parted and take us to different places.

Afterwards I remembered that strange journey, half our family in one carrier and the rest in another, the soldiers protected by their tin hats while our heads were bare, and I recognised just how vulnerable we had been. With the Anyanya gunning for the army, to travel in an army vehicle was like an invitation to be shot at. And yet we felt protected, almost insulated from fear, never doubting God was with us. After nine hours or so our convoy reached Juba at about 2.30 a.m., the first time we had ever covered the Mundri to Juba journey without breakdowns or punctures! We could feel how relieved the soldiers were to have arrived without incident as they drove us to the group of CMS houses. In a flash John and I were out of our separate Bren gun carriers and running towards each other, to be together again and to hold hands with our children as we made our way to the lit-up verandah. There, waiting for us, were Christopher Cook the Mission Secretary with his wife Davie, now living in the house where we had stayed with Brian and Eileen de Saram on our arrival five years before, and Ken and Betty Ogden who were staying in the house next door while they worked on the completion of Juba Cathedral. All of them were jubilant to see us safe and well. Patrick added to the atmosphere of relief when, wide awake after sleeping on my knee for most of the journey, he waved from the verandah and shouted 'Car! Car!' as the soldiers drove off. Christopher, like Brian before him, maintained good relationships with Government officials and would do all he could to help us; he would leave the affairs of the Mission in good order and hand over the last of the CMS property to the Sudanese Church which by then had 57 trained and ordained pastors and two Sudanese Assistant Bishops. We six, the Cooks, the Ogdens and John and I with our three children were the only remaining CMS missionaries in the South. The expulsion order applied to us and also to 272 Roman Catholic expatriate nuns and priests of the Italian Verona Order. Within a week all of us were gone. No expatriates remained in Juba and the South. Burdened and oppressed by the doom and suffering we knew lay ahead for the people and country we had come to serve and grown to love, the flights of expulsion had taken us to Khartoum and then out of Sudan.

A year later, in August 1965, Bishop Gwynne College, Mundri, where we had worked for five years, was destroyed utterly by Government forces; students and staff escaped by fleeing into the bush and after trekking through the forests sought places of safety in Uganda. It was a terrible time in Southern Sudan - fear, suffering and many deaths. It is estimated that following the massacres by the

Government army in Juba in July 1965 the population there fell from 40,000 to 4,000. Due to widespread military violence against civilians throughout the South, as many as 350,000 Southern Sudanese fled to exile in neighbouring countries.

By that time we were at the beginning of ten years on the staff of Bishop Tucker College in Uganda. Just as darkness fell one evening we were surprised to see three battered cars rolling up, packed full of men, women and children. All were weary and hungry after long months of walking through the bush to safety, foraging for food and constantly afraid of being pursued by the army. Safely over the border into Uganda, they were helped by the Church with money to travel by bus and the public taxis now at our house. We saw the anxiety and bewilderment and then the faces light up in recognition. They had known us in Mundri; for them there was no doubt God was looking after them; it was by His plan we went to Uganda after our expulsion from Sudan the year before; we were there to prepare a place for them. We set about making an enormous cauldron of ground-nut soup and went to the village shop for a dozen big loaves of bread. Tonight they would eat and have water to wash and a good sleep in safety. God could be trusted for their next step also. We touched each other repeatedly to make sure we were really together again, we hugged and talked and exclaimed and gave thanks and praised God. At last all twenty seven of them settled down for the night, packed into the small staff house next door to ours which happened to be vacant and available.

They were right in trusting that we would help them. For the next eight years John, Vice-Principal, tutor and librarian at Mukono, was also, as Commissary for Bishop Oliver Allison of Sudan, involved with the Sudanese Church people who were pouring as refugees into Uganda. Sudanese clergy, including the two Assistant Bishops, needed support and suitable places to exercise their ministry; students whose College had been destroyed needed to complete their ordination training, and John helped to find places and funding for them in Theological Colleges in Uganda, Kenya, and Nigeria.

Though at times they were unhappy and despairing, impatient over delays in meeting their needs, our Sudanese friends did not waste the years of their exile. For example, Sapana Bennsion used his accountancy skills within the Church of Uganda, Benaiah Poggo was an effective pastor to a settlement of Sudanese refugees in Bugerere not far from Mukono, and Levi Hassan helped to staff a special course in Mbale to prepare Sudanese men for ordination. All of them longed to be back in Sudan. They were filled with anger about the state of their country and blamed the Arabs, as they called the Northerners, who were ruling it.

Canon Ezra and his family were among the number who arrived in those three taxis. They lived as refugees in Uganda for the next seven years. Ezra continued his work of translating the Old Testament into Moru, but returned to his home in Mundri in 1972 when a period of relative peace followed the Addis Ababa Agreement. That peace broke down in 1983 and even more ferocious warfare resumed in Sudan. The United Bible Society tried to persuade Canon Ezra to move to Nairobi where he could continue his translation work in safety and be supported by the Society, but Ezra felt unable to desert the church in Mundri and chose instead to remain with his own people in Sudan.

On Good Friday 1991, with his wife Hana and two of his daughters, Canon Ezra was in a large party being forcibly conducted on foot by Sudan Government soldiers on the road between Mundri and Juba (the same road on which we travelled in Bren gun carriers with the army in 1964). They were caught up in crossfire between the Government soldiers and an attacking contingent of SPLA (Sudan Peoples' Liberation Army) forces. Among the forty killed in the gunfire were the saintly Canon Ezra and his daughter Cecilia.

POSTSCRIPT

".... the effect of the missionary endeavour was to enable African culture, dignity and values to survive sustained assault, and it does so to this day . . .
"Missionary work has been as much abused in Sudan as anywhere. Working under the harshest conditions, often with minimal resources, and often with minimal results to show for their effort, it would be easy to dismiss the missionaries as of little significance, were it not for the dramatic and vital growth which has taken place in all areas of church life since their departure in 1964."
    - Andrew C. Wheeler *From Mission to Church in an Islamizing State: the case of Sudan 1946 – 64*, in *Christian Missionaries & the State in the Third World*, published James Currey, Oxford, 2002.

THE SUDAN CHURCH ASSOCIATION
Registered Charity No. 290607
exists to support The Episcopal Church of Sudan by prayer, financial assistance and international awareness of the Sudan situation.

Membership, £10 minimum subscription, includes the Sudan Church Review, an attractive and informative colour magazine which members receive every Spring and Autumn.

Profits from the sale of this book will go to The Sudan Church Association. Further contributions would be welcomed by
                The Hon. Treasurer
                Sudan Church Association,
                Church House,
                Crane Street, Salisbury, SP1 2QB